SECURITY AND CO-OPERATION IN EUROPE:
THE HUMAN DIMENSION, 1972–1992

T0348099

SECURITY AND CO-OPERATION IN EUROPE: THE HUMAN DIMENSION, 1972–1992

Alexis Heraclides

Routledge
Taylor & Francis Group

LONDON AND NEW YORK

First published in 1993 by
FRANK CASS & CO. LTD

Published 2014 by Routledge

2 Park Square, Milton Park, Abingdon, Oxfordshire OX14 4RN

711 Third Avenue, New York, NY 10017

First issued in paperback 2014

Routledge is an imprint of the Taylor & Francis Group, an informa business

British Library Cataloguing in Publication Data

Heraclides, Alexis
  Security and Co-operation in Europe:
  Human Dimension, 1972–92
  I. Title
  327.116

  ISBN 978-0-714-63484-5 (hbk)

  ISBN 978-1-138-88193-8 (pbk)

Library of Congress Cataloging-in-Publication Data

Heraclides, Alexis.
    Security and co-operation in Europe : the human dimension,
  1972–1992 / Alexis Heraclides.
      p. cm.
    Includes bibliographical references and index.
    ISBN 0-7146-3484-0
    1. Conference on Security and Cooperation in Europe (1972 :
  Helsinki, Finland)—History. 2. Human rights—Europe—History—20th
  century. I. Title.
  JX1393.C65H47   1993   92-19256
                                           CIP

Typeset by Regent Typesetting, London

To my father

*and to all the other diplomats and scholars who
toiled for a new vision of security
and co-operation in Europe*

CONTENTS

Contents

ACKNOWLEDGEMENTS

This book is the product of several years of active involvement in the CSCE process in what came to be known as its human dimension. Through these years I have benefited from the insight and views of several colleagues, insiders of the CSCE. With the risk of committing the gross error of omitting some of them, I should like to mention those to whom I am particularly indebted for without them I would not have gathered the courage and enthusiasm – or taken the risk – to start writing this book. They are Harris Nielsen from Denmark, Harm Hazewinkel and Ann de Bil Nachenius from the Netherlands, Ambassador J. Laurent and Werner Bowens from Belgium, the late Sir Anthony Williams and Philip Hurr from the United Kingdom, Ambassador Ekkehard Eickhoff from Germany, Ambassadors Max M. Kampelman and Samuel Wise from the United States, Thelma Duran and Tony Mannix from Ireland, the late Ambassador Pan de Soreluce from Spain, Ambassadors Nicos Karandreas, Constantin Tsamados and George Alexandropoulos from Greece, Ambassador Christoforos Yiangou from Cyprus, Ambassador Antonio Armellini from Italy, Ambassador Helmut Tuerk and Dr Stefan Lehne from Austria, Ambassador Nils Eliasson from Sweden, Ambassador Count Mario von Ledebur-Wicheln from Liechtenstein, Ambassador Andre Erdos and Szuzza Hargitay from Hungary, Ambassador Evariste Saliba from Malta, Boyko Noev from Bulgaria, Ambassador Ekrem Guvendiren from Turkey, and the journalist Roland Eggleston.

Needless to say, none of the above bears any responsibility for my assessment and reading of the CSCE–human rights dimension, which is intended as a dispassionate scholarly study based on primary and secondary sources.

I would also like to mention a few other individuals for whose support and assistance I am very grateful. They are Emil Golemanov, Vassilis Bornovas, Mania Telalian and George Dimitriadis.

Last, but certainly not least, I am particularly indebted for the support and suggestions provided by my father, Ambassador Dimitris Heraclides and, of course, to the Greek Foreign Ministry for allowing me to consult its archives.

A.H.

ABBREVIATIONS

RCBMs	Confidence-Building Measures
CDE	Conference on Confidence- and Security-Building Measures and Disarmament in Europe
CHD	Conference on the Human Dimension
CFE	Conventional Armed Forces in Europe
CPC	Conflict Prevention Centre (of the CSCE)
CSBMs	Confidence- and Security-Building Measures
CSCE	Conference on Security and Co-operation in Europe
CSFR	Czech and Slovak Federal Republic
CSO	Committee of Senior Officials (of the CSCE)
EC	European Community
EPC	European Political Co-operation (of the European Community)
FRG	Federal Republic of Germany
GDR	German Democratic Republic
IGO	Inter-governmental organization
MBFR	Mutual and Balanced Force Reduction
MPT	Multilateral Preparatory Talks (at Helsinki)
NATO	North Atlantic Treaty Organization
NGO	Non-governmental organization
NNA	Neutral and Non-Aligned CSCE participating states
N+N	Neutral and Non-Aligned CSCE participating states
OFE	Office of Free Elections (of the CSCE)
UN	United Nations
'9'	Nine member-states of the European Community
'10'	Ten member-states of the European Community
'12'	Twelve member-states of the European Community
'15'	Fifteen member-states of NATO
'16'	Sixteen member-states of NATO
'35'	Thirty-five participating states of the CSCE

TABLE OF CSCE MEETINGS, 1972–JULY 1992

Note: Various preparatory meetings are not included. Of the several meetings of the new institutions set by the Charter of Paris of November 1991, only those of the CSCE Council are mentioned.

Multilateral Preparatory Talks, Helsinki (Dipoli)
  22 November 1972–8 June 1973
CSCE (Phase 1), Helsinki
  3–7 July 1973
CSCE (Phase 2), Geneva
  18 September 1973–21 July 1975
CSCE (Phase 3), Helsinki
  30 July–1 August 1975
First CSCE Follow-up Meeting, Belgrade
  4 October 1977–8 March 1978
Meeting of Experts on the Peaceful Settlement of Disputes, Montreux
  31 October–11 December 1978
Meeting of Experts on Co-operation in the Mediterranean, Valletta
  13 February–26 March 1979
Scientific Forum, Hamburg
  18 February–3 March 1980
Second CSCE Follow-up Meeting, Madrid
  11 November 1980–9 September 1983
Conference on CSBMs and Disarmament in Europe (CDE), Stockholm
  17 January 1984–19 September 1986
Meeting of Experts on the Peaceful Settlement of Disputes, Athens
  21 March–30 April 1984
Seminar on Co-operation in the Mediterranean, Venice
  16–26 October 1984
Meeting of Experts on Human Rights, Ottawa
  7 May–17 June 1985
Commemoration of 10th Anniversary of the Final Act, Helsinki
  30 July–1 August 1985
Cultural Forum, Budapest
  15 October–25 November 1985

Meeting of Experts on Human Contacts, Bern
15 April–27 May 1986
Third CSCE Follow-up Meeting, Vienna
4 November 1986–19 January 1989
Negotiations on CSBMs, Vienna
6 March 1989–November 1990
Negotiations on Conventional Arms Forces in Europe (CFE), Vienna
6 March 1989–November 1990
Information Forum, London
18 April–12 May 1989
First Meeting of the Conference on the Human Dimension, Paris
30 May–23 June 1989
Meeting on the Protection of the Environment, Sofia
16 October–3 November 1989
Conference on Economic Co-operation, Bonn
19 March–11 April 1990
Second Meeting of the Conference on the Human Dimension, Copenhagen
5–29 June 1990
Committee for the Preparation of a Summit Meeting in Paris, Vienna
10 July–November 1990
CSCE Summit Meeting, Paris
19–21 November 1990
Meeting of Experts on the Peaceful Settlement of Disputes, Valletta
15 January–8 February 1991
Symposium on the Cultural Heritage, Cracow
28 May–7 June 1991
First Meeting of the CSCE Council, Berlin
19–20 June 1991
Meeting of Experts on National Minorities, Geneva
1–19 July 1991
Third Meeting of the Conference on the Human Dimension, Moscow
10 September–4 October 1991
Seminar on Democratic Institutions, Oslo
4–15 November 1991
Second Meeting of the CSCE Council, Prague
30–31 January 1992
Fourth CSCE Follow-up Meeting, Helsinki
24 March–June 1992
CSCE Summit Meeting, Helsinki
July 1992

PREFACE

The Conference on Security and Co-operation in Europe (CSCE) is in many respects a unique enterprise. It has not been a traditional inter-governmental organization (IGO), but a continuing process of meetings concerned with implementation reviews and the production of documents. The documents contained commitments which few states regarded as obtainable before their adoption, let alone of any value or enforceable once adopted on paper. As such, the CSCE was not always taken seriously by many a participating state, scholar or journalist, and not least by the superpowers of the day, the United States and the Soviet Union. Those governments that took it seriously had different and conflicting objectives, which they could not easily achieve in that unruly conglomerate of so many participating states, each and every one equipped with the power to veto.

Yet, at the end, all were somehow caught up by the force of things. Ultimately it was the 'power of words', of the human rights commitments in the CSCE, that did the trick – a law unto itself. The new commitments acquired a dynamic of their own, expressing a collective yearning for a better world, which would do away with traditional high-handed inter-state politics which engendered a world bent on *diktat*, on power or the myth of power and all that it begets.

One could argue that the CSCE accomplished very little, that it was no more than a venue of confrontation, at most a device to register a meagre harvest in the realm of East–West politics: a pledge of co-operation and mutual respect in the midst of misunderstanding and actual lack of true mutual respect between East and West – what could be a worse travesty? Seen from a different viewpoint, the CSCE produced much that was worthwhile, becoming one of the precipitants of the dramatic changes in Eastern Europe and then, in its own right, one of the cornerstones of the new world order and of the 'new European architecture'. The reality, whatever it may appear to be in the eyes of the beholder – scrupulous Popperian, or Protagorean/Kuhnian – is probably somewhere in between. The creature known by the acronym CSCE was, in its function as standard-setter, a catalyst of events and trends which one could not abridge, at best a device for erecting the vision of a 'new Europe' based on democracy, peace and unity, at worst a vehicle for undoing the 'other side'.

Irrespective of what it was or ought to have been in the Cold War, the

CSCE has today evolved into what scholars call a regime, and is apparently in the process of developing into a 'diplomatic-security' system and perhaps an international organization.[1] What is clear is that in the last two years it has changed from a forum of East–West confrontation to a framework aimed at tackling political problems and pursuing stability in a Europe finally united on fundamentals.[2] Its identity is to be further elaborated at the Helsinki Follow-up Meeting, generally dubbed by insiders as Helsinki-II, thus confirming its potential seminal importance.

In this study we try to set forth the essentials of this important, though until recently little known, inter-governmental forum – the only existing pan-European one – with special emphasis on its output and esoteric negotiating procedures. In taking stock of the Helsinki process during the period 1972 to 1991 one aspect comes inescapably to the fore: the 'human dimension'; and it is from that vantage point that we approach our subject matter. In this exercise we touch upon the paradox of a fairly traditional diplomatic conference's ability to achieve results even within a very adverse East–West climate of Cold War.

A.H.

'Our delegation believes in the importance of words.'
Ambassador Max M. Kampelman
Head of the United States Delegation
Madrid Meeting, 18 July 1983

'We propose a representative conference ... in Moscow to consider the whole range of problems in the field of humanitarian cooperation ...'
Eduard Shevardnadze
Foreign Minister of the USSR
Vienna Meeting, Opening Statement, November 1986

'A state that cannot stand criticism must do without culture.'
Ambassador Ekkehard Eickhoff
Head of Delegation of the Federal
Republic of Germany,
Vienna Meeting, 26 November 1986

THE CONFERENCE ON SECURITY AND CO-OPERATION IN EUROPE

AN INTRODUCTION: THE CSCE AND ITS MAIN PHASES

The Conference on Security and Co-operation in Europe (CSCE), or Helsinki process as it is more widely known, was officially launched by the signing of the Final Act on 1 August 1975 in Helsinki, at a Summit of thirty-five heads of state or government.

The CSCE was conceived to have as its participating states all the states of Europe and the United States and Canada.[1] The only European state not to participate was Albania which chose to snub the CSCE upon its formation and was then admitted, first as a non-speaking observer (in June 1990) and a year later as a full participant (in June 1991). Europe's micro-states, not state-members of the United Nations (UN), were also included, thereby gaining a voice at the international level: the Holy See, Liechtenstein, San Marino and Monaco, though not Andorra, which is not a state by international law. In September 1991 the three newly independent Baltic states joined the CSCE, the number of participants reaching thirty-eight. And with the disintegration of the Soviet Union and Yugoslavia the number of participating states became forty-eight in January 1992, with the addition of Armenia, Azerbaijan, Belarus, Kazakhstan, Kirgistan, Moldova, Tajikistan, Turkmenistan, Ukraine and Uzbekistan, and with two observers, Croatia and Slovenia.

From the 1970s until the beginning of 1992, on the eve of the Helsinki Follow-up Meeting (Helsinki-II), the CSCE can be divided into two main overlapping phases on the basis of two criteria: (a) framework or form, and (b) the external environment of East–West relations. With regard to framework or form, the first phase is that of a process without institutions, what could be called CSCE-I, from August 1975 until November 1990. The second is the process with institutions, which could be called CSCE-II, from the end of

November 1990 until just before Helsinki-II, which was an in-between period where the old and the new, emerging CSCE co-existed: on the one hand, the CSCE with its traditional meetings aimed at implementation reviews and concluding documents, and on the other, the CSCE with the periodical and extraordinary meetings of its newly acquired permanent institutions. From the viewpoint of the East–West climate, the distinction between CSCE-I and II is less sharp. There exists an in-between period of about a year and a half from the ending of the Vienna Follow-up Meeting in January 1989 to the Copenhagen Meeting (June 1990), which was a 'twilight zone' of transformation from a deflated antithesis along East–West lines for most of 1989, to conciliation, and then to the total irrelevance of the East–West distinction by the next year.

THE PRE-EMINENCE OF THE HUMAN DIMENSION

The CSCE, from the signing of the Final Act in August 1975 until the Paris Summit of November 1990, was dominated by discussions and negotiations on human rights and issues in the humanitarian field, which collectively came to be known in the CSCE by the mid-1980s as the 'human dimension'.[2] Thus CSCE-I could be dubbed the human dimension or human rights phase of the CSCE.[3] The gradual pre-eminence of the human dimension, from 1977 onwards, was an unexpected development. It amounted to a shift from the original inter-state level of rules of conduct between states aimed at promoting *détente* through security, to the level of relations between the individual and the state(s), thus raising the individual to the pan-European plane. Through this mutation process the CSCE was made to stand on its head, if seen from the viewpoint of the originators of the idea of a European Conference, the governments of Eastern Europe, but also from the point of view of traditional state-centric international relations. The CSCE went even further, becoming a trail-blazer on human rights and related humanitarian issues. From 1975 onwards it was mainly the CSCE, among inter-governmental forums, which was the rallying point in the hearts and minds of the oppressed in Europe.

The ability of CSCE-I to carry the banner of human rights and humanitarian questions in Eastern Europe can be attributed to at least three factors. One is the salience of the East–West dimension at the very core of the CSCE. Note that therein lay a dilemma: to respect and come to deal with the East–West divide as a given once and for all, or to do away with one of the two worlds. The tendency of most Western governments during the Cold War was to opt for the latter, with

2

disagreements arising mainly on how best to go about this awesome task. A second factor in the CSCE prominence on the human dimension was that it was a process, and as such almost by definition an ongoing, unidirectional one. It had to come up with concrete results in the form of commitments which would go beyond previous undertakings, the alternative being the end of the process. Thus CSCE provisions could cover more ground and make bolder strides ahead than the UN. At a higher level of abstraction, one can point to a third element, the edge of the political over the legal or legalistic, and I would add, in self-criticism, even the scholarly, which can be tentative and pusillanimous in its striving for objectivity when it comes to situations in the real world regarding human rights violations. But let us start from the beginning, from the origins of the concept of a conference for Europe.

THE ORIGINS OF A SECURITY CONFERENCE FOR EUROPE

It is generally accepted that the Conference on Security and Co-operation in Europe was an offshoot of the brief era of *détente* which reigned between East and West in the first part of the 1970s, a thaw spurred above all by the rapprochement between the superpowers, and by the Östpolitik of the Federal Republic of Germany (FRG) under Chancellor Willy Brandt.[4]

A European conference on security was an old Soviet idea launched in 1954, not long after the death of Stalin, by the Soviet Foreign Minister Vyacheslav Molotov, infuriating Western governments even more, perhaps, than his namesake, a Molotov cocktail, would have. It was a suggestion for what was called a 'Draft General European Treaty of Collective Security in Europe', with the United States and Canada confined to the role of observers. There followed several schemes from the Soviet Union and Eastern European states until 1957, concluding with a proposal by Polish Foreign Minister Adam Rapacki, all brushed aside by the West, particularly in the wake of the Soviet intervention in Hungary in 1956. The Western states regarded the idea as no more than a veiled attempt to further the interests of the Soviet Union and its orbit at the expense of the United States, the European Economic Community (EEC), then in its precarious infancy, and the West in general.[5]

The first elements of the 'human dimension' in the East–West context can probably be traced to the two quadripartite conferences (United States, United Kingdom, France and the Soviet Union) held

3

in August and November 1955, where the three Western states set out a series of proposals on the free flow of information, on establishing information centres, and on the exchange of ideas and persons in the professional, scientific and cultural spheres. Needless to say, it was now the turn of the Soviet Union to say 'no', arguing that this intruded into spheres of exclusively domestic jurisdiction and state sovereignty.[6]

The idea of a conference surfaced again in a statement at the UN General Assembly in December 1964 by the same Polish Foreign Minister as in 1957, the new version including the United States and Canada. This was followed by more concrete proposals on the part of the Warsaw Pact, notably in Bucharest in July 1966, more propagandistically at Karlovy Vary (given the fact that it was a meeting of Communist parties) in April 1967, and more pragmatically in Budapest in March 1969 and reiterated in the same year by the Warsaw Pact in its Prague and Moscow meetings. The NATO position evolved gradually, but, in contrast to the 1950s, several Western countries were no longer averse to the project, provided it would also meet Western interests. The first concrete step in that direction by NATO is considered to have been the one taken at Reykjavik in June 1968, where the Warsaw Pact was invited for 'mutual and balanced force reduction talks' (MBFR).[7]

With the gradual thaw in East–West relations towards the end of the 1960s, the concept of some kind of conference began to gain ground in various Western circles. After the Soviet military intervention in Czechoslovakia, Leonid Brezhnev, apparently feeling more confident (as Sovietologists have claimed),[8] picked up the idea with renewed fervour and tried to render it more palatable to the West. Initially NATO reacted with caution, the United States being the most opposed. In May 1969 there appeared a Finnish memorandum offering Helsinki as the venue for hosting such a conference, the Finns doing their utmost to reassure Western countries that this was at their own initiative and not done at the behest of the Soviet Union. By December 1969 it was obvious that a conference was in the offing, as NATO set forth in its Brussels meeting four prerequisites for its convening: the full participation of the United States and Canada in what would be a conference *for* Europe, not a European Conference; substantial progress on the German issue, particularly with regard to the status of Berlin; the opening of MBFR talks (a United States *sine qua non*); the inclusion of other issues, notably the free circulation of persons, information and ideas. In this last condition one finds the seeds of the 'human dimension' as an essential element of the future conference.[9]

The next two or three years saw several developments, notably the bilateral treaties signed between the FRG and the Soviet Union, Poland and the German Democratic Republic (GDR), as well as the Quadripartite Treaty on the status of Berlin. Thus one by one the various obstacles were overcome, leaving only the MBFR question open. The United States under the sway of Secretary of State Henry Kissinger did not attach any particular significance to the future security conference, but only to the prospective talks on conventional arms, hence 'linkage' with MBFR was stressed, something which Moscow wanted to avoid. As one Kissinger aide put it at the time, 'we sold it [the conference] first for the German–Soviet treaty, we sold it for the Berlin Agreement, and we sold it again for MBFR'.[10] Finally, with agreement on initiating the MBFR talks, NATO gave its consent for 'multilateral preparatory talks' (MPT) at its Bonn meeting of May 1972.

At this juncture, it is of interest to highlight the main Soviet motives and goals for a European security conference. They were apparently the following:[11] to have the Western and other states accept the existing frontiers in Europe; to legitimize the existence of the GDR; to acquire a *droit de regard* on Western European affairs; to preserve the Soviet hegemonic position in Eastern Europe and to have this fact recognized, at least indirectly, by the West; to drive a wedge between the United States and Western Europe, limiting United States influence and, possibly, Finlandizing Western Europe; to counteract the strengthening and consolidation of the West; to weaken EEC integration; to demilitarize the FRG; to gain economic and technological benefits from co-operation with the West. As Robert Legvold aptly put it at the time, the ultimate Soviet objective was 'to strengthen not diminish, to transcend but not to transform, the separate political-economic systems of Europe's two halves ... a medium of healing Europe's economic division while sealing its political division'.[12] Though the guile of Soviet foreign policy need not be overestimated, with the benefit of greater insight on Kremlin thinking in the 1960s and 1970s, it can be said that the above is, by and large, an accurate assessment of Soviet perceptions regarding the convening and possible outcomes of a security conference.[13]

In view of the Soviet origins of the CSCE, the final convening of a conference could be seen as a triumph of Soviet persistence. It brings to mind Kissinger's postulate on the main asset of Soviet diplomacy during the Cold War: that it was 'extraordinarily persevering; it substitutes persistence for imagination ... Like drops of water on a stone, Soviet repetitiveness has the tendency sooner or later to erode the resistance of the restless democracies.'[14] Not surprisingly, the

5

Conference and the Final Act were portrayed in the West, not least in the United States, as a victory of the Soviet Union and the Eastern bloc. George Ball, noted for his acumen on other questions (particularly on the Arab–Israeli dispute), called the Final Act 'a defeat for the West', Raymond Aron referred to the 'comedy of Helsinki', while the playwright Eugene Ionesco spoke of 'a new Munich', and others talked of 'a second Yalta'.[15] Ironically, this view was reinforced by the Soviet Union, which hailed the results as a success for their side, 'a victory for socialism' and peace, and as a triumph for its leader, Leonid Brezhnev.[16]

Today it is more than obvious that the above definitions of the situation constituted a misjudgement of considerable proportions by both superpowers, a fact pointed out at the time by some commentators, including those examining the Final Act from a 'soft law' perspective.[17] Probably the deeper reason for this conjecture was the implicit adherence of the United States and the Soviet Union to the state-centric/power-politics approach, the dominant Realist Paradigm in international politics (Henry Kissinger himself being one of its most eminent second-generation proponents). It is a partial view of the world which attaches little or no consequence to the power of human values, to the rising influence of non-state actors internationally, or to the ability of individuals and groups to effectively question non-legitimized authority, as pointed out from the late 1960s and early 1970s by a minority of eminent theorists of international relations in their penetrating critique of Realism/power politics.[18]

THE HELSINKI TALKS AND THE CSCE PROCEDURAL RULES

THE HELSINKI TALKS

The Multilateral Preparatory Talks (MPT) started as scheduled on 22 November 1972 with the participation of thirty-two European states (in addition to Albania, Monaco did not take part at that stage) and the United States and Canada. The talks took place in Helsinki's suburb of Dipoli, and concluded eight months later by producing a deceptively modest, sparsely written document of some thirty pages entitled 'Final Recommendations of the Helsinki Consultations', known in the CSCE, from its colour, as the 'Blue Book'.

The negotiations were difficult and laborious. It took considerable time for them to pick up, given the diametrically opposed views and expectations, the novelty of the forum for all concerned, the lack of detailed previous planning, the number of participating delegations and, perhaps above all, the unusual situation of having to abide by the strict application of the consensus procedure which was to be the hallmark of the CSCE. In fact, bridging of the opposed viewpoints on the contentious issues was brought about only in the last weeks of the talks, even though the major proposals were already on the table by January 1973.[1]

The various themes that were introduced were placed into three so-called 'baskets', a useful noncommittal term suggested by the Netherlands delegate and elaborated by the Swiss delegate at Dipoli.[2] Basket I dealt with the principles guiding the mutual relations of the participating states, as well as with security aspects, Basket II with economic and related matters and Basket III with what came to be called 'co-operation in humanitarian and other fields'.

In Basket I the most difficult question was formulating the main subjects of the principles. Initially, the Soviet Union and the other Eastern states called for a convention, essentially for a concise text of norms which would have at its core the inviolability of frontiers, followed by non-interference in internal affairs, non-use of force, sovereign independence and territorial integrity, to which would be added co-operation on economic, technological and cultural matters, as well as a mechanism for the continuation of the conference. A related idea was to have a set of legally binding principles, to be followed by a political document. However, any form of *lex specialis* for Europe was unacceptable to the West, not least to the '9' states of the then European Community (EC) and to the United States, which did not foresee ratification by Congress. In the end this question was left open for the Conference. Another lesser matter was which international document would be the main source for the principles section. The Western states indicated the relevant UN Declaration on Friendly Relations, adopted by the UN General Assembly only a few years earlier, in 1970, as the most obvious source for the new set of principles. But the Soviet Union was not of the same view, hence it was decided that the UN Declaration would be the main, but not the only source.[3]

With regard to actual commitments, the Western delegations favoured a longer list of principles which would include human rights as well as self-determination, and argued that the inviolability of frontiers was not a principle in its own right, but one subsumed under other principles, such as the non-use of force and territorial integrity. Among the Neutrals and Non-Aligned (NNA, N+N or N−N, as they are known in CSCE jargon), Switzerland introduced a principle dedicated to the peaceful settlement of disputes (one of the few 'dynamic' 'forward-looking' principles, as Switzerland was to point out). In the end the package deal was to include the inviolability of frontiers, as a separate principle, but also human rights and self-determination, though the West could not get through another idea, the inter-relationship of the principles, aimed at strengthening the human rights principle. The elaboration of each principle was left for the conference, but for good measure, when agreement was reached, Ireland, Spain and Italy submitted a written interpretative statement, stating that the inviolability of frontiers should not be read as excluding the changing of frontiers through peaceful means. Belgium and the Netherlands made similar statements orally, but curiously enough not the FRG, which had been the real protagonist on this vital question.[4]

Outside the principles, negotiations on security in Basket I were limited to the military aspects of security, mainly to 'Confidence-Building Measures' (CBMs) (after the Madrid Concluding Document of 1983 renamed 'Confidence- and Security-Building Measures', CSBMs). Two CBMs were indicated: prior notification of major

8

military manoeuvres and exchange of observers by invitation under 'mutually acceptable conditions' (the famous 'MAC'). But, as expected, the main difficulties arose when it came to initiating and formulating Basket III, where the positions between Eastern and Western delegations seemed unbridgeable.

The Basket III issues of human contacts and information were regarded by the West, particularly by the '9' members of the EC, as the area that could seriously challenge the Eastern political systems, and could gradually lead to their transformation. Thus, it was seen as the most critical issue for the future conference. This, however, was not the view of the United States, which stood aloof, not regarding this exercise as a realistic one in the sense of it being instrumental in bringing results by engendering commitments or change in the actual comportment of the Eastern states. But for the other Western countries, Basket III was the main negotiating counter against the Soviet Union's obsession with recognition of the post-war boundaries in Europe.[5] It was, therefore, presented by the West as the main condition for agreeing to the Conference, by stressing a 'linkage' between progress in Basket III and progress in the other two baskets, and delaying agreement on the other two baskets. Finally, the Soviet Union accepted the inclusion of Basket III. Apparently, this was done because of Brezhnev's commitment to and the personal prestige which hinged on the convening of the conference, but it was also felt that the matter could be kept within bounds, with little added in the future negotiations. This Soviet concession was convenient for Western governments anxious not to give the impression of a 'second Yalta'. Of course, the wording was a compromise (the preamble linking this chapter with 'full respect for the principles', that is even with those that could be used as justification for non-compliance) and, as such, it hardly suggested the major Western victory involved or the fact that the Soviet regime had made a fatal mistake in giving in to its inclusion.[6]

One particular proposal under Basket III which appeared belatedly is worth mentioning, the one by Yugoslavia on 'the rights of national minorities and regional cultures', an issue destined to become central in the CSCE from 1987 onwards, and the only one within the wider human dimension area which at that time could not be placed on an East–West level. Submitted only a week before the closing of the Helsinki talks, it was supported mainly by the Eastern delegations, while the Western delegations were either lukewarm or hostile to the idea, with the United States being among the leaders of the 'anti-minority' camp. The final solution was a compromise, leaving out the concept of 'rights of minorities' and speaking in terms of the 'contribution that national minorities or regional cultures could make' within the framework of respect for the principles (that is, for all the principles).[7]

Another major problem at Dipoli was the question of a follow-up to the conference. The Soviet Union and the entire Eastern bloc (including unruly Romania) were strongly in favour of an institutionalized follow-up to be handled by what was termed a Consultative Committee. On this they were supported by several other states, notably Yugoslavia, Switzerland, Austria and Spain (then under Franco's rule). But the NATO countries were decidedly against any form of institutionalization, for they feared that it would facilitate a *droit de regard* on the part of the Soviet Union.[8] They maintained that a permanent organ should come only after tangible results had been reached in the main conference, and, above all, after the new undertakings had been implemented. According to Ljubivoje Acimovic, a fundamental drawback to the proposal as drafted was that instead of focusing on implementation it suggested a body to 'oversee peace and security', a kind of 'institutional watchdog for the territorial and political status quo in the continent', parallel to the UN Security Council.[9] The final outcome was once again a compromise solution, whereby the principle of a follow-up was mentioned, but the matter left open for the Conference to decide.[10]

By late May 1973 the document was all but ready, with the remaining unresolved questions being of a procedural nature. The French idea of a three-stage conference won approval, with a ceremonial beginning and ending. Geneva was chosen for the main negotiation phase, instead of Helsinki or Vienna. But the Maltese delegate withheld consensus for several days – in what was to become a ritual in the CSCE for the next ten years – by insisting on the inclusion of 'Arab coastal states of the Mediterranean' in the Conference. The 'Final Recommendations of the Helsinki Consultations', the Blue Book, was agreed upon on 8 June 1973, and officially adopted by the foreign ministers of the participating states at the official opening of the Conference in Helsinki from 3 to 7 July 1973.[11]

Today, almost twenty years since the adoption of the Blue Book, it is of interest to note the dominant view at the time of the delegates at the multilateral consultations (the 'Dipoli Mafia' as they were sometimes called in jest in CSCE circles). The Western delegates were equivocal and, in general, guarded in their assessment, and this despite the considerable progress made in injecting the future document and the ensuing inter-state process with Basket III and human rights issues as elements in friendly relations, something well beyond any other document from the UN or in the international law of human rights. The

Soviet Union and its allies, however, appeared to be more satisfied, apparently not being aware what they had got themselves into.[12]

THE CSCE PROCEDURAL RULES: THE 'BLUE BOOK' AND THE RULES THROUGH PRACTICE (1973–91)

The 'Blue Book' adopted at Helsinki in 1973 contains a detailed agenda of the Conference which encapsulates within some twelve pages (between paragraphs 13 and 52) the three chapters or 'baskets', including in the first chapter (Basket I) the principles, ten in number, listed only by their agreed titles. The question of institutionalization, or some other form of ensuring continuation, formed the last chapter on the agenda, sometimes called Basket IV, entitled 'Follow-up to the Conference', comprising a single paragraph (paragraph 53). Only one matter which later created a whole chapter of its own was not included, the Mediterranean, which as a result has not been called a basket and thus has not gained 'basket status' as it were (the Mediterranean is mentioned in the preambles to chapters I and II of the Blue Book).

But it is the rules of procedure which have made the Blue Book a lasting and vital CSCE document from 1973 until the Helsinki Follow-up Meeting. In its paragraphs 54 to 59 and 64 to 88 one finds the CSCE's Bible on procedural rules and on the CSCE's general philosophy. Like many a phrase in scripture and other venerable texts, such as the UN Charter, its assertions are at times ambivalent, cryptic or even contradictory (and one could claim that therein lies part of their mystique). One reason for this was that several of the procedural rules of the Blue Book were in fact meant only for the forthcoming Conference and not necessarily for its aftermath, whatever that might be (or not be for that matter).

The five basic 'sacred rules' of the Helsinki process as set forth in the Blue Book are the following:

1. The right of all European states, as well as of the United States and Canada – but not of any other state – to become participating states or observers (paragraph 54).
2. Participation on the basis of equality, 'outside military alliances', 'as sovereign independent states', that is the non-recognition of alliances as participating officially *en bloc* in the conference (paragraph 65).
3. The consensus principle, defined as 'the absence of any objection' (paragraph 69) – that is, the adoption of documents, mandates, agendas and other decisions as long as all agree.

11

4. The possibility to ask for 'formal reservations or interpretative statements concerning given decisions to be duly registered by the Executive Secretary and circulated to the participating States' which 'must be submitted in writing to the Executive Secretary' (paragraph 79).
5. The presidency to be on a rotational basis, with the exception of the opening and closing stages of meetings which are to be presided over by the host country (paragraph 70), and a limited technical role for the Executive Secretary of each meeting (paragraphs 74–6).

The laconic nature of the procedural paragraphs of the Blue Book left ample room for the development of more concrete rules either by explicit agreement, or through practice by the participating delegations, or on the part of the executive secretaries at consecutive meetings with the tacit agreement of the participants.

The issue of participation, a non-issue until recently, proved thorny from 1990 onwards, first with the request for observer status and later full participation by Albania, then with the Baltic republics, and soon after with the putative states of the former Soviet Union and Yugoslavia. To begin with, becoming a participating state or an observer was an option, 'a right', offered to any sovereign independent European state as well as to the United States and Canada, but this (according to paragraph 54) only until 25 June 1973, which was the latest that the Finnish Government could be informed of the willingness to participate. Apart from Albania, which did not express the wish to take part, all states chose full participation. Paragraph 54 is, however, not clear as to what should happen afterwards. Given the 'sunset clause', the dominant view in the CSCE has been that from that date onwards participation or observer status is no longer a right, but has to be cleared through a consensus decision. This was confirmed first in the case of Albania, and then in subsequent CSCE decisions on participation.[13]

Albania's first request for participation as an observer (as a non-speaking observer) created uneasiness at the start of the Copenhagen Meeting on the Human Dimension in June 1990, when the matter was virtually thrown at the participants by the Danish Foreign Minister chairing the plenary session, to the embarrassment of most foreign ministers present. It was such a summary use of the consensus procedure, and without forewarning, that some doubted whether the consensus procedure had actually been used.[14] However, the practice followed in the next CSCE meetings has established that observer status requires a consensus, as Albania, in each new meeting, has had to ask for observer status anew, which was granted after a consensus procedure.[15]

Furthermore, according to the prevailing view in the CSCE, participation, particularly as a full member (a participating state), implies formal adoption or at least a readiness to accept and implement existing CSCE commitments. On this the Blue Book is ambiguous. It states (paragraph 54) that an observer 'may decide later to accept these decisions or some of them', and adds a useful clause: 'under the conditions defined by the Conference'. Although strictly speaking this provision does not necessarily imply that the observer by accepting the decisions would become *eo ipso* a participating state, it can be read as allowing the CSCE participating states, if they so wish, to set conditions for those joining afterwards. Again the Albanian case established the process. When Albania became a participating state in the course of the Berlin Meeting of the CSCE Council (comprised of foreign ministers), on 19–20 June 1991, this was only achieved after it had formally stated its adoption of the CSCE documents and its willingness to implement them, as well as to accept and assist a rapporteur mission in its territory. This was also the procedure adopted with the ten former Soviet republics, which had to sign a letter to this effect, including the acceptance of rapporteur missions.[16]

Thus at this stage in the CSCE, just before Helsinki-II, four basic rules can be discerned regarding participation. First, a candidate eligible for observer status or participation should be a sovereign independent state recognized by the international community, or, put differently, a state by international law. Thus, the original requests by the Baltic republics for observer status or participation while in their secessionist phase, in 1990 and in the first part of 1991, were not accepted for they were not regarded as eligible by reason of not being independent states. Subsequently, this was also the case with Armenia, which asked to become a participating state, and Georgia, which wished to become an observer (in October 1991 during the Moscow Meeting).

A second rule regarding participation or observer status is the need for a 'decision', meaning approval, via a consensus procedure.

A third rule (which some have challenged) is that the decision on observer status, and particularly on participation, should be made at a ministerial level, as has been the case until now with all new CSCE participant states.

A fourth rule is that independent statehood as such does not imply automatic participation (or observer status), which would have meant relegating the consensus procedure to a mere formality. The new members must state their acceptance of existing CSCE documents and their readiness to implement them. There is also scope for more substantial conditions to be taken into consideration, namely that the state in question should meet some essential prerequisites, notably in the human dimension.

Related to this is the question of recognition. Note that the '12' EC member-states, in mid-December 1991, set a number of conditions for recognition of new states in Eastern Europe and the former Soviet Union, though the '12' apparently have not been very scrupulous in adhering to them.[17] The setting of conditions may seem high-handed and a sign of bygone days, akin to the old 'civilized nations' clause, but it is worth pointing out that today recognition as such is not 'constitutive' of statehood (as some eminent international lawyers claimed several decades ago) but a purely 'declaratory' political act. States are under no legal obligation to afford *de jure* or *de facto* recognition to other states. Clearly, the setting of conditions would be even more acceptable when it comes to an inter-governmental forum, which is entitled to set rules for those wanting to join the 'club'.[18]

With regard to secessionist entities, they are not to be regarded as independent states, so long as their unilateral declaration of independence is opposed by the 'mother' state and does not lead to extended international recognition, as in the case of the Turkish Republic of Northern Cyprus and of Croatia and Slovenia before their overwhelming recognition by other states. The main reason against recognition in international law is that only 'non-self-governing territories' (that is colonies, protectorates and trusteeship territories) are 'self-determination units', that is, entities entitled to the right to independence to be sought even unilaterally.[19] Regions which constitute parts of the metropolitan territory of an independent state cannot legally become independent by the seizure of independence, but only by way of partition, that is, with the consent of the state concerned. In practice, however, several initial secessions developed into partitions, as the central government gave, however reluctantly, its consent (for example, Syria's secession from the UAR in 1962 and Senegal's from the Mali Federation).[20]

In addition to secession, the dissolution of an empire or federation is an admissible way of creation of statehood, being in effect a form of partition, what could perhaps be called 'multi-party' or 'multi-actor' partition, as seen in the disintegration of the Soviet Union, and perhaps in the future with Ethiopia. And since recognitions as such are political acts, whatever the number of recognitions secured, the entity in question may still not be regarded as a state if it does not otherwise bear the main marks of statehood (control of territory and others, including recognition as a secondary aspect), as seen in the case of Palestine, which has been recognized by almost one hundred states up until now.

Before the acceptance of the ten former Soviet republics in the Prague CSCE Council Meeting of January 1992, there had been intense debate among the participating states as to which course to follow. Was the CSCE strictly to apply the international law on successor states, which would have meant that all entities emanating from the former Soviet Union would be eligible for participation? Or was it to stick to paragraph 54 of the Blue Book, which states that '*European* states, the United States and Canada shall be entitled to take part' (emphasis added), and then turn to cartographers and historians of culture in order to try to define where Europe ends? Both the Soviet Union (with its substantial Asian territory) and Turkey (whose main bulk is in Asia Minor, and which is not European culturally or in religion) were defined as 'European states'. The obvious technical reason for this is that part of their territory lies in Europe. In the case of several former Soviet or even Russian components, they are not only geographically Asian, and spatially far removed from Europe's main concerns, but are also culturally and socially strikingly different from Europe, not least in their political culture.

In the end it seems that two arguments prevailed for their inclusion in the CSCE. One was that this was the best way to inject the Islamic Asiatic republics with pluralist values, the principles of democracy, human rights and the rule of law, instead of letting them be a law unto themselves, as it were. Once in the CSCE family they would face the implementation reviews and mechanisms of implementation which had proved so effective in dealing with the communist world of Eastern Europe. Furthermore, if not included, they were bound to veer towards Iran or other Islamic republics. And, after all, it was the Asian states themselves which had opted for being part of the 'European club' (though they may be the first to regret it and perhaps to leave it). There was also a technical difficulty involved in accepting some former Soviet republics but not others. Thus the CSCE crossed the Rubicon and opened up a 'new frontier' for itself, for better or for worse. What is clear is that in the CSCE from 1992 onwards, it will hardly be possible to speak in terms of a 'common European culture' as stated in the Charter of Paris of November 1990.

What 'outside military alliances' – the second procedural rule – has led to in practice will be examined at a later stage. At this point, suffice it to note that though representation as a bloc is prohibited, as seen by the official submission of proposals in the name of individual states (with the exception of the European Community, which is not an alliance), in practice it is one of the essential ways whereby the consensus-building process is being achieved in the CSCE.

Let us now move on to the most revered procedural rule, the third, the CSCE *Grundnorm*, the consensus principle, without which no decision can be reached.[21] Consensus, as defined by paragraph 69, is 'the absence of any objection'. As such it is not tantamount to unanimity, which implies accepting every part of a document or all aspects of a question. A state may choose to withhold its rejection, but afterwards it is bound by the decision reached. The subtle distinction between unanimity and consensus can be seen by the possibility of making reservations or interpretative statements in the CSCE.[22]

Erika Schlager has cogently summarized the generally known advantages of this procedure as follows: that from a practical viewpoint it is easier for negotiators to refrain from saying 'no', rather than being obliged to say 'yes' (and being on the record for doing so); that it protects the smaller states, any one of which is in a position to block or permit the adoption of a decision; that it is an incentive for states to participate, particularly for smaller ones, and protects the numerical minority from 'the tyranny of the numerical majority'; and, most important of all, the consensus rule does not permit any state to absolve itself of implementing the various commitments by arguing that the decision was imposed upon it.[23]

Yet, as we shall see when we examine the real world of multilateral CSCE negotiations, matters are not as ideal as that. Participating states have often had to accept commitments they detest (and then have tried to avoid implementing them), because they found themselves in a minority of one, or of two or three, or in 'bad company' (say with Ceauşescu's Romania), or because they lack convincing arguments. Another negative aspect of the consensus approach is that a state can abuse the rule of consensus by blocking a decision or by withholding its consent in order to obtain something it cannot otherwise get. Furthermore, new commitments are by necessity the outcome of a compromise, and as a result are unlikely to satisfy those with very ambitious goals. On the other hand, it has been possible, in most instances, not to follow a strict 'least common denominator' approach. Thus, on the whole, this procedure has had, until now at least, more advantages than disadvantages for the CSCE and for the Western approach.

Finally, it is worth noting that as far as procedures, agendas and other decisions are concerned almost 'anything goes' and can be altered as long as it is cleared through consensus in the course of a meeting by the chairman of the day – except if it is decidedly against a decision taken at a higher level.[24] It is perfectly legitimate to change even parts of an agenda or grid set by a follow-up meeting,[25] or bend the consensus approach in a new mechanism. But too revolutionary initiatives are unlikely to gain consensus on substantive issues, for instance a move to abandon the consensus principle in a meeting.

The fourth CSCE procedural rule – on formal reservations or interpretative statements – has been a cause of considerable confusion and misunderstanding in CSCE meetings. In the absence of a distinction between the two, the obvious rule of thumb on this is to follow the Vienna Convention on the Law of Treaties. In the CSCE all sorts of motions of this type have appeared, a source of considerable disorder. Often reservations have been called interpretative statements, for obvious reasons. What could be called counter-reservations are simply called statements or interpretative statements. Many reservations, interpretative statements or motions are merely designated by the delegation concerned as statements 'made under paragraph 79' of the Rules of Procedure.

Yet, despite the disparate list of 'paragraph-79 statements', through the years one can deduce some emerging rules from established CSCE practice. First, at the substantive level, interpretative statements should not amount to reservations. Second, a paragraph-79 statement should not go as far as not to adhere to a large segment of a concluding document, thereby, in effect, not giving consent to a document. A reservation or interpretative statement cannot go as far as to place a blanket reservation or doubt an essential element of a document (and this reinforced by the letter and spirit of the Vienna Convention). The best example of an unacceptable reservation amounting to a lack of consensus is Romania's regarding the human dimension of the Vienna Concluding Document.[26] Third, participating states should refrain, unless absolutely necessary, from resorting to a '79 statement', avoiding it particularly in the human rights domain.

The formal procedure for '79 statements' is that they have to be 'duly registered by the Executive Secretary' and 'circulated' to the participating states. In practice, this means that the statement should be officially given in the course of the meeting, under the agenda item in question and after the decision for the adoption of a document, by requesting in front of all other delegations that it be placed in the 'Journal' of the day under paragraph 79 of the Rules of Procedure.[27] This openness permits other delegations to be informed of its content and, if they so wish, question its validity by formally voicing non-acceptance and having this registered, as was the case with Canada's and Austria's rejection of the Romanian reservation mentioned above, and Greece's 'counter-reservation' at the Belgrade Preparatory Committee of 1977 and at other meetings.[28] It follows from this that any announcement which does not proceed in this fashion should not be regarded as a formal reservation or interpretative statement at the level of all the participating states, even though the state concerned may so define it. This was the case with a Turkish interpretative statement on the minorities chapter of the historic Copenhagen Document (June 1990), which was not announced, and came to be known only after the meeting closed, when it was circulated as an information document.[29]

Finally, the fifth procedural rule, the rotational basis of the presidency, is meant to symbolize the principle of the equality of rights among participating states.[30] It also has a practical consequence. It limits the role of the chairman in comparison to other inter-governmental forums which have a permanent presidency throughout a meeting or session. When a difficulty arises the Executive Secretary (who sits to the right of the chairman) is available to the chairman for advice. Even during the Cold War, it was only in rare instances that a chairman would abuse his role or not take heed of the advice of the Executive Secretary. Thus, in CSCE meetings the Executive Secretary is, in effect, the true chairman, despite his limited 'technical' duties.

To conclude this chapter on procedural rules, it is obvious that there is a need for new, more precise, rules of procedure, particularly now that the CSCE is institutionalized, with a profusion of new mechanisms.

3

THE HELSINKI/GENEVA
CONFERENCE AND THE FINAL ACT

HELSINKI AND GENEVA

On the basis of the mandate set up in the Blue Book, the Conference was held in three stages with the participation this time of thirty-five states (Monaco joined). The official, largely ceremonial beginning and ending – with the signing of the Final Act – were convened at Helsinki, on 3 to 7 July 1973 and on 31 July and 1 August 1975 respectively, while the actual negotiations took place in Geneva, from September 1973 until July 1975.

The Helsinki–Geneva Conference on Security and Co-operation in Europe was in many respects unique, being neither a meeting to draft a fundamental legal text, such as the Conference on the Law of the Sea, nor a meeting to conclude a peace treaty after a war, such as the Vienna Conference of 1815, with which it has sometimes been compared. The participants found themselves in a new, very complex and unpredictable setting. Kalevi J. Holsti has captured the Geneva negotiations well by saying that it was 'not a tidy affair ... uncertainty, ambiguity, shifting interests and improvisations were the rule', as the sense of direction and meaning developed gradually through the negotiation process itself.[1] To use the imagery of Victor-Yves Ghebali, the drafting exercise was *une négotiation gigogne*, 'a kaleidoscope' of interlinking minor games implicating a multiplicity of structural or *ad hoc* coalitions.[2] Indeed, theoretically at least, one could be faced with a 'one against all' situation, one against thirty-four delegations.[3]

Already, from the initial five-day ceremonial opening, it was obvious that the Geneva second stage would be more difficult than anticipated in the closing stages of the Helsinki consultations. The message was clear from the opening statements of the Warsaw Pact foreign ministers at Helsinki that their aim would be to cling to their former positions which they had revised or abandoned at Dipoli so as to allow the much-desired conference to take place. Not even the ceremonial first phase was spared difficulties, as the Soviet Union pressed for a communiqué, which the West would accept only if it was purely factual. Then Malta refused to give its consent to the communiqué by re-opening the issue of the Mediterranean states, asking that the foreign ministers of Algeria and Tunisia be given the floor (in which it was supported by Spain). To complicate matters further, Israel also asked for the floor. Particularly indignant about the Maltese action was Soviet Foreign Minister Andrei Gromyko, who, to the alarm of the other participants, went so far as to suggest bypassing the consensus principle and adopting the communiqué without Maltese consent. In the end a compromise formula was devised and the communiqué was issued.[4]

The substantial second phase of the conference began in Geneva at the Palais des Nations on 18 September 1973, and ended, after arduous negotiations, some twenty-two months later, on 21 July 1975. The procedure followed was the most complicated and cumbersome ever to have been pursued in the CSCE process. It comprised a Co-ordinating Committee, the principal supervising body, three main commissions, corresponding to each basket/chapter, and five working groups. The three commissions/baskets were subdivided into eleven sub-commissions and one special working organ (on peaceful settlement of disputes), roughly corresponding to the various sub-chapters of the document.

In Geneva the most active, and in this sense the main architects of the Final Act and of the CSCE process, were the following: the Soviet delegation and the other delegations of the Eastern bloc, above all Romania, which saw in the conference a more independent role for itself (indeed Romania, contrary to the other Warsaw Pact delegations, distanced itself from the Soviet Union, and in matters other than Basket III acted as a neutral or non-aligned state); the then '9' states of the European Community (within the newly adopted institution of European Political Co-operation), which were the principal authors on human rights (Principle VII of the Final Act) and Basket III, notably the Netherlands (the toughest negotiator among them), Denmark, France (which played a leadership role in Geneva), Italy, the FRG, Belgium and the United Kingdom; the neutral and non-aligned states (NNA), which initiated with great difficulty what was to be throughout CSCE-I their role as bridge-builders, notably Austria, Switzerland, Sweden and Finland (the most guarded and equidistant of the NNA), with Yugoslavia active on a wide range of issues apart from national minorities, and Malta vociferous on the Mediterranean dimension. In contrast to Canada, which showed considerable interest, the attitude of the United States was more indifferent than at Dipoli, and the USA distinguished itself, as one author has put it, as 'an observer rather than as an active participant',[5] though it should be stressed that Washington lent its considerable weight on some very difficult subjects.[6]

We will now examine the Geneva phase of the Conference partially, with regard only to the human rights dimension, and other questions with a bearing on this, such as the normative character of the document, the fundamental decalogue of principles, and follow-up.

The debate on the normative character of the document took place with less intensity than at Dipoli, for it was obvious by then that a large majority of participants, including both blocs, was prepared to opt for a morally rather than a legally binding document. The main line was that the document would be compelling politically and morally, but not legally. What really mattered at the end of the day was not its legal or non-legal character, but the substance of the commitments. This was the view put forward in the first phase of the negotiations by, among others, the '9' (though France initially toyed with the idea of a minor legal document which would not require ratification), Greece, whose delegate stressed the morally and legally binding nature of the document, and the Eastern bloc. However, as various delegations put forward pet projects or supported certain texts, some taking the form of legally binding instruments – in particular Switzerland with its 'Draft Convention on a European System for the Peaceful Settlement of Disputes' – the matter took some time to be resolved.[7]

It was the United Kingdom and the United States which championed the idea of the document being cast as a 'Final Act', implying that it would not be legally binding (which is not necessarily the case, as seen with the Final Act of the Congress of Vienna, which is a treaty). But grey areas still remained which kept the United States, in particular, apprehensive. For good measure, the United States, the United Kingdom and the FRG initiated a clause regarding the non-susceptibility for registration of the Final Act under Article 102 of the Charter of the United Nations (which was finally included), to which the Soviet Union, Romania and Switzerland objected on the grounds that such 'negative' language was inappropriate and would denigrate the status of the final document.[8]

THE TEN PRINCIPLES

The texts to follow each of the ten principles as set out in the Blue Book led to hectic drafting exercises in the First Sub-Committee with almost every word or comma being negotiated at length. The Soviet delegation had not anticipated this, and was taken aback by the extended elaboration of the principles that took place.[9] The ten principles retained the titles agreed in the Blue Book, as follows: Principle I, 'sovereign equality, respect for the rights inherent in sovereignty'; Principle II, 'refraining from the threat or use of force'; Principle III, 'inviolability of frontiers'; Principle IV, 'territorial integrity of States'; Principle V, 'peaceful settlement of disputes'; Principle VI, 'non-intervention in internal affairs'; Principle VII, 'respect for human rights and fundamental freedoms, including the freedom of thought, conscience, religion or belief'; Principle VIII, 'equal rights and self-determination of peoples'; Principle IX, 'co-operation among States'; Principle X, 'fulfilment in good faith of obligations under international law'.

The principle on sovereign equality caused few problems of substance between East and West, but ended up including two new elements in addition to established UN language on the matter. They constituted two of the main compromises of the whole Final Act and were the outcome of protracted negotiations, both provisions intended for other sections of the final document. One was the right to determine one's 'laws and regulations' – to which the Soviet delegation wanted to add 'customs' as well – together with a state's right to choose 'its political, social, economic and cultural system'. The second was the well-known clause on the inviolability of frontiers (to be examined in its more proper context of Principle III, below).[10]

The Soviet Union and the other Eastern delegations did their utmost to place the internal law clause in the preamble of Basket III, arguing that all commitments in Basket III should be subject to a state's 'laws, regulations and customs'. But this blanket safety clause did not go through owing to Western and Neutral reaction. The final solution, known as the 'Finnish compromise' – because it was introduced by the Finnish delegation – made a general reference to all the principles in the Preamble of Basket III and added to Principle I the reference to the right of a state to determine its laws and regulations. The compromise was acceptable to the Neutrals and to the West only when it was agreed that a qualification be added, which was placed under Principle X, that '[i]n exercising their sovereign rights, including the right to determine their laws and regulations, they will conform with their legal obligations under international law' and 'pay due regard to and implement the provisions of the Final Act'.[11] Thus, as has been claimed, the overall solution largely nullified the gains to the Soviet Union.[12]

The negotiations on the second principle, threat or use of force, were also difficult, though the reading of the text does not suggest, as

Harold Russell points out, 'how much anguish was expended in arriving at this rather traditional result'.[13] This principle was one of the fields where two battles were fought. One was the issue of the Brezhnev Doctrine. The other was the question of Cyprus, for it was during the Conference in Geneva that Turkish military intervention in Cyprus and the subsequent occupation of a large area of the island took place. On the first question one of the main protagonists for a strong text was Romania, under its very able and articulate chief delegate, Valentin Lipatti. Given the acute problem in Cyprus, Greece was also active in pursuing a strong text (and was in contact on this with the Romanian delegation) and, assisted by Cyprus, tried to inject into the concept of 'pretext' a reference to use of force and invasion. On the other side, the Turkish delegation wanted wording that would permit military occupation on the basis of international law, which according to them would include the 1960 Treaty of Guarantee on Cyprus, the legal grounds on which Turkey had justified its action. Not surprisingly, both Turkey and the Soviet Union rejected the notion of 'pretext'. The eventual compromise on this question was reached in the final hours of the conference and was based on a Greek formula.[14]

It has generally been acknowledged that one of the most critical elements in the whole document was the inviolability of frontiers, which together with human rights and Basket III were the most contentious issues and the main claim of the Final Act to covering new ground in standard-setting. To the Soviet Union it was apparently 'the key to European security' and to a successful outcome of the Conference.[15] At the time, most outsiders to the CSCE considered the principle as a major defeat for the West and as ratifying the frontiers in Europe as they had emerged from the Second World War, including, of course, the annexation of the Baltic states. The Soviet Union was jubilant at its inclusion as a separate principle. In fact the worst possible consequence of this principle, and of the Final Act as a whole regarding frontiers, was that it was a recognition of a state of affairs that had already existed long before the adoption of the Final Act.[16]

Upon closer examination it is obvious that, contrary to Basket III and the human rights principle, the inviolability of frontiers, once accepted as a principle in its own right, shrank instead of expanding to meet the various voluminous drafts submitted by the Soviet delegation. Indeed, the final text on frontiers turned out to be the shortest in the principles section, only four and a half lines in all, while the human rights principle ended up being by far the longest text among the ten principles. In fact, it does not depart from earlier international arrangements on frontiers and adds nothing more to the recognition of existing frontiers in Europe.[17]

The inherent difficulty with the inviolability principle was how to marry two contrasting concepts: on the one hand, the ban on any change to frontiers sought by the Eastern countries, and on the other, the concept of peaceful change to frontiers, which was an equally new concept at the international normative level, whose main proponents were, for obvious reasons, the FRG (German reunification) and the '9', who were concerned with the possibility of future European integration.[18] It soon became clear that the Soviet delegation was not, in fact, against the notion as such, but could accept its inclusion so long as it would not be part of Principle III. Then, on the suggestion of the Spanish delegation, it was provisionally registered as a 'floating sentence'.[19]

The FRG had been careful to table a reservation permitting it to reopen the question of the wording of the floating sentence, for it felt that the draft severely limited the possibility of change of frontiers by imposing no less than three conditions for it to take place: international law, peaceful means, and agreement.[20] The FRG appealed to Secretary of State Kissinger to lend the weight of the United States at a high level, and the final agreement came after some six months, following repeated contacts between Soviet and United States delegates, including contacts between Kissinger and Gromyko. The most complete version of the various exchanges and drafts, involving the placement of commas and the words 'only' and 'international law', appears in an account by John J. Maresca, one of the United States delegates at the time. The last FRG proposal suggesting an alteration to a Soviet draft (in which the Soviets had changed a previous United States draft by agreeing to drop the word 'only') was simply to change the place of a comma, thereby rendering the mention of international law parenthetical, implying that international law is basic, to be taken for granted, and not a condition. Finally, it was decided to put this sentence under the principle of sovereign equality as one aspect of a state's right to its foreign affairs, in spite of a sharp reaction on the part of Romania.[21]

As for the inviolability of frontiers itself, there were no major difficulties between East and West, for Western countries also agreed that there should be no assault on frontiers. Thus Principle III ended with two short sentences as follows:

> The participating States regard as inviolable all one another's frontiers as well as the frontiers of all States in Europe and therefore they will refrain now and in the future from assaulting these frontiers. Accordingly, they will refrain from any demand for, or act of, seizure and usurpation of part or all of the territory of any participating State.

The Soviet delegation was careful to translate 'assault' into a Russian word with a broader concept (*posegat*). There was also some difficulty with the Soviet suggestion to include the word 'demand' in the second sentence. It was upon Yugoslavia's insistence that the inviolability principle was said to cover in the first sentence 'all one another's frontiers as well as the frontiers of all states in Europe', so that it could cover borders with Albania as well. This was strongly supported by, among others, those states with frontiers outside Europe, that is the United States, Canada and Turkey.[22] Finally, so as to retain the balance between the two concepts on frontiers – inviolability and peaceful change – but also in order to highlight the principle on human rights, the 'Guiding Principles' section concludes with the proviso that '[a]ll the principles set forth above are of primary significance and, accordingly, they will be equally and unreservedly applied, each of them being interpreted taking into account the others.'[23] The original grounds for such an idea are to be found in an early Greek proposal on 'the indivisibility and interdependence of the principles'.[24]

The main difficulty regarding the fourth principle, territorial integrity, was that several Western and NNA delegations were in favour of extending it beyond acts which involved the use of force. The concept of 'unity' was added to territorial integrity at the insistence of Yugoslavia, which, even in those days, feared separatist tendencies in its midst. The final sentence of this principle, on the unlawfulness of occupation and acquisition of territory (strongly supported for differing reasons by, among others, the United States, Romania, Greece and Cyprus), was the result of a British compromise solution to two strongly-worded proposals by Cyprus, on non-recognition of illicit territorial acquisitions, and Romania, on a ban on occupation, which was strongly opposed by the Soviet delegation.[25] It ran as follows:

> The participating States will likewise refrain from making each other's territory the object of military occupation or other direct or indirect measures of force in contravention of international law, or the object of acquisition by means of such measures or threat of them. No such acquisition will be recognized as legal.

Note that the Soviet Union mistakenly concluded that the use of the word 'will' made reference only to future situations, thus absolving it of its annexation of the three Baltic states. In fact 'will' is the standard wording for political texts such as the Final Act, corresponding to the use of 'shall' reserved for legal instruments.[26]

The fifth principle, the peaceful settlement of disputes, was one of the major disappointments of the Conference for most Western states, notably for Italy, Greece and for the initiator, Switzerland, whose proposal was an ambitious one providing for elaborate procedures for a compulsory peaceful settlement of all international disputes. The Eastern states considered that such a line infringed on state sovereignty, while more than one Western state was not prepared to entertain new voluntary methods for settling international disputes. It is of interest to note that despite the two specialized intercessional meetings that followed, one in Montreux and the other in Athens, and two important concluding documents from follow-up meetings (the Madrid and Vienna Documents), it was only at the Valletta Meeting of January 1991, that is in the aftermath of the adoption of the 'Charter of Paris for a New Europe', that a breakthrough was achieved, but even that was not as far-reaching as the original Swiss concept in Geneva, which comprised no less than sixty-one articles.[27]

The attempt to formulate a meaningful statement on the sixth principle, non-intervention, was a tightrope exercise for the West and the like-minded NNA delegations, in that it had to strike a balance by, on the one hand, banning any form of intervention along the lines of the Brezhnev Doctrine and, on the other, not providing the ideal excuse for preventing criticism and diplomatic initiatives for the violation of human rights and undertakings under Basket III. The West, assisted by the Neutrals, tried to do this by putting the emphasis of non-intervention on coercive action, that is along the classical approach followed in international law. However, the end result is not as clear as they would have wished. The second and third paragraphs can be seen as definitions of interventions along the coercion line, but can also be interpreted as illustrations of extreme cases of intervention which are unacceptable. The last paragraph of Principle VI refers to terrorism and engages participating states to 'refrain from direct or indirect assistance to terrorist activities, or to subversive or other activities directed towards the violent overthrow of the regime (*sic*) of another participating State'.[28]

The seventh principle, on human rights, was lengthy and elaborate despite a stringent all-Eastern reaction (here with Romania well in the Eastern boat). This principle, together with the eighth principle, on self-determination, will be examined later.

Negotiations on the text for the ninth principle were hectic because 'co-operation among States' touched on some of the fundamental differences between the two worlds. The Soviet Union and its allies tried to inject it with their philosophy of peaceful co-existence with co-operation as the duty of states, while the West was adamant in adding the individual to the process of co-operation. Despite Soviet resistance, it was finally decided that persons, institutions and organizations, in addition to governments, had 'a relevant and positive role to play in contributing toward the achievement' of the aims of their co-operation. Thus the individual and his or her activity were a factor in improving co-operation, in other words in enhancing good neighbourly relations, mutual understanding and peace.

The tenth principle, on fulfilling obligations under international law, was a source of some difficulty not only between East and West but also within the Western camp, due in particular to the appearance of restrictive French drafts which came to be supported by the Soviet Union. One of the main obstacles was differences among participants as to the sources of international law. The adopted text divides obligations under international law into two categories, those arising from the generally recognized principles of international law, and those arising from treaties or other agreements. This obscured the real problem, which is how the first category of sources becomes binding. According to Western countries, it is binding if it is generally accepted by a large majority of states, while for the Soviet Union and its allies some kind of acknowledgement, however tacit, was needed from *all* states.[29]

The principles section ends with a series of paragraphs intended to tie up various loose ends, and to emphasize further the importance of the principles. On the whole, the principles section was substantial in that it did not strictly adhere to the lowest common denominator and did not become, as the Soviet Union had wanted, simply a solemn acknowledgement of the Soviet position and their territorial gains in Europe. This will become more evident as we examine the principle on human rights. In fact, as Luigi Ferraris, a participant and commentator, has pointed out, 'in practice there was an attempt to attain the maximum allowed and realistically achievable within the present state of international relations'.[30]

THE PRINCIPLES OF HUMAN RIGHTS AND SELF-DETERMINATION

The human rights dimension or individual dimension is covered in the Final Act by Principle VII, by Principle VIII on self-determination (the only generally accepted human right of a collectivity), by the mention of the role of persons in Principle IX on co-operation and, of course, in

Basket III. The most protracted and difficult negotiations for texts as far as the human dimension was concerned were those in Basket III, particularly the provisions on human contacts and information, but, strangely enough, not so much in Principle VII on human rights, which contained equally explosive commitments for the Eastern countries. This is not to say that agreement on Principle VII was swift. It took some three months and the largest number of sessions in the negotiations on principles for this to come about. The successful outcome was attributable to the concerted efforts of the West and the NNA, in particular to the delegations of Switzerland, the United Kingdom and Italy, to the Holy See on religious freedom, and to Yugoslavia regarding the paragraph on national minorities. Moreover, the Soviet Union was not as intransigent as had been expected. Apparently, after it became obvious that they could not succeed with a short text, the view prevailed that the mention of the UN Covenants with their well-known safety clauses and the balance between the two generations of human rights would be sufficient protection.[31]

Apart from national minorities, the following proposals proved particularly difficult to agree upon: religious freedom, proposed by the Holy See and strongly supported by the great majority of delegations; information about human rights and the participation of individuals and organizations in the promotion of human rights, proposed by the United Kingdom; protection against arbitrary arrest and safeguarding the spiritual and physical integrity of the individual, proposed by Switzerland; the banning of actions against human rights by one state against individuals of another state, proposed by Cyprus and reformulated by Switzerland as a ban on reprisals violating fundamental human rights.[32]

The proposal on religious freedom was drafted very broadly by the Holy See to include full enjoyment 'alone or in community with others, of freedom of thought, conscience, religion or belief'. The Soviet delegation could not easily accept a third appearance of religious freedom (it already appeared in the title of the principle and in the first paragraph, which also included a non-discrimination clause mentioning religion). They tried to limit religious liberties to freedom of worship and not to include 'thought' or 'belief', even though this placed them in the awkward position of having Western delegates arguing for the rights of non-believers as well. The final compromise was reached after a series of contacts between the delegates of the Holy See and the Soviet Union, with the final wording being that 'the participating States will recognize and respect the freedom of the individual to profess and practise, alone or in community with others, religion or belief acting in

28

accordance with the dictates of his own conscience'. The Soviets tampered with the Russian translation, making 'belief' appear as 'faith', paying no heed to Western complaints.[33]

The British proposals ended as the following brief formulation, which was a Maltese compromise wording to save the concept: 'They confirm the right of the individual to know and act upon his rights and duties in this field.' The Swiss proposal on personal liberties and the ban on arbitrary arrests were lost, save for a mention in the last part of the second paragraph on the effective exercise of human rights: that they are 'essential' for a person's 'free and full development'. The Cypriot, later Swiss reformulation on reprisals came at the beginning of the sixth paragraph with the obscure formulation that '[t]hey will constantly respect these rights and freedoms in their mutual relations …'.[34]

The proposal on national minorities was part of a wider Yugoslav proposal, one aspect of which was introduced within the context of Principle VII. In contrast to the state of affairs in the CSCE since the mid-1980s, the concept was now not very popular. The delegations of several countries fought against the proposal or were instrumental in weakening it, including Greece, France, Belgium, Bulgaria, Spain, and to some extent also Portugal, the United Kingdom, Romania and Turkey. Support, lukewarm rather than enthusiastic, was voiced by the Soviet Union, Hungary, the GDR, Austria and Italy. One of the first delegations to stand against the inclusion of minorities was that of Greece, which suggested that the great sensitivity of the matter would not permit the negotiators to arrive at a generally acceptable formulation.[35]

When it was finally agreed to cover the issue of national minorities, Yugoslavia proposed the following wording:

> The participating States respect the interests of national, ethnic and linguistic minorities and their right to free development, in such a way that such minorities might contribute to free development, of friendship and co-operation between the countries and peoples concerned.

Yugoslavia as well as Turkey was attached to the concept of 'national minority', which they regarded as referring to minorities whose wider nation already had an independent state of its own or whose 'brother' nation formed a component part of a federation. Others, like the Soviet Union, were in favour of the concept of 'ethnic group'. Italy preferred a reference to 'minorities' in general.

Three elements in the Yugoslav draft were generally unacceptable. First was the obvious collective character of the right, drafted by Yugoslavia as rights of a minority as a whole; second was the element of 'interests'; and third the wording derived from the familiar Yugoslav concept of minorities as bridges of friendship between countries (a concept supported also by the Turkish delegation). Greece produced a counter-proposal, nullifying the essence of the Yugoslav paragraph, as follows: 'The participating States respect the legitimate interests of people belonging to national minorities already recognized by bilateral treaties or by international legislation.' The initial compromise text was somewhere between the two extreme positions, more appropriately worded along human rights lines, not 'interests':

> The participating States will respect the rights of persons belonging to such minorities to equality before the law, will afford them with the full opportunity for the actual enjoyment of human rights and fundamental freedoms and will, in this manner, protect their individual and collective interests.

The final wording on national minorities included the cryptic phrase 'on whose territory national minorities exist', and, in view of the French difficulties with 'collective interests', the Greek formula of 'legitimate interests' was taken on board.[36]

The principle of self-determination of peoples was championed first and foremost by the FRG, which saw it as a *sine qua non*. The obvious aim was to facilitate future German reunification. Bonn's emphasis was on what is termed 'external' self-determination, the right of peoples to independence or union. The Soviet Union regarded the inclusion of self-determination in a European setting as absurd, since there were no colonies (with the exception of the *sui generis* case of Gibraltar) and all states/peoples were already independent. Multinational states such as Canada and Yugoslavia, but also more ethnically homogeneous ones such as Greece, called for the inclusion of a 'balancing element' that would not extend, however unintentionally, self-determination to national minorities or give licence to the dissolution of federal states.[37]

The Greek delegation suggested the term 'inalienable' be added to the principle, to render it constant and not 'once and for all', also proposing that self-determination should not lead to the violation of human rights (having in mind its proposal on the interdependence between the principles).[38] The need for constant choice was stressed by other Western delegations, particularly by the Netherlands, but was resisted by the Soviet Union on the basis that there can be no advance blessing to any change, for some changes could be unacceptable, such as, it argued, changes for the worse.[39]

The Soviet delegation presented a short draft which covered only one aspect of self-determination as it appears in UN texts, the 'internal' one, and this only in part, the right of peoples to choose their government and political and social system. There followed a French draft which filled in the missing aspect of 'internal' self-determination, namely enjoyment outside interference from without. But it was Yugoslavia and the Netherlands that offered more thorough texts which went further than the relevant UN provisions on self-determination. Yugoslavia's draft included the thrust of both the 'internal' and 'external' aspects, stressing, among others, the 'universal significance' of the principle and the 'eradication of any form of subjugation or of subordination contrary to the will of the peoples concerned'. The Netherlands draft contained two innovative elements: self-determination as the right of a people 'to choose, to develop, to adapt or to change' its political and other systems without interference, and the element of 'respect for human rights'.[40]

The Hungarian delegation provided a compromise draft which was a good attempt at balancing the various divergent views. The element of 'external' self-determination dear to the FRG was included in the term 'all nations have the right to formulate their own internal and *external* political status' (emphasis added). The Soviet Union was granted the colonial dimension it wanted, by a reference to 'suppressing of any form of racial and national oppression of people in all parts of the world'. The element of freedom of choice wanted by the West and the Neutrals was also included. But the text, upon closer examination, appeared static, in the sense that all the European nations had exhausted the basic element of self-determination, and it now remained for them to develop as they chose.[41]

The United Kingdom delegation presented another compromise text. With the assistance of the Canadian and Italian delegations, the elements of 'inalienable' and 'constant choice' were presented as 'all peoples, always have the right, in full freedom, to determine, when and as they wish, their internal and external political status, without external interference'. The Soviet delegation could accept this, though it made sure that the word 'always' was translated into Russian so as to mean 'now and henceforth', thus excluding actions such as the Soviet intervention in Czechoslovakia in 1968. However, it was not satisfied with the formulation on the colonial aspect, which had followed the Yugoslav phrase, the 'elimination of all forms of opposition against

31

peoples'.[42] Finally, a compromise was reached between Yugoslavia and the Soviet Union which reads very oddly at the end of Principle VII, as follows: 'they also recall the importance of the elimination of any form of violation of this principle' – this is mere tautology.[43]

There remained the question of how to formulate the 'balancing element', for there was general agreement on quelling secession and external support to secession. Negotiations were informal, taking place outside the official sessions among the various interested delegations, mainly Greece, Romania, Spain, Canada and Cyprus. The Greek delegation came up with a strong wording on the banning of the total or partial dismemberment of a state based on the UN Friendly Relations Declaration of 1970, which did not go through largely because of strong opposition from the FRG.[44] Since it was an attempt to address different and controversial problems under one umbrella, progress was not immediate. However, the final phrase was simple enough. It was a reference to the UN Charter and the norms of international law, 'including those relating to territorial integrity of States'.[45]

BASKET III

Negotiations in Basket III, and particularly those on human contacts and on information, were the most protracted and arduous of the whole Geneva Conference. They started on 28 March 1973 and ended over two years later on 8 June 1975, and at times put the whole CSCE enterprise in jeopardy. The thrust of Basket III was simply unacceptable to the East, who could not go beyond notions of bilateral co-operation on specific humanitarian cases and on cultural, educational and other exchanges mainly between government institutions.[46]

In these negotiations the Eastern bloc, sensing the danger, was markedly more cohesive than in any other drafting committee. Romania, though still making a point of speaking on its own, was fully in line with its Warsaw Pact allies. So, equally, was Hungary, which had frequently taken a more liberal line in Basket II (Hungary and Poland gave the impression that they were more flexible than the rest of the Eastern delegations). A characteristic illustration of the negative attitude of the Warsaw Pact members towards Basket III, and also Principle VII, was the fact that in the closing speeches given at Helsinki by their heads of state or government on the adoption of the Final Act (Phase III of the Conference), no mention was made of Basket III or Principle VII.[47]

Basket III, particularly its first two chapters, was chiefly an achievement of the '9'. This is not say that the '9' and the NATO group were not without their differences, particularly as to tactics, namely how far to push the Eastern delegations without risking the total collapse of the talks. For the '9' the Conference was their first major opportunity to make their mark as a cohesive group in foreign policy (on the basis of the Davignon formula for co-ordinating their foreign policy in what was known as European Political Co-operation, EPC). Among the '9' those particularly active in Basket III were the Netherlands, the most hard-line of the negotiators on the Western side; Denmark, mainly concerned with human contacts; the United Kingdom, somewhat more flexible and mainly responsible for information; Italy, somewhat more subtle than the Netherlands, but almost equally firm; France, which in its attempt to play a leadership role in the '9' throughout the Conference, tried to limit the differences within and across blocs in Basket III; Belgium, which was firm; and the FRG, which then and throughout the Cold War was characterized by a cautious step-by-step approach on the human dimension.[48]

The polarization between East and West limited the role of the NNA delegations as potential bridge-builders. This was probably partly because most of the NNA delegations were, rightly, seen by the East as ideologically committed to the Western approach on Basket III questions.[49] According to one assessment, among the NNA the most pro-East was Yugoslavia, the most pro-West were Austria, Sweden and Switzerland, while the most equidistant of all was Finland.[50]

When the talks began, the Soviet Union tried to avoid discussions altogether, using various delaying tactics, such as that negotiations could not commence before some vital issues in the First Sub-Committee on principles were finalized. When this line could bear no more fruit, they switched to a demand for one consolidated text in Basket III, which would have the character of a recommendation and not an agreement and the need for a preamble which would include sovereign equality, non-intervention in internal affairs and respect for internal legislation. The West reacted by, among other things, stressing the need for a substantial text of commitments opening new avenues and methods of co-operation, which if need be would lead to changes in internal legislation. They also attacked the selective presentation from the 'Guiding Principles', which, they argued, consisted of inter-related norms, equally worthy of respect.[51] The obvious *quid pro quo* evident by March 1974 was for the West to give in to a preamble, and the East to accept that reference would be made to all the principles as the basis of co-operation in this field. However, the 'all-embracing package' suggested by the Finnish delegation, which in effect did not go very far in diluting the essence of the following text, took several more months to materialize, being accepted in late July 1974.[52]

But then came the difficult question: to what extent would the acceptance of the preamble mean tangible progress in the text which followed. Western hopes were soon to be frustrated, as the Soviet and other Eastern delegations resisted one text after another, particularly in the human contacts and information sub-chapters, and tried to base agreement on a strict interpretation of the consensus procedure, which would amount to either rejecting provisions or watering them down considerably. Talks reached a dangerous stalemate as late as spring 1975. The Soviet delegation appealed to Western delegations for agreement 'now or never', giving the impression that a breakdown was possible. Kissinger descended on several Western European capitals trying to impress on his colleagues that the CSCE had to be settled as soon as possible. However, the policy of the Western states to continue to push the East as far as possible and not to give in too soon prevailed.[53] Progress was finally made from 29 May 1975 onwards, under the co-ordination of the Austrian delegate for human contacts and the Swiss for information, with sessions stretching sometimes well into the night in 'the room of miracles', as it was jokingly called.[54]

THE QUESTION OF CSCE FOLLOW-UP

The question of follow-up which had bedevilled the initial discussions during the MPT was also a cause of considerable concern in Geneva. At Geneva the Soviet Union played second fiddle, having abandoned the idea of encouraging anything permanent or a special organ, apparently wary about how the whole CSCE enterprise was developing, with its substantial emphasis on human rights and humanitarian issues (Basket III). The United States, and to some extent France, did not even favour a follow-up. The final compromise was the result of the persistence and tenacity of smaller states in all three groups, the NNA as a whole and Romania, supported by Norway, Spain and Canada.[55]

A Yugoslav proposal submitted in March 1974 envisaged a so-called 'Continuing Committee', to be established with the aim of co-ordinating, initiating and reviewing activity linked with the implementation of CSCE decisions and initiating further co-operation by periodic meetings of representatives of states. Denmark, the EC country most concerned with continuation, supported a 'technical secretariat', while the FRG advocated *ad hoc* experts' meetings. (It is interesting to note the similarity between these ideas and the institutionalization in the

CSCE since November 1990.) In April 1974, a Danish compromise proposal expressed the views of the '9' and the NATO group (with a lukewarm France). It called vaguely for 'unilateral, bilateral and multilateral measures to implement decisions', and for a meeting of high officials of the participating states to review progress in implementation and in improving relations, and then to submit proposals, including possible additional meetings of experts or a new conference. Romania stressed the need to include in any institutionalized follow-up some sort of implementation of the decisions reached. Ironically, for those days, the West was resolutely against this, the main reason apparently being that it feared that the East would use the lack of a permanent organ as an excuse for not implementing Basket III and confidence-building measures.[56]

The final outcome was nearer to the Danish/'9' approach, which was more palatable to the two superpowers. The idea of 'new measures' (that is, new standard-setting) was taken out, but the other worthwhile ingredient of the CSCE, an implementation review, was included. The preamble of the Follow-up chapter reflected the views of the NNA, and the operative part the views of the '9'. It declared the 'resolve' to proceed to 'a thorough implementation of the provisions of the Final Act', 'the deepening of their mutual relations' and 'the development of the process of *détente* in the future'. The question of continuity and follow-up had gained a foothold, 'albeit in an indirect way',[57] since the 'first' meeting was to take place in Belgrade, which implied that there would be more such meetings. Note also that at least one more lesser meeting was assured after the Belgrade Follow-up, that on the peaceful settlement of disputes.

The Geneva phase of the conference finally concluded its task at 3.44 p.m. on 21 July 1975.

THE FINAL ACT: SIGNIFICANCE, NORMATIVE CHARACTER AND CONTENT

The Final Act, or Helsinki Final Act as it is more commonly known, was adopted by signature by the 'High Representatives', that is the heads of state or government, of the thirty-five states on 1 August 1975.

The Final Act was in many respects 'without any precedent in diplomatic history',[58] 'an unusual document which defies all comparison'.[59] J.E.S. Fawcett has graphically described it as having 'the body of a treaty, the legs of a resolution, and the head of declaration of intent', and concludes that 'those who refer to the Act as the Helsinki

Agreement are legally inexact but politically correct'.[60] It is unique in the 'number of problems it deals with, the diversity of principles expounded by it, the multitude of rules it expresses, and the programs it formulates',[61] and, not least, in the solemnity with which it was drafted and the manner in which it was adopted, all indicating the importance attributed to its undertakings.[62] The Final Act was not a document of commitments made under pressure in order to meet an urgent need, but an expression of the political will and common aims of the participating states, irrespective of ideological and other major differences. Thus from the normative viewpoint, the document, in being a product of international negotiations on the basis of a consensus procedure, contains only what the participants 'wanted to be included'[63] (even though, as any CSCE negotiator knows only too well, this is 'legal reality', not reality).

It is generally accepted that the Final Act and the subsequent CSCE documents are not legally binding in the sense that they do not give ground for a claim for reparation or for judicial remedies for non-performance.[64] They are, however, 'authoritative and controlling for the parties'.[65] The provisions contained in the Final Act are binding politically and morally and legitimate peaceful 'political action to obtain performance'.[66] It is a document of 'soft law', of a 'programmatic character',[67] a 'program for peace',[68] as seen from its content and wording but also from the various statements made by heads of state or government on its adoption.[69] Failure to fulfil such obligations entails loss of prestige and credibility and runs counter to the aims of friendly relations.[70] On the other hand, it can hardly be claimed that the Final Act is devoid of any 'legal effect'.[71] Indeed, the commitments therein are of 'great legal significance',[72] equipped with a unique juridical power,[73] either by having to be related to or interpreted by reference to relevant international law principles, or as evidence of emerging rules of customary international law, or authoritative interpretations and clarifications of ambiguous international norms.[74] The signatory states are obliged to implement the Final Act and subsequent CSCE undertakings, unilaterally, bilaterally by negotiations with other participating states, as well as multilaterally.

The themes of the Final Act of the CSCE are placed under three main chapters (the three baskets) and two smaller ones. Basket I bears the somewhat misleading title of 'Questions Relating to Security', and deals with two distinct issues, the 'Declaration of Principles' and security matters, basically with CBMs (Confidence-Building Measures).[75] Under the principles chapter, and following the ten principles, is a sub-chapter which deals with the principle of peaceful settlement of disputes, which has no real substance and concludes that a meeting is to be scheduled after the follow-up (the Belgrade Follow-up).

Basket II is entitled 'Co-operation in the Field of Economics, of Science and Technology and of the Environment'. The title of Basket III is 'Co-operation in Humanitarian and Other Fields', and it includes four sub-chapters: 'Human Contacts', 'Information', 'Co-operation and Exchanges in the Field of Culture' and 'Co-operation and Exchanges in the Field of Education'. The most important chapter, 'Human Contacts', includes the following sub-chapters after the preamble: 'Reunification of families', 'Marriage between citizens of different states', 'Travel for personal or professional reasons', 'Improvement of conditions for tourism on individual or collective basis', 'Meetings among young people' and 'Sport'. Also included were three separate paragraphs without titles worth mentioning, which were distinguished from the rest of the text by way of asterisks: on contacts, meetings and exchange of information between 'religious faiths, institutions and organizations', under 'Human Contacts'; and on 'national minorities and regional cultures', under the sub-chapters on culture and education.

The ten principles of the Final Act are by their very nature of a higher order than the remaining commitments (harder soft law, as it were). To draw a parallel from internal law, the Principles function more or less as the constitution, the rest as laws and other measures. All ten are principles of international law, most are no less than peremptory norms (*jus cogens*), for instance, the non-use of force. This distinction is also suggested by the fact that other CSCE commitments following the section on principles are phrased in more lenient terms, and now and again denote their adherence to, or inspiration from, the Principles.

The Principles are characterized in the Final Act as being of 'primary significance' in guiding relations between participating states. Furthermore, they 'will be equally and unreservedly applied, each of them being interpreted taking into account the others', which implies *a contrario*, as Emmanuel Decaux points out, that an insistence on one principle should be avoided, for it will create an imbalance.[76]

The ten principles differ in several respects from the seven principles of the UN 'Friendly Relations Declaration' of 1970, by among other things: (a) introducing two new principles of inter-state relations – human rights obligations and the inviolability of frontiers; (b) splitting one principle into two, namely non-use of force and territorial integrity, thereby highlighting the latter; and (c) including or excluding elements from the principles existing in both texts, thus placing greater emphasis on some aspects and less on others.

THE HUMAN DIMENSION IN THE FINAL ACT

The core of the human rights dimension of the Final Act and of subsequent CSCE documents until the Vienna Follow-up Meeting which adopted the all-embracing concept of 'human dimension' was Principle VII and the 'Human Contacts' chapter of Basket III. But, generally speaking, Principle VII and the whole of Basket III were regarded, particularly by legal experts, as 'the human rights undertakings' proclaimed by the Helsinki Final Act. Another, until recently neglected, issue within the wider human rights dimension is self-determination as enshrined in Principle VIII, a question of seminal importance in today's Europe and one, I would argue, in urgent need of further elaboration.[77] On the whole, the dual approach to the human dimension, one via Principle VII, the other through Basket III, was a more or less deliberate manoeuvre, which served the Western side well in the CSCE during the Cold War.[78]

As is well known, human rights are not very prominent in the UN Charter, hence the need for the pace-setting Universal Declaration of 1948, and the array of legal instruments initiated by the UN Commission on Human Rights. Yet at the time of the Helsinki/Geneva Conference on Security and Co-operation in Europe, the case could still be made in favour of domestic jurisdiction and non-interference. By and large, there was at the time 'no resolution of these diverse views and no authoritative definition of the human rights obligations of states' under the UN Charter.[79] Simply, most states appeared to support the view that 'a consistent pattern of gross violations of human rights',[80] such as apartheid and other forms of racial discrimination, genocide, slavery, or torture, in addition to being violations of particular conventions with regard to the state-parties, were also violations of the UN Charter, if not of customary international law, binding on all states.[81]

Thus, it was in the Helsinki Final Act, and in the CSCE process that it spawned, that respect for human rights was first recognized unequivocally, at the multi-state level, as 'an essential factor for peace', as one of the main norms of friendly relations and co-operation between states, as against a rigid interpretation of the norm of non-intervention in internal affairs.[82] With the Final Act there was a basis for arguing that concern for human rights was not to be interpreted as a violation of the principle on non-interference in domestic jurisdiction, but as a legitimate international concern.[83] With the Final Act the basis was set for seeking information, exchanging views, negotiating or making diplomatic representations to a participating state about its compliance or non-compliance, and monitoring such compliance,[84] which many years later led to the adoption of the CSCE human dimension mechanism. However, as Walter Tornopolsky points out, in the Final Act the main emphasis is on conforming with universal human rights requirements, irrespective of the system of government. It is 'conformity to standards, not conformity to methods'.[85] (This limited, permissive approach was abandoned after the adoption of the Copenhagen Document in June 1990.)

Non-intervention as it appears under Principle VI of the Final Act follows, by and large, the traditional international law approach of 'unlawful dictatorial interference' (not all-embracing, as conceived by Soviet legal experts in those days), that is, one which is backed by the threat or use of force. It is based, according to Gaetano Arangio-Ruíz, on coercion, be it military, political or economic, 'with the wrongful purpose of securing undue advantages for the intervening State'.[86]

Principle VII expresses the Western approach to human rights, which stresses the pre-eminence of civil and political rights ('first generation rights'). In this respect, and in that it keeps safety clauses to an absolute minimum, it follows the line of the UN Universal Declaration of Human Rights.[87] Economic, social and cultural rights are mentioned only in passing, and this has been the case with subsequent CSCE documents, despite repeated attempts by the Eastern bloc to correct the imbalance.[88]

As for Principle VIII, on equal rights and self-determination of peoples, it is not as innocuous as it appears at first sight, but breaks some new ground when compared with the relevant provisions in the UN Charter (articles 1 and 55), with the 1966 UN covenants on human rights (article 1) and, particularly, with the UN Friendly Relations Declaration of 1970. According to Antonio Cassese, who specializes in the legal aspects of self-determination, the Final Act 'gives a definition of self-determination that breaks new ground in international relations'.[89] Its originality is not to be found in the 'external' aspect of self-determination – there its basic merit is its comprehensiveness – but in the 'internal' aspect, where it allows for 'the permanent possibility for a people to choose a new social and political regime, to adapt the social and political structure to meet new demands'.[90] It is a 'continuing right', to be exercised in 'full freedom', meaning when human rights are respected, in this case mainly freedom of expression.[91]

Basket III is drafted in less committing language and is replete with escape clauses, as a result of the well-known Eastern opposition to it, but this in no way diminishes its great significance. Contrary to Principle VII, which 'restates classical absolutes', Basket III contains 'more modest undertakings'.[92] In this distinction between the two aspects of the CSCE human dimension one can see the difference between the 'absolute' approach, which was to be spearheaded in the future CSCE process by the United States, and the 'gradualist approach' embodied in Basket III, which was to be the line followed by most Western European states, and most of all by the FRG.[93]

Generally, Basket III commitments can be seen as the applied side of Principle VII, and are for the most part 'narrower in scope and more specific in terms of the goals they attempt to achieve'.[94] To follow our previous analogy between constitutional norms and laws and regulations, Principle VII could be seen as the constitutional norm and Basket III its detailed applied aspect, the rules and regulations.

Thus, to conclude, the human rights dimension of the Final Act and of the CSCE it initiated is one of its main claims to perpetuity: first, by upgrading human rights commitments in the realm of inter-state relations as a matter of legitimate international concern; second, by imposing through the years more exacting commitments than those existing in the international law of human rights; third, by functioning as a time bomb – or as a 'Trojan horse', as the Eastern states had complained – introducing into the European context, and notably in Eastern Europe, respect for human rights, and keeping up the momentum, even at the risk of destroying the whole process and marring East–West relations.

On the whole, the Final Act was 'profoundly Western in letter and spirit', as Vojtech Mastny has argued, and in exchange for pledging its respect 'for the geopolitical realities Moscow deemed essential for its security' made 'domestic conduct a legitimate subject of international scrutiny', hardly a reason for the Soviet Union to feel triumphant at the outcome.[95]

THE CSCE DURING THE COLD WAR
(1975–86): AN OVERVIEW

IN THE DOLDRUMS

The CSCE ran into dangerous waters soon after its inauguration because of the decrease in what had been known as *détente*, and the reason for the Conference in the first place. Following the failure of the first Follow-up Meeting in Belgrade, in 1978, the CSCE was in the doldrums, so much so that one was tempted to follow Herbert Marcuse's view on acronyms,[1] that their main function is to conceal and forget goals which they cannot meet – in the case of the CSCE, 'co-operation', 'security', 'Europe'. Yet perhaps, above all, it was the looming shadow of the Soviet Union associated with the origin of the idea for a security conference which had nearly given the new-born process a kiss of death. But die it would not, though it almost went into oblivion. In fact, after Belgrade and despite an even worse East–West climate, by the 1980s it had found a way to produce far from negligible results in the form of new commitments, while at the same time pursuing its implementation review that rendered non-compliance increasingly difficult to uphold.

To be fair, this relative lack of interest in the CSCE was not completely unjustified, particularly as regards the period from 1978 until 1987, from the Belgrade Meeting until halfway into the Vienna Follow-up Meeting. This bad image can be attributed to several inter-related reasons. One was the fact that even though there had been no use of force against a CSCE participating state since the signing of the Final Act (the last being the military interventions of the Soviet Union and Turkey, in Czechoslovakia and Cyprus respectively), this 'no war' situation could hardly be seen as having led to the creation of a putative 'regime' in Europe, let alone of a security system, in spite of the exacting *décalogue* of principles which prompted some analysts, mainly from Eastern Europe, to define it in such terms. Remember the fears of intervention in Poland in the early 1980s and military intervention by a

CSCE state, the Soviet Union, in a non-CSCE state, Afghanistan. The two alliances reinforced their arms arsenal and rearranged their battle positions, at the same time reformulating their strategic doctrines – the United States in particular, whose barrack-room scientists were bent on making nuclear war acceptable, as if the war of ideas could be a gladiatorial struggle where might would be right. (Fortunately for beleaguered mankind, the force of ideas has more than once proved more powerful than power politics, senseless leaders and the cold steel of arms.)

Related to this was a second factor, the actual extent of East–West polemics during CSCE meetings, mostly prompted – it should be admitted – by the uncompromising, often virulent Western attacks on Eastern practices. A third factor compromising the CSCE was that not only was there a lack of a common value system, but neither was there any prospect of accepting the other side, let alone any emerging degree of respect for the other side's world-view. A fourth reason is particularly relevant to the most controversial area, the human dimension: that the commitments in this sphere for the most part were not implemented by the Eastern countries. In fact, they *could* hardly be implemented by the Eastern states without undermining their whole edifice. Another factor prompting lack of interest was probably the particular output and style of the whole affair, notably CSCE's frustratingly slow pace, long duration and arcane procedures in negotiations for texts, and what seemed in comparison modest results in new commitments, at least until the mid-1980s.

CSCE AND *DÉTENTE*

The coming of the CSCE represented, as one author has put it, 'an institutionalization of *détente*'.[2] The professed objectives of the Final Act and of the process it spawned were to promote 'better relations among themselves' and 'to make détente both a continuing and an increasingly viable and comprehensive process'.[3] The CSCE was there on paper in order to uphold and foster *détente*. Yet it could do no such thing. *Détente* proved evanescent, for it was only skin deep. There was no firm ground in the European cosmos on which to build untrammelled relations across the East–West divide. Thus the ink was hardly dry on the signatures of the thirty-five heads of state or government (some of them famous, others infamous, including those that lasted in power the longest, Jivkov and Ceauşescu) than *détente* gave way to a more bitter East–West clash, what some came to define as the Second

Cold War. The CSCE, like all other inter-governmental forums with superpower participation during the Cold War, reflected, in one way or another, the existing East–West conflict, but this was even more the case for the CSCE. Indeed, the CSCE was mainly an attempt at a dialogue between opposing blocs, rather than deliberations among sovereign and independent states 'outside military alliances', as was stipulated, with a tinge of idealism, in the Helsinki rules of procedure. As East faced West in the CSCE, with twenty-three out of the thirty-five participating states belonging to one of two rival blocs, it became the international forum *par excellence* where East confronted West.

Yet, as the CSCE process somehow continued and did not come to a halt, many came to accept the conventional wisdom that talks between East and West in such meetings, however non-existent the dialogue, were somehow better than no talks at all. This notion was implicit in the original reasoning behind the idea of a conference within the East–West divide. However, around the CSCE's tenth anniversary, the conclusion of most thoughtful commentators was against the argument that stressing incompatible difficulties was a useful exercise. It could hardly be claimed that the CSCE spurred greater inter-governmental co-operation across the East–West divide. Even traditional theorists, proponents of the Realist Paradigm in International Relations such as K.J. Holsti, concluded that 'the CSCE has been a source of inter-national conflict, not a mechanism for either coping with it or trans-cending it'.[4] This was also the assessment of one of the foremost international relations specialists on human rights, the late R.J. Vin-cent.[5] One could not but reach the conclusion, in those days, that the CSCE was not only a dreary diplomatic conference, but worse, that it fanned the flames of the Cold War with remarkable abandon.

However, as Mastny has pointed out (to his credit, even before the Vienna Meeting which started in November 1986), 'these appearances are deceptive of the actual performance of a mechanism that is in important ways more productive than the mechanism of the United Nations'.[6] Mastny, and a few other scholars and delegates at CSCE meetings, were more optimistic about the positive results of confronta-tion, at least as far as Western interests were concerned, clearly implying that the loser was bound to be the communist world, as one CSCE undertaking after another piled up against it. Yet such an optimistic view was not based so much on the actual facts at the time, but perhaps above all on sheer faith, or what others would call ideology or ideological faith. (Note, incidentally, that within the evolution of scientific knowledge, faith is regarded, notably by Thomas Kuhn, as the ultimate reason for switching *en masse* to a new scientific paradigm if the older one is found wanting and is being challenged by alternative paradigms.⁷)

CSCE AS A PROCESS: A TALE OF SEVERAL CITIES

The CSCE, in being a process comprised of several distinct, associated and interlinked meetings, is a tale of several cities. Before 1990 the CSCE was an institution without institutions. Until then, all attempts at institutionalization were regarded as anathema, particularly by Western participants. The CSCE, said the purists, 'is a process', no more, no less, rightly pointing out that therein lay its main power.

Of course, therein also lay a danger. From 1975 until the Paris Summit, the continuation of the Helsinki process, though often taken for granted, was not totally assured since it was based on the concluding document of each new follow-up meeting. This was particularly the case until the adoption of the Madrid Concluding Document, which, *expressis verbis*, recognized the principle of 'regular' further meetings.⁸ The rationale was that the process would continue only as long as it could produce results; it had to deliver, otherwise it could be terminated. For most Western states concrete results meant above all two things: on the one hand, new, more detailed commitments, particularly on security, human rights and humanitarian issues (what was officially called, somewhat cryptically by Western delegates, 'a balanced approach', a well-known CSCE phrase meant for different things on different occasions, to suit a variety of concerns); on the other hand, the various commitments had to be lived up to, notably those on the human dimension. Otherwise, over the CSCE hung a Damoclean sword, however invisible. The process could be brought to a halt by the refusal to consent to another follow-up.

As we know, this did not happen, even though the majority of Eastern countries did not ameliorate their human rights position until the late 1980s. Ironically, however, as the years went by, this came to be the secret wish of several Eastern rather than Western states. Certainly, one reason for the acquiescence of the hard-liners among Western states was that the various CSCE meetings provided an invaluable opportunity for putting the Eastern countries in the dock. This was the approach of the United States, which saw this as its main goal in the human dimension field. Indeed, the United States tended to regard new standard-setting as largely unnecessary and perhaps even as endorsing non-compliance, by 'substituting new provisions for carrying out previous agreements'.⁹ But most of the other Western states rightly attached greater importance to the adoption of more exacting

44

standards, in order to build up the original pro-Western Helsinki edifice on the human dimension. This last development could in the short term alleviate the plight of some individuals or groups and was the main preoccupation of the FRG, which has traditionally spearheaded the moderates within NATO and the European Community, assisted by France, Denmark, Ireland, Greece and Spain. In the long term, such undertakings could also have destabilizing effects on Eastern political systems.[10]

Under the original, pure-process-type non-institutionalized CSCE which existed until the Paris Charter (November 1990), four broad categories of meetings were held: main conferences; follow-up meetings; important intercessional meetings between follow-ups, usually called conferences, such as the Stockholm CDE Conference or the Conference on the Human Dimension; and smaller intercessional meetings. This fourth category comprises 'meetings of experts', such as the Athens Meeting of Experts on the Peaceful Settlement of Disputes, or simply 'meetings', such as the Sofia Meeting on the Protection of the Environment, as well as lesser events, often designated as forums (which include in the delegations specialists in the relevant fields), such as the Budapest Cultural Forum and the London Information Forum, or symposia, such as the Cracow Symposium on the Cultural Heritage, or seminars, such as the Oslo Seminar on Democratic Institutions. Under the Paris Charter a new category of meetings was added.

Up to 1992 four follow-up meetings had been convened. However, let us first examine the CSCE *modus operandi* in general.

OFFICIAL DELIBERATIONS DURING THE COLD WAR

In the CSCE, business is conducted at two distinct levels, in an almost schizophrenic fashion: at the formal official level of meetings in plenary and in official committees (usually called working groups or working bodies), and at the level of unofficial informal meetings. The first was decidedly and painfully confrontational. The latter level was by contrast relatively cordial and businesslike, and even when it could not produce results it brought forth two elements, each with an inbuilt dynamic. One was the reality of divergence, two separate paths not able to meet but going along with candour and professional mutual regard in most instances. The other was a widespread feeling of frustration with the divergence, with the clash, an inbuilt, pent-up reservoir for change to a better world.

Official deliberations during the Cold War era of CSCE-I were characterized by the inevitable East–West clashes and negotiations on an East–West basis with the NNA acting as bridge-builders. In the sphere of human rights and related issues the West had an obvious edge, since the majority of the NNA were imbued with the same values on such matters. Another characteristic was the considerable degree of cohesion within the Western and Eastern camps, and, at times, even within the NNA in their attempt to present a unified front and add more weight to their bridge-building endeavours.

At CSCE meetings during official sessions, there was always a role for the skilful diplomat, the 'Cold Warrior', the orator and *prima donna*, and even a place for the more contemplative delegate. But whatever the style or argument, the overt, scarcely disguised aims for most members of the two alliances during official sessions remained the same: how best to undo 'the other side', indicating its shortcomings, and how to defend one's own state more effectively. This was the reigning spirit within the respective caucus sessions of the two blocs. Needless to say, the human dimension was the area of greatest debate and dispute, for it was chiefly here that the divergence between the two systems unfolded. As matters came to a head in CSCE meetings there was no mincing of words, but rather words were used which, contrary to the old saying, inflicted far greater pain on one's 'bones' than any 'sticks or stones' could ever hope to do. A case in point was that of various United States delegations at CSCE meetings, with their penchant for scathing attacks on the Soviet Union for its human rights record by mentioning actual cases ('naming names') in detail (such as the fate of specific Helsinki monitors, of specific *refuseniks*, of Soviet Jews, abuses in psychiatric practices and so on). Other Western delegations followed suit, notably Canada, the United Kingdom and the Netherlands – and, at times, Italy, France and others, but with less emphasis on detail, and a more diplomatic turn of phrase. The FRG approach did not lack 'punch', particularly as time went by, but was decidedly more subtle, and did not favour 'naming names'.

For their part, the Soviet and other Eastern delegations would blame the United States and NATO countries in general for warmongering, for 'whipping up hatred' (a favourite Eastern phrase), and for responsibility for the arms race. They would in retaliation cite the plight of the homeless, the jobless, the Blacks, the Hispanics and the Indians in North America, violence in Northern Ireland and other matters. A well-known speciality of Eastern delegations, particularly of Soviet delegates, was to generate procedural debates that could go on for hours, the obvious aim being to limit the time available for the painful implementation reviews. The Soviet Union and the other Eastern countries started to react to Western, and increasingly even Neutral, criticism with more elaborate and sophisticated arguments from the Bern 1986 Meeting onwards, and particularly during the Vienna Follow-up. This was less obvious in the case of Czechoslovakia. As for Hungary, noteworthy for its polished interventions, it was simply not criticized by the West after the 1985 Ottawa Meeting.

The other basic characteristic of CSCE-I, the considerable level of internal bloc cohesion, is a tendency hardly in evidence among the NATO camp in other international forums, notably in the UN system. Here social scientists would not fail to notice one of the Simmel–Coser postulates in operation – that the existence of an external foe, and an awesome one at that, tends to breed internal cohesion.[11] Indeed, until 1989, it was only in rare instances that a member of one alliance would criticize directly, by name, another member of the same alliance. When this was done, the tone tended to be subdued and words were used with great care, in contrast to clashes at the UN and elsewhere, notably between Greece and Turkey. Another interesting outcome of bloc unity, often missed by commentators on the CSCE, is that if an issue, whatever its merits, could be placed within the East–West divide, it could automatically count on the active support of most of its allies together with maximum publicity (for instance, the Turkish–Bulgarian clash which began in the Ottawa Meeting and ended at the Sofia Meeting on the Protection of the Environment in the autumn of 1989). On the other hand, questions not congenial to the divide could not muster much support and were seen by Western and some neutral states as almost irrelevant to CSCE concerns, notably the Cyprus problem, the plight of the Kurds or that of the Albanians in Kosovo. The far from satisfactory human rights records of Yugoslavia or of Turkey throughout the Cold War were rarely if ever mentioned. This approach, though justified given the centrality of the East–West conflict, was hardly an accurate reflection of the human rights reality in Europe as a whole; in effect it presented the CSCE as decidedly 'lopsided'. This allied cohesion and lack of intra-alliance conflict further defined the CSCE as a venue of East–West confrontation.

Given all of the above within the CSCE, and the prevailing Cold War atmosphere, it is perhaps a miracle that somehow there was an output, in the form of noteworthy documents, in a few key areas covered by the CSCE, such as the 'human dimension'. Of course, the very first miracle was the initial introduction of the concept of human rights and of Basket III.[12] Apart from the sheer determination of most Western states in this matter, another factor which proved crucial was that the Soviet Union, on more than one occasion was in a weak negotiating position at the Helsinki–Geneva conference, by virtue of being a *demandeur*. Thus, in the end, Moscow had to give way on matters it heartily disliked. The Soviet Union could not boycott the process, much as it threatened to do so. It was 'hooked'. The West, on the other hand, was seldom eager to end up with a document. As for the United States, which did not attach great importance to the CSCE or to new standard-setting commitments (a position that has worried its much more involved allies), it was drawn into the affair, particularly from 1980 onwards, because of the opportunities offered by the reviews of implementation. But perhaps above all in the difficult years, the ability of the process to produce new commitments was due to the dynamic of the process itself. This was the result of the other CSCE, the unofficial one, which gave the Helsinki process a life of its own by way of tangible results in the form of new commitments.

THE UNOFFICIAL DELIBERATIONS: MULTILATERAL NEGOTIATIONS

The implicit rules of multilateral negotiations rest on two pillars: on the rules of procedure and on the climate and structure of relations between CSCE participating states at any given time. Provided there is some prospect of ending up with a document, a CSCE meeting becomes informal, going underground as it were. Official meetings are largely supplanted by informal talks in the so-called 'contact groups', 'informal groups', 'drafting groups' and 'friends groups', and often during coffee breaks.

The informal, open-ended groups are structured on the basis of a set of implicit rules. The office of chairman is permanent (not rotating as in the official meetings) and until 1989 it was by definition held by a member of one of the NNA delegations, usually by a Neutral such as Finland, Switzerland, Austria or Sweden. The chairman's duties as 'co-ordinator' are to register agreement or lack of agreement on texts, and to offer suggestions for compromise language, orally or in the form of non-papers. In these informal groups, the deliberations remained, until 1989, mainly a negotiation between Eastern and Western delegates, who sat for the occasion facing each other across the table, with NNA delegates placing themselves in between. The co-ordinator and the other NNA delegates acted as bridge-builders and con-ciliators. Negotiations were almost always laborious, though the negotiators were spared the rhetorical flourishes which abounded in the plenary and other official sessions. Of course, this is not to say that there were no clashes during negotiations for texts. There were occasional angry outbursts, walk-outs, filibustering, silence on one side of the table, and other ploys in the war of nerves, as well as personal feuds (or a rapport) across the table between adversaries. In the Cold War days, almost every proposal, phrase, word or comma, however secondary, would be treated with caution and placed within the wider negotiating gamut if it came from 'the other side', particularly on issues in the human rights dimension. Indeed, there were several dummy proposals (texts simply aimed to counteract proposals from the other side), red herrings or 'negotiating fat' within a proposal or phrase, not to mention the array of 'propagandistic' proposals – those simply intended to point an accusing finger – which had no chance of being included in the final text.

Until 1988 the inclination of both Eastern and Western delegations was for 'win–lose' and damage control, rather than for 'positive-sum' and gains to all sides.[13] Two classic approaches used in other negotiating settings – package deals and splitting issues (dealing with the easiest first in order to produce results quickly and generate momentum)[14] – could be discerned at times. However, these were rarely deliberate manoeuvres, but rather depended on circumstances, the proposals involved, the strategy set by the heads of delegation in the caucus meetings of the two alliances, as well as the tactics and pace which the co-ordinator would try to inject into the deliberations with the assistance of the other NNA delegates. Usually the most effective way to avoid ending up with the lowest common denominator (which means not including a proposal on an issue or ending up with a weakly phrased commitment) was to make trade-offs with other difficult texts in other paragraphs or chapters of the final document being drafted. But this device was not always available, or immediately obvious, particularly if it involved a text in another contact group, and, in any event, the tendency was to leave the crucial horse-trading until the very end. At informal meetings a delegation, sensing that a consensus was evolving, could block consensus by not permitting a text to be tabled as 'accepted language', or by reserving its position and allowing the text to be registered in brackets or through other devices. This brings us to the sacred consensus principle of the CSCE.

In practice, the consensus principle has rarely amounted to a power of veto on a CSCE document as a whole. Although several participating states have toyed with the idea of withholding consent to a document or threatened to do so (such as Greece in 1974 in an attempt to deal with the Turkish military intervention in Cyprus[15]), very few have actually proceeded on that course after realizing that they are isolated in a minority of one or are in 'bad company'. The few exceptions through the years include the United States in the Bern Meeting (1986), and Romania in the Budapest Cultural Forum (1986) and in the Sofia Meeting on the Environment (1989), whose draft document Romania accepted after Ceauşescu's fall. There is also the case of Malta which withheld consensus for an extended time in Geneva in 1975, in Belgrade in 1978 and in Madrid in 1983. The behaviour of Malta, as well as Romania, particularly with regard to the CSCE Conference on the Human Dimension, suggested a CSCE *à la carte* and raised the spectre of the possibility of ostracism from the process.

In view of the difficulty of a single state blocking consensus on its own, withholding agreement has been used far more frequently and effectively by the various caucuses of states (the EC, the Western, the Eastern and the NNA). However, if a delegation is making a stand on its own, the pressure from its partners or allies is overwhelming, particularly if the rest have genuinely tried to accommodate its needs by providing different forms of compromise language. Consensus evolves in stages in a 'consensus-building process',[16] first in the various caucuses (in the case of the EC, first among its member-states and then in the NATO group), which are informal and officially non-existent (as are the open-ended contact groups for that matter), then in the open-ended informal groups and then officially at the plenary, where, as pointed out above, reservations can also be made. Until the end of the Vienna Follow-up, members of the EC or NATO refrained from putting forward proposals or supporting the proposals of others outside their group if these did not obtain agreement within their own group.

Now let us go into the details and intricacies of the various post-1975 CSCE meetings, focusing, of course, on questions of the human dimension.

BELGRADE AND MADRID

THE BELGRADE FOLLOW-UP:
THE ABORTIVE MEETING

The Belgrade Follow-up Meeting, the shortest of the follow-up meetings during the days of the Cold War, lasted five months (4 October 1977–9 March 1978) and was a failure. It did not produce a document of substance, with new commitments, and was far more confrontational than one would have expected given the climate of East–West relations at the time, which was somewhat better than in the next seven or eight years. But perhaps the greatest failure of Belgrade was that the CSCE was found not to be immune to failure. A standstill in what was essentially a process was a threat to its very existence. However, from the CSCE human dimension perspective, there was one far from negligible gain: the implementation review focusing mainly on human rights. Introduced in Belgrade for the first time, it was not rejected by the Warsaw Pact countries and thus gained a foothold as one of the basic features of the Helsinki process and one of its claims to effectiveness.

In the Preparatory Meeting (15 July–10 August 1977), which produced the 'Yellow Book' – the agenda of the main meeting – agreement did not come easily, but the atmosphere was businesslike, with few signs of the confrontation and lack of dialogue which were to follow. The Eastern countries were evasive on the question of follow-up, with the West hardly more enthusiastic. This was to be mainly the concern of the NNA and Romania.

The Belgrade Meeting has been registered in CSCE history largely because of its hard-hitting implementation review, which went on for some eight weeks and continued during the official presentation of proposals. This review of practices was novel, not only in the Helsinki process, but also in the history of diplomacy.[1] It was a kind of tribunal, unique in the protection of human rights, going much farther than the relevant discussions in the UN and other forums. Human rights came to dominate the Belgrade Meeting and caused an acute and bitter East–West confrontation. In this the United States delegation was at the forefront, making scathing comments on human rights abuses in the Soviet Union and elsewhere in Eastern Europe, notably in Czechoslovakia and the GDR. In fact, Belgrade was seen by the new Carter administration as the forum *par excellence* in which to launch human rights as an axis of United States foreign policy. Also critical of Eastern practices were Canada, France, the United Kingdom, the FRG, the Netherlands, Belgium, Norway and Luxembourg and the Neutrals, mainly Sweden, Austria and, to a lesser extent, Switzerland and the Holy See. The focus on human rights was not unrelated to a growing general sensitivity to human rights violations among Western peoples, spurred, among other things, by the appeals and declarations of 'dissidents' in the East, notably in Czechoslovakia (Charter 77) and the Soviet Union, who had found in the Helsinki provisions a rallying point and a ground to denounce their governments' human rights abuses.[2]

Much of the blame for the meeting's failure has been laid on one delegation, or to be more precise on one delegate, the United States chief delegate, Justice Arthur Goldberg, whose confrontational style was meant to personify Carter's new approach. This line was not shared by the US Department of State, but was the dominant thinking in the White House, conceived by the National Security Adviser, Zbigniew Brzezinski, and key members of the US 'Commission on Security and Co-operation in Europe'. This independent body, created by Congress in 1976, has played an important role in Washington's CSCE policy,[3] and had concluded that there was considerable merit in following a 'confrontationist approach'.[4] Goldberg, a judge and an activist on civil rights and Jewish matters, had direct access to the White House, bypassing not only the diplomats in his delegation but also the State Department, and was in contact with the Israeli Prime Minister, Menachem Begin, who sent him information notes on the Jews of the Soviet Union. He was a source of embarrassment to his delegation on more than one occasion, for not only did he clash with the Soviet delegates but also, in the NATO caucus, with his Western counterparts. He was not on good terms with his own delegation either, particularly with the diplomatic staff under Ambassador Sherer, with whom he was hardly on speaking terms.[5]

The harsh polemics which were to be the trade-mark of Belgrade were first initiated not by the United States but by France[6] and Canada, with the United States curiously appearing almost tentative in the beginning. Of the communist countries, only Romania was spared criticism (contrary to what was to happen some ten years later).[7]

Eastern delegations reacted with the non-intervention argument, and at times threatened to walk out of the meeting, but then they engaged in counter-attacking Western states, thus, in effect, accepting the logic that such criticism was legitimate in the CSCE. The United States approach may have ensured the ultimate failure of the meeting, but in the meantime there was little indication that either bloc was 'in a mood to accept the ideas of the other side'.[8] Equally, there were few signs that the Soviet Union, under the ageing Brezhnev administration, and its allies were prepared to implement, however gradually, the various 'Western' human rights commitments agreed in the Final Act, or to accept more such commitments, which would have meant widening the scope of the criticism against them in future meetings. Indeed, the opposite seemed to be more true.

However, despite the adverse climate, as many as one hundred and nine proposals were officially submitted. Most of the proposals on human-rights-related issues coming from Eastern countries were counter-proposals of a propagandistic nature, so much so that not even the Eastern delegations cared to include them in their version of a concluding text. In January 1978, the delegations started the multi-lateral process for a document. Over a period of some five months, in a complicated and time-consuming exercise, daily negotiations took place in all sorts of groups, in plenary, in the five official committees, in the 'Subsidiary Working Bodies' (one to each basket, plus the Mediterranean and the follow-up), as well as informally in 'drafting groups', 'contact groups' and in less informal meetings containing fewer delegations.[9]

The most active group in the negotiations was the highly coherent '9' of the EC who presented the NATO caucus with various *faits accomplis*, frustrating Canada and Norway, which were both actively involved in the meeting, and raising complaints from Goldberg about lack of co-ordination between the EC and NATO caucuses. France tried to play the leader of the '9' as in Geneva, but was less successful, showing an exaggerated sensitivity in distinguishing the '9' from NATO, and often not even participating in the NATO caucus. Particularly energetic among Western delegations were those of the Netherlands, the FRG, Belgium, Norway, France, Canada and Luxembourg. Italy was less active, while Ireland appeared to act more as an NNA state. At Belgrade, the NNA came to the fore as a more distinct and coherent group in assuming their role as bridge-builders. Most active and effective among the Neutrals were Austria and Sweden, and among the Non-Aligned Yugoslavia played an important role. The Eastern bloc – with the exception of Romania, which continued on its familiar

independent track – was particularly cohesive, with the Soviet delegation in full control and Czechoslovakia and the GDR 'more Catholic
than the Pope'.[10] Hungary and Poland, however, at times appeared
more independent.[11]

The fact that on many issues agreement was reached indicated that
given better circumstances outside the meeting, or at least inside, the
CSCE could be capable of producing something of substance and
build on the Helsinki commitments. However, a worthy overall document proved impossible, even though the NNA and several Western
states thought it might be obtained on the basis of trading concessions
in Basket II for more commitments on human rights and human
contacts. The various drafts for a concluding document that appeared
(an early draft by the '9' plus Canada, Norway and some NNA; several
Soviet drafts; a compromise French draft; and finally a Western
proposal for a document submitted for the record but without French
co-sponsorship) were not generally acceptable and could not function
as a basis for negotiating the final text. When it became obvious that not
much could be done, Canada floated the idea of a three-line document,
of the type 'we met, we talked and we agreed on meeting again'. The
NNA made a last attempt with a substantial but short (four-page)
document, with no mention of human rights. The Soviet delegation
indicated that they could accept this with minor changes, but the West
would have none of it.

When it became clear that the CSCE was hanging from a thread if
no document was produced which would provide for another follow-
up, the West and NNA delegations decided on a 'bare-bones' text. The
only two among the '35' to have difficulty with this approach were
Romania and Yugoslavia, which being the host country had higher
hopes for the document emanating from its capital. Denmark proposed
a short three-page draft on behalf of '16' delegations (the '9' plus the
remaining seven NATO members), which was to become the basis of
the concluding document. At the last moment, Malta, taking advantage
of the consensus procedure, withheld its consent until it obtained an
experts' meeting on the Mediterranean in Valletta and an agreement to
discuss Mediterranean security in the next follow-up.[12]

It is generally accepted that the main achievement of the four-page
Belgrade Document, adopted on 8 March 1978, were the reaffirmation of the undertakings of the Final Act (and of the commitment to
détente) and, in particular, the actual continuation of the process by
agreeing to another follow-up meeting (to take place in Madrid from
11 November 1980 with a preparatory meeting commencing on 9
September), and by scheduling three specialized meetings – a meeting

on peaceful settlement of disputes in Montreux, a scientific forum, and a meeting on the Mediterranean in Valletta. Thus, the CSCE was endorsed and, in a way, 'institutionalized' as an ongoing multilateral process.[13]

The Belgrade failure is attributable to several factors. No doubt Goldberg and the confrontational approach placed on the 'delicate fabric' of the infant CSCE burdens it had difficulty in carrying.[14] A far too great emphasis on one aspect – human rights – could hardly be called a balanced approach, and caused an 'upsetting of the balance'[15] which led inevitably to 'an ideological and propaganda-type debate'.[16] Thus, in the wake of Belgrade, as Karl E. Birnbaum has concluded, the CSCE process was 'far from safeguarded'.[17] However, it was not only the CSCE that was in danger, but also, and more importantly, what remained of *détente*, or rather the existing 'pseudo-*détente*'. As the Greek ambassador, Dimitris Heraclides, eloquently said at the time, 'one wonders whether the slogan of *détente* constitutes the international substratum of the CSCE or has turned into a Faustian garment for the retention, at an international level, of a collective illusion'.[18]

THE MADRID FOLLOW-UP:
THE TORMENTED MEETING

The Belgrade failure placed a huge burden on the next follow-up meeting – no less than to breathe life into a moribund CSCE by coming up with a 'qualitatively different' result.[19] The intercessional meetings had not gone well, with the surprising exception of the Hamburg Scientific Forum, which ended up with a worthwhile document on scientific co-operation that included human dimension elements, for example, respect for human rights as 'one of the foundations for a significant improvement in their mutual relations, and in international scientific co-operation at all levels'.[20]

According to the conclusion of one of the collective studies of that period, the future of the CSCE lay 'in the hands of the superpowers', who could wreck or paralyse it if they continued to be actively involved in the same fashion.[21] On that score prospects were dim. The Soviet Union cultivated the view that its support of the CSCE endeavour should not be taken for granted; and in the United States, the presidential elections had brought victory to Ronald Reagan, who had previously expressed doubts about the 'expediency of American participation' in the CSCE.[22]

The Madrid Meeting was held at a time when East–West relations had plummeted to their lowest level since the 1960s. Among other factors were the Soviet military intervention in Afghanistan, the Polish crisis, the prospect of a Soviet intervention in Poland, the imposition of a state of emergency in that country, the clamping down on human rights activists in Eastern Europe and the Soviet Union, and the continued repression in Eastern bloc countries. If to this bleak picture one adds the advent of the 'new right' in the United States, with its simplistic 'empire of evil' Reagan spirit, and the issue of the deployment of Pershing and cruise missiles in Europe, then it was clear that Madrid would have to work miracles if it was to lay the Budapest ghost to rest.

Above all, the life of the CSCE was dependent on the construction of a substantive document, replete with commitments on human rights and human contacts, while at the same time not letting the East off the hook on their grave shortcomings in this sphere. These were two aims at odds with each other, as had been seen in Belgrade.[23] Quite surprisingly, both were achieved, though the main goal, a substantial document, seemed unattainable for most of the time in Madrid. Despite various threats to quit, to call for an adjournment (by France and Switzerland, in particular), or not to go ahead with 'business as usual' (by the United States on at least two occasions), the meeting somehow plodded on, month after month, with several recesses in between, for 'no result' was simply inconceivable.[24]

It was not only the future of the CSCE that hung in the air, with no one daring enough to take the blame for wrecking it, which did not allow for the luxury of a Belgrade-type outcome. Despite the menacing clouds outside the conference and the recurrent thunderstorms within, there were from the very beginning the seeds of a comprise, an inbuilt *quid pro quo* which could bear fruit once the time was ripe, as in the Helsinki–Geneva talks. The participating states could exchange a disarmament conference for concessions on the human dimension. The situation was, however, more complex than in the original MPT and CSCE meetings, for while the Soviet Union was in the position of *demandeur*, the West was by now deeply involved in the CSCE affair, and could not push things to the point of collapse. Furthermore, there was a willingness on the part of the NNA and several Western states to try to accomplish something worthwhile on military security as well.[25]

The Preparatory Meeting was a sign of things to come, lasting nine weeks instead of the expected two or three weeks, the Soviet Union and its allies wanting less than in Belgrade, the West more, but content also with a result along the lines of the Belgrade Yellow Book. The main points of contention were the implementation review and the vital question of follow-up. The Soviet Union wanted only two weeks devoted to implementation, to overlap with the introduction of new proposals. On follow-up, the NNA and the West strongly favoured the making of a commitment at an early stage, while the Soviet Union saw it as contingent on a 'successful' outcome of the meeting – a reversal of the positions of East and West in Helsinki–Geneva. The Soviet delegation was so adamant on this question that it gave the distinct impression that it had come to Madrid with the aim of 'scuttling' the CSCE process. Thus, as early as November 1980, with deadlock in Madrid and with the Polish crisis in the background, the CSCE 'seemed to hang in the balance'.[26]

At the Preparatory Meeting, the EC countries were less coherent than usual. This may have been due to the weak Luxemburg presidency, and/or to the able but persuasive stance of the United States delegation, assisted by the tough negotiating attitude of the United Kingdom, the Netherlands and, surprisingly, even the FRG. Among the other Western delegations, Italy and Canada took a similar stance, while France, Belgium, Denmark, Ireland, Norway and Greece were more accommodating. Spain and the three most active Neutrals, Austria, Switzerland and Sweden, played the mediating role, though they were seen as too pro-Western by the Eastern delegations. Among the Eastern states, the most intransigent were the Soviet Union, the GDR, Czechoslovakia and Hungary, while Romania, Poland and Bulgaria appeared somewhat more flexible.[27]

The end of the Preparatory Meeting has by now passed into CSCE lore as one of its most bizarre episodes. The date scheduled for the main meeting was 11 November 1980, but on the previous night no agreement on the agenda had been reached. It was then that a new CSCE contrivance was discovered, the old parliamentary device of stopping the clock. This was done at two minutes to midnight on 10 November. Talks continued into the early hours of the morning and throughout the next day, but still with no result, partly due to the role of the Hungarian chairman, who remained in the chair since it was still, fictitiously, the 10th. When it was agreed to start the clock again, negotiations continued but without success. However, the Spanish Foreign Minister had made it clear that, in order to keep to the time set for the official meeting, he would open the meeting on 11 November come what may. Thus, with the agreement of the participants, he declared open the main meeting at fifteen minutes to midnight on the 11th, and after a few minutes closed it. Negotiations continued, with agreement finally reached on 14 November on a compromise proposal of the NNA. Meanwhile, the foreign ministers were placed in the curious position of making their opening statements even though the continuation of the conference was not assured.[28]

The main architects of the compromise were Switzerland and Spain, the host country. The agenda adopted, which was proposed by Austria, Sweden, Yugoslavia and Cyprus, came to be known as the 'Violet' or 'Purple' Book (from its colour). It was less than had been achieved in the 'Yellow Book', though it retained the same basic structure: five weeks for implementation (not eleven as in the Yellow Book, but not two as the Soviets had wanted), and without automatic or explicit rules for follow-up meetings (the agenda included only the discussion of 'other meetings'). Thus the Soviets, with their tough bargaining stance, seemed to have it their way on paper but, as is often the case, success can be its own worst enemy.[29]

Once open, the Madrid Follow-up had no assured future for most of its existence.[30] The review of implementation that took place until the Christmas recess was mainly concerned with human rights violations in Eastern countries. Castigated for their record were the Soviet Union (for its human rights abuses and for the Afghanistan affair), Czechoslovakia and the GDR, less so Poland and more mildly Hungary and Romania. Although the review was 'frequently heated, at times tempestuous',[31] by and large the Eastern countries endured, by comparison with Belgrade, 'a much more frank and specific barrage of criticism', in many respects due to the United States chief delegate, Max M. Kampelman, noted for his 'candid eloquence' and lack of excess, based on the premise of not being 'rude or unnecessarily offensive'.[32] Indeed, at times it appeared that the British representative was sharper in his criticism of Eastern practices.

The Soviet delegation reacted by condemning the West as having opted for a 'verbal bull-fight',[33] but, on the whole, it responded in a more relaxed and resigned manner than in Belgrade, where it had over-reacted at the most minute criticism.[34] The United States was joined in its condemnation of Soviet practices by a wider range of countries than in Belgrade: by all of the NATO countries (with the exception of Greece), as well as by Austria, Sweden and Switzerland, and also by the Holy See and even San Marino.[35] The United States referred to specific individual plights, 'naming names' as it has done consistently at CSCE meetings;[36] to which the Soviet delegation retorted with accusations of 'gross and massive violations' of human rights.[37] Needless to say, as in Belgrade, there was no real dialogue between East and West, whereby shortcomings would be explained and a readiness to change indicated, though the West apparently tried to steer such a course by attempting to be self-critical from time to time.[38]

In Madrid eighty-seven proposals were officially submitted.[39] This was less than in Belgrade, but the proposals were on the whole more substantial and down to earth, covering all the CSCE spectrum (those of the West being less one-sided than in Belgrade). The two main clusters of proposals were on human rights/human contacts and on military security. The Eastern delegations were strong advocates of the latter and though they showed some readiness to give in on human rights as part of an overall bargain, they were very reticent to begin with, probably for negotiation purposes, but perhaps also in the belief that they could get away with relatively few concessions. The '10' of the EC attempted, where possible, to submit proposals as a group, but with France wanting to present proposals on its own as well.[40]

The principal Soviet objective in Madrid was for the CSCE to convene a 'Conference on Military *Détente* and Disarmament in Europe', to include items such as nuclear-free zones, a nuclear freeze and the abolition of the neutron bomb (called the 'capitalist weapon', devised 'to waste' people but leave property intact).[41] This goal was a major part of Brezhnev's 'Peace Programme for the 1980s', adopted in February 1981 by the 26th Congress of the Communist Party of the Soviet Union.[42] On the other hand, the Soviet delegation made it clear to Western delegations that it was not prepared to pay any price for such a meeting since, after all, it was an all-Europe *desideratum*.[43] However, as Max Kampelman had deduced early on in Madrid, from his numerous discussions with the Soviet delegates, the Soviet craving for a disarmament conference was deep and based on a variety of reasons, which meant that they would be prepared to pay a considerable price for it (needless to say the tough United States negotiating posture in Madrid was based on this premise).[44] Furthermore, the security conference conceived by France and some other Western and Neutral states was different from what the Soviet Union was proposing. It was to focus mainly on CBMs, not on disarmament as such. And this hardly made the West a *demandeur*, for the fear remained among Western delegations that an ambitious security conference, however carefully mandated, could shift the overall CSCE balance away from the human dimension. Thus it remained a Western leverage and the one that ultimately carried the day in Madrid.[45]

The basic proposals under Principle VII were a meeting of experts on human rights comprised of official delegates and private groups, proposed by Canada and co-sponsored by the United States and Spain; measures concerning the need for progress in the effective exercise of human rights, including protection of monitoring activities, presented by the '10' members of the European Community and co-sponsored by the other Western delegations, which was one of the flagship proposals submitted by the West; bilateral human rights round tables, proposed by the United States and co-sponsored by Denmark and Norway; proposals on freedom of thought, conscience, religion and belief, by the Holy See; on the right of workers to form free trade unions, by the Western countries; and the Eastern countries' proposals on the right to work, education, on acceding to the UN covenants on human rights and other matters.

Under Basket III the main proposals were family meetings, facilitating reunification of families and marriages, and simplifying emigration procedures, proposed by the European Community and other Western countries; a meeting of experts on family reunification, proposed by the United States (which emanated from the US Commission's staff)[46] and co-sponsored by Canada, Denmark, Greece and the United Kingdom; and organizing a cultural forum, submitted by France, and, separately, by Yugoslavia.[47] A vital proposal outside the human dimension which is worth mentioning was the French proposal on convening a conference on disarmament in Europe, whose emphasis was to be on CBMs, which had NATO blessing and was to be the basis of the final outcome;[48] and there was also the proposal by eight Western delegations on terrorism, which formed the basis of the relevant text adopted.

The Madrid Meeting was to finish if possible by as early as 5 March 1981, but it dragged on with as many as five phases of deliberations as follows: submission of proposals, from January until April 1981; the start of the actual multilateral negotiations, which was a stalemate, from May to July 1981; a second phase of negotiations with no results, from October to December 1981; a major deadlock from February to March 1982, which ended with an agreement on the longest adjournment in CSCE follow-up history, of almost nine months; continued diplomatic clashes in November and December 1982; the last span of negotiations from February to July 1983, where wrapping up the conference was delayed for almost two months by Malta.

In broad outline the negotiation setting was similar to that in Belgrade, with the Eastern and Western states on either side and the NNA as bridge-builders. In February 1981 the official committees, the Subsidiary Working Bodies, were replaced by drafting groups, where proposals received a second reading, but most of the drafting took place in experts' contact groups. Contrary to Belgrade, the '9', later the '10' (Greece joined the European Community in January 1981), worked closely within the NATO group with the United States delegation, France participating regularly within NATO and more rarely trying to assume an independent role. The United States delegation was comprised of diplomats, congressmen and staff members of the US Commission, and despite the change in Administration (from Carter to Reagan) did not undergo substantial transformation. The most notable change was that the role of Chairman of the US Delegation was switched from Judge Griffin Bell to the co-chairman of the delegation, Max M. Kampelman, the prominent Washington lawyer and well-known Democrat (one of the very few Carter appointees to remain in place), who had been in charge during the Preparatory Meeting. Kampelman's role in Madrid, contrary to that of Goldberg in Belgrade, was a very valuable one, to the extent that he can rightfully be regarded as one of the main architects of the difficult but successful conclusion. He adapted well to his CSCE job, earning the respect of other delegates for his candour and eloquence, and not least for making it a point to consult constantly with his Western colleagues with a view to attaining a common Western stance.[49]

The Eastern bloc was disciplined and cohesive, as in Belgrade, with the exception of Romania which again paddled its own canoe, appearing on several issues as a non-aligned country. The Soviet contingent suffered no less than three changes in its head of delegation, but it was mainly controlled throughout by its deputy, the able Sergei Kondrashev.[50] Malta did not always work with the NNA, while the Holy See, which is not an NNA member, sometimes joined the group. The protagonists among the NNA in a more successful role as bridge-builders than in Geneva or Belgrade were Switzerland and Austria, headed respectively by ambassadors Edouard Brunner and Franz Česka, who were, it seemed, in a kind of competition with each other, representing respectively the tougher NNA and the more subtle approach.

One of the difficult issues was the security conference, particularly as to the zone of application, a delicate matter which now and again tested the United States' patience, especially given France's propensity to take initiatives without due NATO consultation (notably in the summer of 1981).[51] Human rights issues initially received less attention, but the West made it clear that they would not accept a security conference without substance on human rights and human contacts. The NNA prepared a first draft of a concluding document by 31 March 1981, a thirty-five page text on topics on which some provisional agreement had been reached, which tilted to the Western side on Basket III in particular. The reaction of both East and West was one of reserve, due among other things to negotiation tactics. In the months that followed there was little movement, and as this phase ended in July 1981, prospects for an outcome by the next phase were dim.[52]

The next much more ambitious and complete NNA draft was prepared by the Austrian delegation and supported by Switzerland, Sweden, Finland and Cyprus (not at that stage by Yugoslavia), and was circulated as a non-paper on 10 December 1981. At the level of the EC caucus, the initial reaction to the Austrian draft was by and large positive. The FRG delegation especially stressed the need to exploit the momentum created by the Austrian initiative and, if possible, to reach initial agreement by Christmas. Apparently, only the United Kingdom (the '10' presidency at the time) and the Netherlands found the draft disappointing. At the NATO caucus, the general reaction was that the main problem lay in the issue of zone application, on which the West should stand firm so as not to extend it. On the human dimension there were differing views, but on the whole the draft was characterized as positive. The United States delegation insisted on the inclusion of a ban on radio jamming and, particularly, on the addition of the issue of Helsinki monitors.[53]

However, this otherwise substantial draft concluding document was to become a casualty of events in Poland.[54] By an unhappy coincidence it had been circulated on the very day that martial law was established. The event cast a shadow over the deliberations in Madrid and was to plunge the CSCE 'into the worst crisis of its existence'.[55] The draft concluding document was tabled officially a few days later (RM.39), with NNA co-sponsorship, including Yugoslavia, but not Switzerland. The Swiss delegation stated that for reasons extraneous to the Madrid Meeting (i.e. the Polish situation) it was not prepared to discuss the draft in detail and suggested the resumption of discussions in February 1982.[56] At the official level the British delegation, on behalf of the '10', characterized the draft as positive and expressed readiness to regard it as the basis of discussions in the next year with the aim of improving some points. The United States was more reserved, while the Soviet Union said that it found several worthwhile elements but also a number of omissions. The last days of the meeting before the Christmas break were dominated by references to the Polish situation, though not in extreme terms.[57]

In January 1982, the meetings of EC foreign ministers and the extraordinary meeting of NATO foreign ministers decided on an early resumption of the Madrid Meeting at foreign minister level in order to discuss the Polish situation. However, technically this could not be done in those days, when no permanent CSCE organs existed to assess whether consensus existed on a point. Therefore, the United States launched the idea of Western and like-minded NNA foreign ministers arriving and delivering speeches on Poland and Afghanistan at the outset of the next session in Madrid.[58]

When talks were resumed after the long Christmas recess, Secretary of State Alexander Haig and all the Western foreign ministers, including those of Switzerland, Austria and Sweden, descended on Madrid. Haig was very sharp about Poland, Afghanistan and other human rights violations, and was supported by all the Western countries (with the exception of Greece, then under the newly formed Papandreou government),[59] as well as by Switzerland (which, incidently, called for the immediate interruption of the Madrid Meeting), Austria and Sweden. The ministers left Madrid having experienced one aspect of the CSCE, procedural harassment, and being witness to a six- or seven-hour procedural debate, as the Polish delegate in the chair, assisted by the Soviet representative and some others, refused to give the floor to any foreign minister after 1.30 p.m., the time scheduled for the plenary of that day.[60]

After the foreign ministers had left, some Western delegations, and most of all the United States, were not in the mood for compromise or for business as usual, but favoured a long adjournment. This was also the view of Switzerland. However, the majority of Western delegations favoured going back to the business of drafting. It was one of the most difficult moments in Western alliance cohesion in Madrid, which was finally overcome with the United States delegate's approach carrying the day.[61]

However, an adjournment was, technically, virtually impossible, for there was need for consensus, that is Soviet consent to it, and at the time the Soviet delegation was at its most businesslike, pushing for a final document. It was one of the rare occasions in the CSCE during the Cold War where the Soviet delegation was ready to go ahead with drafting, while the Western delegations were stonewalling in the plenary sessions. The next days were tense, a veritable war of nerves. The final outcome was attributable to United States ingenuity, NATO solidarity and firmness and, finally, a timely Swiss–Austrian intervention.

The technical difficulty was resolved by a United States idea, supported by the FRG and British delegates and sold to the other NATO partners. The plan was to refuse approval of the weekly working schedules of the drafting groups. 'Eloquent silences' followed.[62] For session after session, Western delegates stayed silent to

Eastern calls for further drafting sessions. The Soviet Union on its part would not give its consent in the plenary to adjourning the meeting (such a decision could only come by consensus in the plenary). With the exception of Switzerland, the NNA wanted to continue, but since that would not be productive, given the heavy atmosphere and resolute Western opposition, Austria intervened to break the deadlock between East and West by proposing a few more sessions of the plenary and the drafting groups (in which the West continued their silence). Meanwhile, Switzerland convinced the NNA of the need to adjourn, and then put the proposal to the '35', to which the Soviet Union would not initially give its consent. The last day (12 March 1982) of this phase was one of mutual recrimination. There followed a nine-month recess.[63]

This episode in CSCE history, from December 1981 until March 1982, prompted by the Polish situation, indicated something of particular importance. It demonstrated, as Mastny points out, 'how deeply the Helsinki consciousness had become ingrained in European thinking on security'.[64]

During the interim period there were extended consultations between the Western states on how to proceed. The international situation was not getting any better, on all fronts that mattered to the CSCE. In addition to Poland, there was also the protracted crisis of leadership succession in the Kremlin, which obviously would prevent a breakthrough in Madrid. Switzerland began to entertain the possibility of a Belgrade-type document. The United States was against business as usual, favouring a long two or three years' recess. But this time it was the more subtle approach which carried the day. The '10' and the majority of NATO members urged the resumption of talks on the NNA draft document, but with the addition of a series of new and substantial requirements to it, including trade union rights (with Poland in mind). This appealed to the United States delegation, which finally agreed to go ahead.[65]

The next round was resumed on 9 November 1982. The Western amendments requested finally totalled seventeen in all, some more substantial than others, including trade union freedoms, the right of all peoples to freely determine their political status, and the role of Helsinki monitors. There were also several under human contacts and information, as well as two proposals for experts' meetings – one on human rights proper (the original Canadian proposal) and the other on human contacts. The Canadian and Western European delegations, assisted by Switzerland and Sweden, were at the forefront of the negotiations at this point, but there was no progress in the drafting groups. The session ended on 18 December 1982. All were aware that the next one had to be the last and were doubtful if a substantial outcome was still possible.[66]

In the next round, which began on 8 February 1983, things moved slowly in more informal settings – in six so-called 'mini-groups' consisting of three representatives from each of the three groups (East, West, NNA) – but progress was made. Finally, the NNA took the plunge and issued a revised draft on 15 March 1983. The Western delegation appeared unsatisfied. They stated that the draft favoured the Eastern side and that its own amendments, where included, were so weak as to be almost imperceptible; the human contacts meeting had been omitted, as had the ban on jamming, the amelioration of conditions for journalists, the right to strike and several others. The United States, in particular, insisted on a totality of the original Western amendments. Apparently, however, this attitude was basically a negotiating stance.[67] In fact, not only the FRG and the other moderates but also the United States were satisfied with the new NNA draft.[68]

After two weeks the West scaled down its demands, insisting on only some of the amendments, notably the human contacts meeting, strengthening the mandate for the human rights meeting, ending jamming of radio stations and other small amendments on CSBMs and on monitors. For six whole weeks there was no move, both sides standing steadfast. Then came a breakthrough; on 3 June Romania stated that it could accept the amendments desired by the Western side. Both superpowers, the Soviet Union in particular, were now under pressure to agree to the proposed compromise. On 17 June 1983, at a reception, the Spanish Prime Minister, Felipe Gonzalez, came forward with a final compromise offer, a 'package' which included taking on board the human contact meeting and starting the Stockholm meeting in January 1984.[69] The idea of some kind of package being presented by the Spanish Prime Minister had apparently been conceived by the United States delegate in discussions with the FRG and Spanish delegates.[70] It was (and was meant to be) a proposition to which the Soviet Union could hardly say 'no'. Predictably, there was a general readiness to accept it as the basis (or 'framework' as the Soviet delegation put it) for agreement. The main points of contention were the date of the next follow-up meeting and the human contacts meeting. Switzerland suggested putting the decision on the human contacts meeting in a chairman's statement, with the intention of reducing its importance. The United States found this difficult to accept, and took some time to answer in the affirmative. Finally, the statement was placed at the end of the Madrid document but was part of it, and when the Bern Meeting took place no Eastern delegation claimed that the meeting was secondary. Final agreement was reached on 15 July 1983.[71]

Regrettably, the document was not adopted for almost two months because Malta once again withheld consensus. This time it was seeking a meeting on security in the Mediterranean. The official reason given was that Malta's aim was to alter the reigning East–West confrontational approach, but the true reasons were probably linked with Prime Minister Dom Mintoff's activities and his attempt to render service to the Arab world. Having previously succeeded with such blackmail tactics in Belgrade, Malta thought it could do so again, but this time Malta found itself on its own, being besieged by all, for no one wanted the Middle East conflict to creep into the CSCE by the back door. Such was the general fury with Malta that some were prepared to go ahead with the adoption regardless of Malta, or so it was impressed on the Maltese, who, seeing the danger, gave in. On 6 September Malta accepted a Spanish face-saving device according to which all states of the CSCE would support Maltese initiatives to strengthen peace in the Mediterranean, but only when they considered it appropriate to do so. This was placed in the Journal, but in fact did not amount to much, for raising such issues in the future within the CSCE was after all Malta's sovereign right, as was the rejection of any such concrete proposal by the other states.[72]

But this was not the end of ill luck for the tormented Madrid Meeting. Not even the adoption of the Madrid Concluding Document could be as happy a self-congratulatory exercise as expected. The reason was the downing of a Korean Airlines passenger airliner with nearly 300 civilians on board by the Soviet air force on 1 September, which the Soviet Union claimed to have been an error in 'standard operational procedures'. Not only did this lead to bitter recriminations in the Palacio de Congresos, but in the resulting saturation reporting of the incident by the media the three-year Madrid achievement passed almost unnoticed internationally. In a way, such an ending was more fitting for the Madrid Meeting, the longest and most frustrating CSCE exercise in the most adverse international climate ever experienced in the CSCE.

THE MADRID CONCLUDING DOCUMENT: A NEW BEGINNING

The Madrid Concluding Document, as it is known,[73] was a substantial document for its time. Even the United States was satisfied, regarding

66

it as a 'significant improvement on the humanitarian provisions of the Helsinki Final Act'[74] and 'a reasonably successful conclusion'.[75]

The Madrid document comprises some thirty-eight pages following the chapters and sub-chapters of the Final Act. In many respects it supplements the Final Act at the standard-setting normative level by additional, more precise and rigorous commitments.

Its most important moves forward are to be found in the human rights dimension under the section Principles and in Basket III under human contacts and, to a lesser extent, under information. Among the other noteworthy provisions are those concerned with measures against terrorism and, of course, the Stockholm Conference on Confidence- and Security-building Measures and Disarmament in Europe, admittedly one of the main achievements of Madrid. In the Madrid document the Stockholm Conference was conceived as a multi-stage undertaking. Starting on 17 January 1984 and based largely on a French proposal, it was to be devoted mainly to CSBMs and was worded in such a way that any attempt to dilute its character by empty rhetoric on disarmament was considerably limited.

In the principles chapter of Basket I, the most extensive part is that devoted to Principle VII: no less than sixteen paragraphs (out of twenty-five in all), twelve of which are of a normative nature, while the other three refer to the convening of the meeting of experts for human rights. Most of the remaining normative paragraphs on principles are concerned with the condemnation of terrorism (four paragraphs including the largest one, based on Western proposals) and measures to combat it. With few exceptions, most of the twelve normative paragraphs on human rights build on and strengthen the Western concept of human rights set by the Final Act. The entirely new elements are trade union rights and equality between men and women.

The link between human rights and good inter-state relations, already existing in the Final Act, is rendered more explicit, and it is stressed that the participating states are committed 'to assure constant and tangible progress' in this field, irrespective of their political, economic and social systems. Commitments on trade unions include the 'right of workers freely to establish and join trade unions, the right of trade unions freely to exercise their activities and other rights', plus the safety clause demanded by the Eastern delegations, in 'compliance with the law of the state', and the counter-safety clause, in 'conformity with the State's obligations under international law'. Among established elements which are reinforced, albeit with certain safety clauses, is religious freedom, covered by three paragraphs in this chapter which are complemented by a provision under 'Human Contacts' encourag-

67

ing 'contacts and meetings' among representatives of religious institutions and organizations.

In the traditionally difficult issue of national minorities there was little move forward, but the need for 'constant progress' was stressed and, interestingly, the cryptic word 'exist' in the Final Act (a hidden safety clause) is left out.[76] The problem of the Helsinki monitors, a major source of difficulties between East and West, could not be stated explicitly but appears indirectly at least twice.[77] Also included were the Western idea of bilateral round tables and, more importantly, the Ottawa Meeting of Experts on Human Rights, whose very acceptance clearly implied that the CSCE participating members no longer regarded such matters as exclusively for internal jurisdiction and not for international concern. Ottawa, of course, could not compete with the Stockholm Conference in importance, but the addition of the Bern Meeting of Experts on Human Contacts and the Budapest Cultural Forum, both within the human dimension sphere, redressed the imbalance to some extent.

The main steps forward under Basket III were in human contacts and information, the subjects of major concern to the West in this chapter. The general assessment of Basket III has been that, on the whole, most of the original Western proposals for inclusion in the human contacts section were 'incorporated, albeit often in diluted form'.[78]

The key words in the human contacts section which strengthened the relevant Final Act provisions were, according to one view, accepting 'to favourably deal with applications' regarding family meetings, reunification of families and marriages between citizens of different states and to 'decide upon them in the same spirit' (the Final Act wording was 'to deal with positive and humanitarian spirit to applications').[79] To that the West managed to insert, according to one calculation, at least five additional elements: to decide on applications for such marriages and family reunification within six months (Final Act: 'as expeditiously as possible'); to refrain from actions against applicants in employment, housing, residence status, family support and access to benefits; to provide the necessary information on emigration procedures; to reduce fees charged on emigration to a moderate level in relation to the average monthly income; and the right to renew applications after reasonably short intervals, aimed against the policy of definitive refusals once and for all.[80]

On information, there were a number of provisions on ameliorating working conditions for journalists, nationals as well as foreign correspondents, and providing better access to foreign media.

Thus, to conclude, on human rights and Basket III the Madrid document kept to the Western standards of not having a mere repetition of existing commitments, not diluting existing commitments, and including items where new wording goes beyond previous commitments. The Madrid Concluding Document can be seen as a new beginning for the CSCE in the human dimension.

Max M. Kampelman, looking back at the Madrid Meeting, concludes that it 'was a major stage-setter for the East–West progress that followed', among other things, for consolidating the Western approach to human rights as a major policy objective towards the Soviet Union.[81] With Madrid the Helsinki process was put back on its feet: results could be achieved even within the coldest of Cold Wars, and harsh criticism of Eastern practices could be pursued without threatening the CSCE with collapse.

6

BETWEEN MADRID AND VIENNA

OTTAWA AND HUMAN RIGHTS:
PARALLEL MONOLOGUES

The three intercessional meetings between the Madrid and Vienna Follow-ups, those in Ottawa, Budapest and Bern, were very characteristic of the spirit reigning at the time, the one of 'parallel monologues', to use an expression of the poet George Seferis from another context. As for the Stockholm Conference it went about its business successfully and concluded in a much more balanced manner, tilting less to the East than the Soviet Union would have hoped for.

The Ottawa Meeting of Experts on Human Rights (7 April–17 June 1985) was the first meeting devoted exclusively to one fundamental aspect of the human dimension, Principle VII, human rights proper. Not surprisingly, the meeting did not produce a document, an outcome anticipated by the Western states whose slogan was 'better nothing than an unsubstantial document', or one that would dilute the essential Western character of human rights and fundamental freedoms as set out in the Final Act and in the Madrid Concluding Document.

The Preparatory Meeting set the course for things to come by reaching agreement *à la Madrid*, that is after the set deadline and by the device of stopping the clock, with negotiations throughout the night, with no agreement next day (7 May 1985), and the main meeting being opened without an agenda. The final compromise came from the NNA group later in the day. The main points of contention had been, as in Madrid, the publicizing of sessions, the amount of time to be allotted to a review debate, and an unusual request by the Eastern delegations, which ended up as a useful element in the final package, to commemorate the fortieth anniversary of the end of the Second World War.[1] In the agenda adopted there was ample time for a review debate (three weeks), with the official opening by Canada and the closing statements being public.

The three-week implementation debate was strenuous, with almost all of the Western bloc states, as well as Austria, Switzerland,

Sweden and Liechtenstein, voicing criticisms of the Soviet Union and other Eastern countries, notably Czechoslovakia, the GDR and Bulgaria. Ottawa is also renowned for the first appearance at an inter-governmental forum of the Turkish–Bulgarian clash regarding the Muslim/Turkish minority in Bulgaria, which lasted until autumn 1989 (at the Sofia Meeting on the Environment). Poland was partially criticized but was able to show that in some areas, such as religious freedoms, its record was a sound one. Hungary's behaviour was low-key. It was evasive but sophisticated in its pronouncements, warding off any criticism. Romania was ably represented and also managed to avoid being criticized until the last moment, when its emigration policies were not left without adverse comments to which it reacted, *inter alia*, with its well-known argument of a 'brain drain' by the West. Needless to say it was the Soviet Union which bore the brunt of Western attacks, particularly by the United Kingdom, the United States, the Nether-lands and more subtly by the FRG, France and Italy.[2]

The obvious Soviet aim regarding the Ottawa meeting was basically one of damage limitation,[3] and in this the Soviet delegation was fairly successful.[4] When they were faced with increasingly harsh criticism in the actual meeting, they went on the attack (after briefly alluding to non-interference), and were well prepared for this, with an extended dossier of 'massive' human rights violations for any state that dared criticize them. They also put forward their concept of human rights 'coherently and vigorously'.[5] These exchanges often went on for hours, but they also had their moments of comedy – for instance, when the Soviet delegate lashed out at the Netherlands for its tolerance of pornography and other such 'crimes', the Netherlands representative reacted with relish by stating, among other things, that the right to work was hardly an individual right but 'a curse' that had befallen man since being evicted from Paradise; or when the Soviet delegation was rendered speechless because it had no appropriate dossier with which to hit back at the sharp attack made by the Liechtenstein representative.

The proposals put forward in Ottawa numbered forty-five in all. The Western proposals which gained an all-Western co-sponsorship covered the following themes: freedom of movement, initiated by Ireland; freedom of religion, by France; the right to know and act upon one's rights, by the FRG; trade union rights, by the United States; the ban on torture, by Greece; and observers at trials, by France. Western proposals which did not get an all-Western blessing included: NGOs, by Denmark and Canada; monitoring, by Norway; human rights inquiries, by the United States; co-operation in human rights matters, by Belgium; psychiatric abuse, by the United Kingdom and the United States; incommunicado detention, by the United States; capital punishment, by the Nordics; national minorities, by Turkey, co-sponsored by the Netherlands and the FRG; and terrorism, by Turkey, co-sponsored by the United States and Spain.[6]

The Eastern delegations tried to match the Western proposals, if not in substance at least in quantity. The evident Eastern strategy was to counterbalance the rights appearing in the CSCE texts with 'second generation' rights, such as the right to work, and, if possible, novel 'third generation rights', such as 'the right to life in peace', free of nuclear war.

The proposals by the NNA included three by Austria, on the banning of torture, freedom of religion and the equality of men and women; the right to know about one's rights, by Sweden; bilateral and multilateral co-operation on human rights matters, by Finland; and four proposals by Yugoslavia on its pet projects of national minorities, ethnic groups (later co-sponsored by Austria), the rights of migrant workers and democratic participation by the people in decision-making ('popular participation' was a favourite subject of Yugoslavia which had been launched in the UN). The Neutrals' flagship proposal on holding regular meetings on human rights (arguing that such matters are of legitimate international concern) was initiated by Switzerland and co-sponsored by Sweden, Liechtenstein and San Marino, to which were later added Austria and from the West, Spain. (In this proposal one can trace the beginnings of the idea for the CSCE Conference on the Human Dimension adopted in the Vienna Follow-up). Finally, the Holy See presented a proposal on the implementation of religious freedom through consultations with the institutions and organizations of the various faiths.

The '10' of the EC were tightly knit and effective under the Italian presidency, the main protagonist being the representative of the United Kingdom, the late Sir Anthony Williams, whose diplomatic skills came to the fore not only in dealing with the Eastern delegations but also in bridging the gap between the United States approach and the more moderate line represented by the FRG, France, Greece, Denmark and Ireland. Thus, though technically speaking all the main decisions on common proposals were taken by the Western group as a whole, following consultations in the NATO caucus – thereby, in effect, submerging the '10' in the '16' – it was the '10' who were the real driving force behind most of the major Western initiatives. In this they had the support of the Canadian delegation, whose role as hosts (together with personality factors) made them unusually moderate.

The Finnish delegation's posture, equidistant between East and West (or pre-East as the Western delegations dubbed it at the time), earned it the role of co-ordinator in the established informal contact group, a privilege of dubious value since agreement on a document was highly unlikely. The Finnish delegate presented a draft which was nearer to the Eastern approach of laying the emphasis on co-operation rather than reinforced commitments on civil and political rights. As a result the text was unacceptable not only to the West but also to the like-minded Neutrals, the Finnish delegation having made the mistake of not consulting first with the other NNA delegations. The Soviet delegation wanted a paragraph-by-paragraph reading based on the Finnish text, noting jokingly in the contact group that the meeting could well end up with a document of two proposals, since there was general agreement only on two items, the eradication of torture and the equality of rights between men and women. Since it was obvious that no detailed document stood a chance, there was no concentrated attempt at real drafting, apart from a short-lived informal drafting group on national minorities under Yugoslav chairmanship, which appeared to suggest a compromise as Yugoslavia seemed prepared to scale down its goals to the lines of a Turkish proposal that was acceptable to the rest, including Bulgaria.

The Soviet Union was intransigent to new commitments that would further reinforce the 'imbalanced' Principle VII, but there was some indication that its very tough stance in the negotiations was not shared by all its allies. When it was more or less obvious that there would be no concluding document the West submitted its version of an ideal document (OME.47),[7] its 'wish list' which included not only the all-Western proposals listed above, but also elements from proposals on which there was no agreement in the '10' or '16', for instance, on psychiatric practices and on terrorism.[8] Like the Western delegations, the Warsaw Pact presented an 'Eastern' concluding document (OME.48).

As time was running out, Austria, with the assistance of Switzerland and Sweden, came out with a short text which was submitted as an NNA draft document. The text was of the Belgrade type, saying that talks had taken place. There was one important element: a recommendation for future meetings on human rights. The Eastern delegations could not accept this idea and suggested an even weaker text. The clock was stopped on Friday 14 May for negotiations to continue throughout the weekend and until the early hours of Monday morning for a last attempt at a document, but to no avail, even though the NNA text came to be supported by the West, since the East would not accept any change in their own short version.[9]

Thus the Ottawa Meeting, the first CSCE meeting on North American soil, ended with no document. In addition to the prevailing climate of East–West confrontation then in full swing, to the difference in philosophies between East and West and to their approaches to the meeting in question, there were also two structural problems involved that hindered the development of a document of substance. One was that the majority of NNA countries supported Western views on human rights, and could thus not be seen as genuine bridge-builders. The other was that the fact of having a meeting devoted only to human rights forestalled any trade-offs in other areas, which would have permitted some 'give' on the part of the Eastern countries. The only logical road ahead, apart from a mere reaffirmation of existing commitments, was that of trading concessions on first generation rights (civil and political rights) with second generation rights (economic, social and cultural rights) – something apparently realized by the Soviet delegation – which are after all barely mentioned in the Final Act or in the Madrid Concluding Document. Of course, this was totally unacceptable to the West for it would have meant transforming the basic character of the human rights dimension of the CSCE and what the whole CSCE stood for in the West.

At the end of the Ottawa Meeting the feeling of disappointment with the state of affairs in Eastern Europe and with what the CSCE – then in its tenth year – could possibly accomplish under such circumstances was intense. Even though the inability to produce a significant document had been foreseen, no document at all was unique at the time in the annals of the CSCE, implying failure. In fact, there was an important positive aspect to this: it was a sign that standards had risen and that putting together just *any* paper, simply for its own sake, in such a vital area of the CSCE was unacceptable – something, incidently, which went down well with the public and with the Helsinki monitoring groups.[10] As most Western states concluded in their *post mortem* assessments of the exercise, Ottawa had not been 'a death knell on human rights in CSCE', as some outsiders believed, but an effective exercise in accountability and, according to Washington, the message had been given to the smaller Warsaw Pact states that improvement in their human rights performance could play a significant role in improving their relations with the West. In fact, as pointed out by one EC state, the Soviet Union had won a pyrrhic victory. Most importantly, Ottawa had established, beyond doubt, that criticism regarding another state's human rights record could hardly be construed as interference, but was a legitimate international concern and states could be placed in the dock and required to justify their behaviour on the human dimension.[11]

In the wake of Ottawa there hung an intriguing question: but now what lies ahead? There could be but three answers: the resurrection of *détente* and co-existence on the basis of some minimal code of conduct – what could be called the 'phoenix effect'; the gradual but relentless triumph of the Western liberal ideological blueprint; or the establishment of the Eastern communist ideology, thereby vindicating the old claim that Marxism–Leninism had an inherent 'historical advantage'.

The outcome of the Ottawa Meeting was to cast its shadow on the ceremonial meeting of 30 July–1 August 1985 at Helsinki for the tenth anniversary of the signing of the Final Act CSCE, which took place with statements by foreign ministers. This was the first major appearance of the new Soviet Foreign Minister, Eduard Shevardnadze (who was very much aware of this fact),[12] who, together with Mikhail Gorbachev, was destined to play a historic role in the human dimension. In their speeches US Secretary of State Shultz and Shevardnadze were extremely critical, the former castigating the Soviet Union for its human rights record, and the latter producing the old argument of non-interference and accusing the United States of being against peace, as demonstrated by its Star Wars project.[13]

In the Budapest Cultural Forum, which took place between the Ottawa and Bern meetings in the autumn of 1985 (15 October–25 November), the possibility of a document was even more remote, given the great number of formal and informal proposals submitted – over 250 in number – and the participation of several eminent personalities who spoke in their own capacity, most, with the exception of those from the East, being highly independent. In the end not even the short two-page factual statement was accepted, due to Romania's withholding of consensus. Thus a second CSCE meeting, again within the human rights/Basket III spectrum, had not produced a text.[14]

BERN AND HUMAN CONTACTS: GROPING FOR A DIALOGUE

It was in the next year, at the Bern Meeting of Experts on Human Contacts (15 April to 27 May 1986), that one could detect for the first time a thaw in East–West relations at the CSCE level. The meeting was less polemical between East and West, to a degree unknown until then in the human dimension sphere since the adoption of the Final Act. No doubt the main factor for this was the attitude of the Soviet delegation. Apparently the nascent Gorbachev administration was already making its mark, however timidly. Indeed, the meeting was moving towards a concluding document which was not achieved because of a last minute *volte-face*, surprisingly, by a Western delegation.

The main meeting, as in Ottawa, was preceded by 'preparatory consultations', the main issues again being the degree of openness and the time to be allotted for implementation. There was also the question of the division of labour in the subsidiary working bodies which were to be established. The United States was for as much openness as possible, while the NNA and the '12' realized that it would be more pragmatic to settle for the Ottawa formula. As in Ottawa, discussions continued well into the night of the last day, but agreement was reached sooner this time, in the early hours of 15 April (the day of the opening of the main meeting). The only change from the Ottawa model (apart from now creating two subsidiary working bodies) was that the closing statements could be longer (seven to ten minutes with the possibility of one whole day devoted to them). Following the opening statements, the Western delegations decided to give a press conference to inform the public. The impression had already been created in the preparatory consultations that this time a concluding document of some substance was possible and was not unwelcome to the Eastern side.

The general debate on implementation was much more restrained and moderate. There was an emerging dialogue of sorts, with the Soviet delegation under Yuri Kashlev (who was to head the Soviet contingent in Vienna also) setting the pace, followed by the Polish delegate Jerzy Nowak. In the implementation review the most telling points were made on the Western side by the FRG and British delegates, as well as by the aggressive Canadian delegate.[15] The United States delegation was headed by a theologian, who was prone to sermonizing the East on how to abide by the right to religious freedom and other values of the Western/US 'paradise'. This patronizing attitude irritated Eastern delegations, but amused other delegations with its 'brothers and sisters' approach (the term was actually used more than once).[16] The Soviet delegation used its ammunition mainly against the United States and Canada. The recurring theme of the whole debate (to be reiterated in the Vienna Follow-up under the item 'human contacts') was on the right of free movement (exit visas) and entry visas (the 'right to entry' according to the Eastern delegations). On this and other matters there were moments of tension, but the most extended and fearsome confrontation was that between the Turkish and Bulgarian delegates on the treatment of the Muslim/Turkish minority of Bulgaria, with the Bulgarian delegation being better prepared this time. The only other major clash was that between Cyprus and Turkey, which lapsed into a lengthy procedural debate.[17]

On the whole, the implementation stage in Bern was probably the most worthwhile exchange of views on the human dimension until then, and, the '12' concluded, 'problems were addressed substantially and in genuine terms', while Eastern delegations resorted to using extreme socialist terminology only in their closing statements.[18]

The total number of proposals was forty-six. The Western proposals were pulled into shape in the '12' and '16' at the experts' level (deputy heads of delegation), both under Dutch presidency (often working from very early in the morning, in what the British delegate dubbed the 'Dawn Patrol'). They submitted twenty proposals in all, addressing specific issues or difficulties that had arisen in the implementation of CSCE undertakings, the basic criteria being to 'add substance to the existing provisions' and 'indicate procedural means to promote their implementation'. Some were co-sponsored by NNA delegations. The Eastern delegations reacted with no less then twenty-two proposals, obviously in order to counterbalance the Western proposals in negotiations. The quality of the Eastern proposals was generally lower than in Ottawa, most of them being poorly drafted, not addressing major problems, and overlapping each other. For the West the most worthwhile Eastern idea was a last-minute Soviet proposal recommending that measures be taken to improve administrative regulations and practices on questions of exit and entry for family reunification and family meetings, which implied a recognition for the first time in the CSCE that there was room for improvement in the way Eastern European states applied CSCE commitments.[19]

It was clear that a concluding document, substantial in several respects, was a realistic aim as the attitude of the Eastern delegations, probably with the exception of Romania, was favourable, completely different to their approach in Ottawa and Budapest. Thus the negotiations for a document (a Report as it was to be called) were not delayed and went on as comprehensively as possible. The main driving force for a document were the '12' (pulling with them Canada and the United States), the main protagonists being the Dutch and British delegations, with important contributions by the very experienced Belgian delegation.[20]

First there were various bilateral contacts between Western *chefs de files* (the initiators of specific proposals) and Eastern delegations on individual proposals to see what could be acceptable if reformulated. Then the Western caucus decided to 'sound out' the Eastern delegations rather more formally regarding the totality of their proposals. A so-called 'sounding group' was set up, comprising the delegations of the Netherlands (the '12' presidency), the United States, the Soviet

Union and Romania, with the Austrian delegate (who was to be the future co-ordinator) present as an observer so that he could be in a position to launch a first draft of a concluding report as a basis for discussion. Soon a contact group (informal and open-ended) was formed under the Austrian ambassador, Rudolf Torovsky. The main negotiator on the Western side (sitting on the right of the table) was Sir Anthony Williams of the United Kingdom (the West's most adroit negotiator), and on the other side of the table, the Soviet deputy head Victor Shikalov and the Romanian delegate, Diaconu.

The negotiations were protracted and difficult but there was a move forward. It was soon clear that it was Romania (sitting as usual at a certain distance from the other Eastern delegations), rather than the Soviet Union, which was taking the harder line.[21] The non-paper presented by the co-ordinator clearly tilted on the Western side (contrary to what had happened in Ottawa). As a result the Eastern delegations became less flexible (the Soviet delegation at one point walking out of the negotiations in protest against the pro-Western tendency of the co-ordinator).

Laborious negotiations continued well into the night, again with the device of stopping the clock. The Austrian and Swiss delegations presented a revised non-paper which was then officially deposited on 23 May as an NNA paper, the 'Report of the Meeting of Experts on Human Contacts' (BME.49). The paper was more middle of the road than the previous one, and seemed to gain support from all sides. Only the Romanian delegation, and to some extent that of the United States, which had not been very active in the contact group, seemed more circumspect, particularly on the question of contact by 'persons belonging to national minorities and regional cultures on their territories with persons in other states with whom they have close affinities'.[22] In this Romania had the support of the Soviet Union, on the grounds that the national minority issue was not included in the 'Contacts' section of the Final Act, and the idea was finally dropped, much to the relief of some Western delegations, who had previously tried within the '16' to omit it from the Western text. A last point of contention – which was given much attention by the media at the time[23] – was that of facilitating exits only to 'participating states' and not universally, which the United States wanted so that Soviet Jews would be able to go directly to Israel. In any event, the conclusion of the contact group was that the Austrian–Swiss non-paper was accepted by all delegations *ad referendum* during the afternoon of 26 May, the date that the meeting was to close (the meeting had been extended by one day). It seemed that at last a document, and a substantial one at that, had been achieved in the CSCE human dimension field in the inter-cessional period between Madrid and Vienna. However, this was not to be, and the problem came from an unexpected quarter, the United States.

The United States delegate announced to an astounded NATO caucus later in the day that the document was not acceptable because it was too weak and was a step backwards from existing CSCE commit-ments. The other NATO ambassadors could barely hide their indig-nation, including hard-liners such as the United Kingdom delegate. Only the Canadian delegate came to the support of the United States. The FRG ambassador, Ekkehard Einchoff, made an impassioned appeal, alluding to some of the topics on which there was a move forward that would be particularly beneficial to his compatriots and their ethnic kin. Then, one by one, the Western heads of delegation took the floor in what was an eloquent presentation of what the CSCE was trying to achieve with its step-by-step approach, hoping to impress upon their inexperienced United States colleague the merits of the document and urging him to contact Washington to convey their views. The '12' decided that the Netherlands presidency should contact the State Department at a high level, while the FRG informed its EC partners that Bonn would make a separate *démarche* to Washington. When the United States stance became widely known, the Soviet delegation and its allies (without Romania) suggested a further delay so as to give more time, but the idea was not pursued in view of the inflexibility of the United States. The strain between the United States and its Western European allies was not improved when Secretary of State Shultz rejected Foreign Minister Genscher's last-minute appeal.[24]

This turn of events was advantageous to the Eastern bloc, which could lay the blame for failure on the United States, and particularly to Romania, which might otherwise have been the one to veto the document in the end.[25] In the closing statements which followed most of the delegations voiced their disappointment at the outcome. The Soviet delegation and the other Eastern delegations attacked the United States for its 'systematic negative attitude' in the CSCE and elsewhere in matters of peace and co-operation, and for following 'an attitude of yesterday' not fit for a changing Europe. The Western states were, of course, far more restrained in their assessments, but they could not hide their frustration with the United States delegation, the only exception being Canada (which did not seem unhappy at the development). The FRG delegate made it clear that he would have gladly left Bern with the document as it was proposed. The United

Kingdom said that it had supported the document with some reluctance, but that the United States assessment had been more pessimistic and 'we can only respect their views'. The Swiss Foreign Minister stated that the NNA document was a move forward but consensus had not been reached because of the opposition of one delegation, which was regrettable. The only distraction during the gloomy closing session was another Turkish–Bulgarian clash, which, however, was fairly brief in comparison to Ottawa's final stage. Thus ended the Bern Meeting, generally regarded at the time as the 'missed opportunity'.[26]

The last-minute *volte-face* by the United States has remained one of the mysteries of the CSCE. What baffled delegates at the time was that the United States delegation had participated in all the phases of the consensus-building process in the NATO caucus and then in the sounding group and contact group, giving no indication of what was to follow. It seems that they must have received last-minute instructions from Washington.[27] Perhaps, as the Swiss complained, the whole affair was partly due to the 'amateurism' of the United States delegation or, to be more precise, of its head of delegation.[28] The decision was probably influenced by Congress and by domestic public opinion, as well as by the desire to send a clear signal to the Kremlin. Moreover, it was also typical of the general approach of the United States to the CSCE and new commitments.[29]

After the meeting, the United States took some pains to explain its decision to its allies by pointing out that the document was full of deficiencies and loopholes and that it diluted commitments made in Helsinki and Madrid.[30] In CSCE procedural terms, the rationale was that 'the overall ambition of the draft document [was] so low that, rather than reflecting true consensus, it reflect[ed] an inability to achieve consensus on substantive issues'.[31] Of even more dubious value was another argument by Washington that 'cynical governments' could argue that they were not bound by previous commitments but only by those in this document (an argument which has, at times, been used in different versions).[32] In fact, as pointed out by the '12' and the FRG in particular, the text really did not fall that short, for it contained several useful formulations which would have made it a stepping-stone for the forthcoming Vienna Follow-up Meeting.[33]

Thus, in one respect, Bern became the opposite of Ottawa, in that this time it was United States, not Soviet, intransigence that carried the day. For a fleeting moment Europe was as one against the 'New World' across the Atlantic, the basic difference between them being the level of commitment to the whole CSCE exercise.

THE VIENNA FOLLOW-UP:
THE ARDUOUS BREAKTHROUGH

FEW EXPECTATIONS

The Vienna Meeting was pivotal for the CSCE. It was where the crucial breakthrough took place which proved to be a turning point in East–West relations.[1] Though a few months shorter in duration than the Madrid Meeting, the time devoted to drafting was longer, which indicates the intensity of the negotiations.

A few weeks or even days before the Vienna Follow-up was about to begin, prospects for a successful outcome were dim. The dominant mood in the '16' (NATO) and '12' (EC) meetings on the eve of the Follow-up was one of pragmatism. The United States maintained that the primary objective of Vienna should be the review of compliance, its chief concern being that if the West pushed ahead with sweeping new commitments these could be used by the East 'to flee forward' from existing obligations (another version of the familiar argument).[2] The moderates correctly pointed out that new commitments did not annul previous ones but, on the contrary, the creation of additional provisions brought more pressure to bear. Yet, in general, even the moderates were sceptical about how far to pursue new commitments since they were seen as largely unattainable.[3] The relative success of the Stockholm meeting raised fears of an imbalance in favour of the military aspects of security. Thus, on the whole, it would not be an overstatement to claim that few participants suspected at the time that the Vienna Concluding Document would ultimately become so substantial in the human dimension sphere, and fewer still could have predicted the momentous events in Europe that were to follow.

The story of the Vienna Meeting is largely the story of our subject matter, human rights, human contacts and the other Basket III issues – in effect, the 'human dimension'. Indeed, it was in Vienna that the concept of the 'human dimension' was officially launched by the West, and was then gradually taken up by the Soviet Union and its allies as a concept and as an acceptable term.

The Preparatory Meeting (September–October 1986) which set out the agenda for Vienna was a sign of things to come, for matters went through smoothly, in contrast to the confrontations and antics of previous meetings, and there was prompt agreement on all the issues that had traditionally bedevilled preparatory meetings, such as the level of openness, the time available for implementation and assuring a follow-up. The first and last plenary meetings were to be open to the public as in Madrid, but so were the plenaries at the beginning and end of each new session. The compromise over the duration was an even simpler matter to achieve although the East had asked for five weeks and the West for eight. There was to be an overlap in the agenda items: with implementation lasting for eight weeks and the submission of proposals starting from the sixth week and to be officially introduced during the seventh week. The follow-up was also solved without problems, unlike Madrid, and it was agreed that the Vienna Meeting would not close without an agreement on the date and place for the next follow-up. The most difficult question proved to be a secondary one, working hours for the meetings – past experience had shown that a chairman could abuse his role by insisting on the cut-off time that had been set, as had happened in Madrid when the foreign ministers were present in February 1982.[4]

The smoothness of the Preparatory Meeting emboldened some among the '12' with ambitious proposals on the human dimension to push them forward within the group, notably Denmark, for a conference on the human dimension, the Netherlands, on a consultative committee, and the United Kingdom, on an information meeting. These ideas did not gain much support at the time, but it was agreed that there was a strong case for some kind of major initiative by the '12' in this field.[5]

VIENNA, 1986: IMPLEMENTATION – BUSINESS AS USUAL

The start of the Vienna Meeting was as impressive as the magnificent Hoffburg Palace where the meeting took place until mid-1987. The foreign ministers' speeches were more optimistic than usual, in what was, after all, the best international climate since 1975. Foreign Minister Shevardnadze created a stir by suggesting that Moscow should be the venue of a conference on humanitarian co-operation.

However, the feeling that something was about to happen in the murky waters of East–West relations was momentary. After the foreign ministers left, the CSCE was back to normal, or what was normal in those Cold War days. Indeed, the implementation debate was characterized by more than the usual number of clashes, reminiscent of the days before the Bern Meeting, with almost all of the Western countries joining the fray. The interventions on human rights and human contacts were often devastating, with the brunt of the criticism falling on the Soviet Union, and then Czechoslovakia and Bulgaria (regarding the Muslim/Turkish minority).

The Canadian ambassador, William Bauer, the hawk *par excellence* of the meeting, pulled no punches (becoming the diplomat the Eastern delegates loved to hate), repeatedly lecturing, almost too eloquently, on the principles of human rights and democracy and on Eastern abuses, and concluding that the Soviet record was 'deplorable' and that 'the new wind which we are told blows from Moscow brings no refreshing change'.[6] The United States chief delegate, Ambassador Warren Zimmermann (Max Kampelman's deputy in Madrid), a more restrained orator, was probably more convincing. Together with his deputy in Basket III, Samuel Wise, and the British delegates, Ambassador Lawrence O'Keeve and Philip Hurr, he allowed Eastern delegations little time to catch their breath. Zimmermann pointed out among other things that there is a 'vital connection between a State's approach toward human rights domestically and its conduct internationally. If a State is pathologically distrustful of its own citizens, is it not prone to a certain paranoia in its foreign policy?'[7]

The Soviet delegates used their familiar arguments against the West, but this time did not mention non-interference and avoided lengthy speeches on their 'exemplary' record. Indeed, they hardly tried to show that such a record existed. The Soviet lead was followed by Bulgaria and Czechoslovakia, while Hungary, Poland and the GDR tried to be as non-confrontational as possible, and Romania kept a low profile. Among the most spirited slogans used by the Soviet delegates were 'Western political hooliganism', 'Cold War stereotypes', 'confrontational escapades' and 'psychological warfare' against the socialist countries now in quest of change. What was conveyed strongly were a sense of hurt pride and the claim that change in the Soviet Union was endogenous, brought about purely by internal circumstances and as a consequence of 'new thinking' from within, and was not the result of pressure or in order to mimic the 'defunct capitalist model'. The main defect in their presentation, apart from a lack of convincing arguments, was that they failed to develop a proper intonation and escalation in the argument, tending to rush on with what they had to say as if to get it over with as soon as possible.

The overall United States assessment (to be more precise, the conclusion of the US Commission) regarding the implementation debate was that the Soviet Union and its allies had come 'under the most concentrated and concerted attack for human rights abuses since the beginning of the Helsinki process in 1975'.[8] What was striking about this, and made Vienna somewhat extreme in its implementation review, was that it had taken place at a time when the Soviet Union and two of its allies, Hungary and Poland, were already taking significant steps in meeting human rights standards in ways well beyond what could be dismissed as mere 'window-dressing'. The Western slogan in Vienna was, in fact, 'no compliance, no need for new commitments'.[9] However, contrary to the general belief at the time, the West was not totally unanimous in this line, but those in the Western camp who were not in tune were not in a position to do much other than watering down some of the '12' speeches, avoiding 'naming names' themselves, and so on. For moderates among the Western delegations, the implementation debate was a necessary evil which had hopefully become a ritual, with little effect on subsequent businesslike negotiations.

Before the delegations left for the Christmas break the West had succeeded in highlighting continuing Eastern abuses, including psychiatric abuse, harassing Charter 77 and the Jazz Section in Czechoslovakia, and much was made of the death of dissident Anatoly Marchenko in a labour camp on 8 December. Thus, the various changes in the Soviet Union (symbolized by the ending of Andrei Sakharov's exile in Gorky and announced by Ambassador Kashlev at a press conference in the Hoffburg Palace), and the Moscow conference proposed by Shevardnadze were overshadowed. Of course, few could then have guessed that this was to be the last review of implementation in the old mode of East–West, the last important meeting with the two sides facing each other like primeval warriors, each one convinced of his righteousness in the wider scheme of things.

However, let us now look at the event that made the Vienna Meeting different from the very beginning, the 'Moscow proposal', the 'preposterous idea' of having Basket III issues, the East's most hated subject, being discussed in Moscow, the 'Mecca of totalitarianism'. The Soviet proposal could be one of three things: a most audacious propaganda stunt and negotiating ploy; genuine and sincere; or a folly.

THE MOSCOW PROPOSAL: THE CHALLENGE

Shevardnadze's idea of a Moscow meeting to discuss all humanitarian (Basket III) issues was probably, in CSCE terms, the single, most influential act that was to lead to a dramatic change and breakthrough in the CSCE. The participants were duly amazed, even the Eastern delegations, and apparently even the members of the Soviet delegation itself. Obviously the proposal was a top-level Kremlin decision. In Vienna only two foreign ministers dared show interest in the idea, no lesser figures than Hans-Dietrich Genscher (FRG) and Leo Tindemans (Belgium). Others, such as the Netherlands and Swiss Foreign Ministers, pointed out the need for a permanent mechanism for implementation, while the Danish Foreign Minister referred to a human dimension conference.

The Moscow proposal was officially submitted a month later (on 10 December 1986 as WT.2) and introduced by Deputy Foreign Minister Anatoly Kovalev. WT.2 was basically an idea with very little content, simply the convening of 'a Conference of Representatives of the CSCE Participating States on the Problems of Humanitarian Co-operation ... in Moscow'.[10] The area was Basket III, seen as the addressing of 'problems' that could be dealt with through 'co-operation'. However, in the preambular part there was reference to human rights as well. Yet from December onwards, and for almost a year, the Soviet delegation could not be more concrete on its proposal, and on several occasions gave a distinct impression that it either lacked instructions or received conflicting instructions or that the Soviet Union had lost interest in its proposal.

After the initial shock of the proposal the West began consultations in earnest about how to react. If it was not what it seemed, basically a clever if risky propaganda stunt, could it mean that for the first time the Soviet Union was a *demandeur* on the human dimension? At first, only the FRG, Greece and, to some extent, Belgium showed sympathy for the idea, while the rest were averse to it.

The United States called the Moscow proposal a propaganda stunt aimed at 'blunting criticism', and a 'cynical' one at that, but at the same time it pointed out the value of the idea for negotiating purposes. The Soviets had 'put themselves on the hook', the USA told its allies, so let them pay a high price for having pulled such a stunt.[11] Washington's answer was soon formulated as 'neither yes nor no', but 'yes' as long as certain stringent conditions were met. These ranged from technical requirements, such as access to the media and human rights NGOs, to more fundamental prerequisites, such as a good human rights record. These demands were upheld almost to the very end of the Vienna Follow-up. The United States' approach contained an element of ambiguity, for it was not clear – negotiation strategy apart – whether the conditions were meant to be an indirect 'no' (particularly in calling for a good human rights record, which seemed simply unattainable within such a short time-span), or whether, in fact, they were really conditions. Plainly, in this ambiguity lay the wisdom of the approach, for it was also aimed at striking a balance between the feelings of Congress and those of public opinion, particularly of the insistent human rights advocates and the directly-concerned ethnic and religious groups in the United States.

Canada was totally averse to the idea at Vienna, especially at the delegation level. 'Going to Moscow', the very city associated with the worse abuses of human rights, was for it inconceivable. France, the United Kingdom, the Netherlands and Norway also saw the Moscow proposal as a political ploy and a propaganda stunt, and felt that accepting it would give a stamp of approval to the continuing violation of human rights. The Netherlands and France, in particular, also believed that this was a public relations exercise which would not include substantial changes and that the West must not fall into the trap set by the Moscow proposal. It was also pointed out that in a Moscow meeting the Soviet Union would, in all likelihood, try to follow its Ottawa and Bern policy of attempting to change the character of Principle VII by including at the same level second generation rights, the 'right of entry' and so on.[12] France's somewhat surprising intransigence appeared less convincing after Paris was flagged as a venue for a human rights meeting in 1989, the year of the two hundredth anniversary of the French Revolution and the momentous declaration on the 'rights of man' – the obvious trade-off being a meeting in Moscow as well. However, among the hard-liners the most elusive approach was that of the United Kingdom, for although officially it did not change its firm decision not to go Moscow (to the place where it felt there were no human rights), on the ground (in Vienna and at EPC level) it was very instrumental in putting forward the elements of an acceptable compromise. The reasons for this approach were not clear: was it a calculated move or was there internal disagreement or pressure from outside, from, say, the United States? Note that on one occasion (in December 1987) the EC partners had witnessed the British dissociating themselves from one of their own 'non-papers', which was a very useful stepping-stone to the final solution, at which point the FRG had said that they would gladly take over the parenthood of the paper.[13]

The moderate camp on the Moscow proposal was led by the FRG, Italy, Denmark, Belgium, Spain, Greece and Ireland (with Portugal siding more with the hard-liners). It could be a ploy, Belgium pointed out, mainly in so far as the Soviets calculated that by suggesting such a proposal they might avoid a great deal of discussion of similar issues in

Vienna and new commitments therefrom. But stunt or ploy, argued the moderates, this was a bold and positive proposal. As they pointed out, the Soviet leaders could not have been so naive as to have made it without realizing its consequences, above all the risks they were taking with such a meeting and the fact that they were thus making themselves a *demandeur*. The FRG's posture may also have been the result of more intimate knowledge of the evolving, genuine 'new thinking' in the Kremlin. Bonn was later to argue that by going to Moscow the West would be rendering a service to the dissidents there and would contribute to a better human rights record, rather than placing a stamp of approval on continued abuse. This was to be the view of no less a figure than Sakharov himself, and of the majority of Soviet Helsinki monitors.[14] However, the Soviet line in Vienna, which often seemed not to be firmly backing the Moscow proposal, gave more ammunition to the intransigent camp in the West.[15]

Among the '12', who were more or less equally divided into moderates and hard-liners, the final conclusion reached by the end of 1986 was that the proposal, if handled carefully, could be advantageous to the West – by encouraging far greater compliance from the Soviet Union; by the setting of conditions for the meeting (with the prospect of progress in implementation plus further technical conditions during the actual meeting); and by functioning as an impetus for the '12' to submit their own more far-reaching and imaginative proposals on future meetings or a human dimension mechanism.[16]

By and large, it was one of those moments, not uncommon in world politics, when misperception and intransigence were able to achieve positive results, for the greater the delay on agreement on this and other important issues in Vienna, the more substantial became the commitments, as 'new thinking' gained a stronger hold in the Soviet Union and East–West relations improved with the passage of time.

THE HUMAN DIMENSION PROPOSAL: THE COUNTER-CHALLENGE

The most immediate practical result of the Moscow proposal was renewed interest in the Danish and Netherlands projects. The United States for its part produced what was called a 'rotating regime of national Helsinki observers'.

The Danish idea, first aired in mid-September 1986 at an EC Ministerial Meeting, envisaged a semi-permanent 'Conference on the Human Dimension' (CHD), to counterbalance similar developments in the military field, with several sessions, ranging from three to eight weeks, which would include, at some stage, participation of NGOs in official delegations. The Conference would deal with general problems and not with individual cases and would submit its agreed recommendations to the post-Vienna follow-up. 'Human dimension' was defined by Denmark as including human rights (Principle VII) and human contacts.[17]

The Netherlands concept which appeared at the end of October 1986 was for what was called a 'Consultative Committee', intended as a mechanism to monitor implementation. It was to meet once a year, but also at the request of one of the participating states, to discuss developments in a particular case behind closed doors, which could lead to on-site inspection. For the next month or so the two proposals were in competition. Denmark emphasized the 'institutionalization' element in the Dutch concept (and its unfortunate choice of name, which was the same as an ill-fated idea regarding follow-up in Helsinki/Geneva). The Netherlands reformulated its proposal by December to a 'consultative mechanism', but still comprising regular as well as special meetings (at the request of a participating state).[18]

Early in December 1986 France came up with an all-embracing approach (based in part on a previous French idea aired during the CSCE tenth anniversary in 1985) suggesting bilateral talks, multilateral consultations and a conference, to be preceded by two preparatory meetings. The conference would be under probation as it were, to take place only if certain conditions, including progress in implementation, were met. The Netherlands was not happy with the French approach, for it ignored the notion of special meetings upon request. Then Italy brought the Moscow proposal more to the fore by setting out basic conditions for its acceptance: an improvement in the Soviet record; a precise mandate suited to the West; and various provisos for an eventual Moscow meeting as to openness and so on. Spain, among others, warned against over-strict conditions for the convening of a Moscow meeting, which would be interpreted as a veiled 'no'.[19]

With three Community proposals on the table there were two ways forward: to chose the most suitable of the three or to try to combine them. Denmark and the Netherlands suggested a merger of their proposals.[20] Portugal favoured a merger of all three with the French scheme as the basis.[21] The FRG (which together with Italy, Spain and Greece was unhappy with the dominance of the negative approach towards the Moscow idea) suggested combining the three proposals and placing them in the form of conditions by, among other things, recommending two pre-conferences, one in the Hague, the other in

Copenhagen, which would not lead automatically to a Moscow conference.[22]

In mid-December seven conditions were suggested by the United Kingdom (the '12' presidency at the time). The main condition was that the host country for a human rights/humanitarian review had to comply with the relevant provisions, and the minor conditions were of a technical nature regarding the convening of the meeting itself.[23] Thus 1986 ended with no agreement among the '12' on either the content or the advisability of having a common '12' or Western proposal as such.[24] The United Kingdom, which was urged to try to come up with a merger of the three ideas, appeared to be dragging its feet. To complicate things even further the United States circulated a non-paper on 'Helsinki Monitors', which was strongly advocated by the US Commission. The '12' – with the exception of the Netherlands – found the proposal unacceptable and felt it would be incompatible with anything that might come from them.

In the following year France took the initiative with a new version of its all-embracing concept, in which can be seen in embryo the basis of the future '12' proposal. There were difficult exchanges at the EPC level but finally a definite text was hammered out. It was agreed that it would be introduced on 4 February 1987 in the name of the '12' by the Belgian Foreign Minister. (The text is almost identical to that of the final proposal.[25]) Then came an unexpected complication. When the '12' informed the '16' of the proposal in Vienna and of their intention to submit it, their NATO allies reacted angrily, particularly Canada, Norway and the United States, which saw it as a breach of Western solidarity. What perturbed them most was that not only had they not been forewarned, but they had not even been invited to contribute to the proposal or modify it. They regarded a '12' proposal which they were expected just to accept as simply unthinkable, particularly on such a vital issue as a human dimension mechanism. The crisis was not easily resolved as the United States, Canada and Norway wanted to 'open up' the whole proposal again. The United States tried to incorporate its own Helsinki monitors proposal but without success as only the Netherlands reacted favourably to this. The crisis, one of the worst in the course of the Vienna Meeting, resurrected an old problem: to what extent could the '12' appear as a separate unit during the Cold War days of bloc-to-bloc interaction, when alliance solidarity was regarded as an asset and the right way to do business?

In the end a few secondary changes were introduced, but problems still remained with two substantial amendments suggested by the United States: to limit the requests for bilateral meetings and special meetings so as not to abuse the system by constant use; and to fix the dates and place of the conference during the Vienna Meeting – with the objective of being able to put greater pressure on the Soviet Union if Moscow was to be the venue – rather than leaving the matter open. The first amendment was unacceptable to the '12', even though it made a great deal of sense. The second was modified to providing for a decision in Vienna on the date of the first meeting, which would be entrusted, among other things, to set a date and place for the main conference. Another compromise was to have Belgium (alphabetically the first, but also the president of the '12') as the main sponsor of the human dimension proposal, with the other sixteen as co-sponsors in alphabetical order.[26]

The proposal was finally submitted as scheduled on 4 February 1987, after a last-minute clash between the delegates of the United States and France. Its title was 'Proposal on the Human Dimension of the Helsinki Final Act' (the word 'conference' was omitted), commonly known by its number, WT.19, or as 'CHD'. It consisted of two parts, the mechanism and the conference. The mechanism comprised four points: (1) acceding to requests for information and representation by the governments of the participating states, and also by 'private persons or groups' on questions 'relating to human rights'; (2) holding bilateral meetings 'in order to examine with a view to resolving them, cases or situations of non-respect for human rights, and humanitarian cases or situations relating to human contacts'; (3) instituting a notification procedure among the participating states to which 'particularly difficult cases or situations' could be referred; (4) giving every participating state 'the possibility of requesting and securing at the shortest possible notice a special meeting of 35 to discuss and resolve specific situations or cases'. The issues which created greatest difficulty not only to the other side, but also to others, including some Western delegations, were point 4, derived from the Netherlands proposal, and the provision in point 1 whereby individuals and groups could also request informa-tion, which virtually permitted individual petitions.[27]

The 'conference on the human dimension of the CSCE' was to consist of a meeting and a conference. The date and place of the meeting were to be decided in Vienna. Its objectives were to evaluate the mechanism, review the situation on human rights and human contacts, and elaborate and recommend 'new measures with a view to improving the implementation of the undertakings entered into'. The meeting would be declared closed only when it had been able, 'in the light of its assessment, to reach a consensus on the date and place of a conference'. The tasks of the conference were to adopt such measures as were recommended and otherwise follow a similar course to the meeting.

THE NEGOTIATIONS ON NORMATIVE COMMITMENTS

When the delegations returned to Vienna on 27 January 1987 to commence the submission of proposals, the atmosphere was more relaxed. The final total of proposals was one hundred and fifty-six, the greatest number ever at a CSCE follow-up meeting. According to one estimate, some sixty per cent of these proposals actually became the subject of negotiations. Interestingly, the seven Warsaw Pact countries submitted seventy-two proposals, more than twice as many as the seventeen Western countries (thirty) and almost three times as many as the nine NNAs (twenty-three). As Stefan Lehne, an author and participant, has rightly pointed out, this was the result of greater co-ordination by the West, two-thirds of whose proposals enjoyed the support of most of them, and because the West tabled only one proposal in the military field, while the East submitted at least a dozen in that area. One other record for the CSCE was the number of 'bloc-transcending' proposals, which amounted to no less than thirty-eight, seven of which included both Eastern and Western delegations. The first to include both Western and Eastern delegations (in fact, one from the East, Hungary), was on national minorities and human contacts.[28]

In addition to WT.19, the Western flagship *par excellence*, the other flagship proposals were on an information forum (of British origin), an economic conference (of German origin), and the proposal on military security. Among the 'textual proposals' (those setting new standards and commitments) included were national minorities, religious freedom, freedom of movement, rule of law, human rights monitors, and various aspects of human contacts and information. The main Eastern proposals, apart from WT.2 on the Moscow conference, were the Polish proposal on a mandate for CDE (Conference on CSBMs and Disarmament in Europe), the proposal by Czechoslovakia for an economic meeting in Prague, a symposium in Cracow on cultural heritage proposed by Poland and a meeting in Sofia on the environment proposed by Bulgaria.

After the bulk of proposals had been submitted and presented there was a standstill, with negotiations not starting in early spring 1987 as originally expected, but during May of that year. One of the reasons for this was that negotiations in the military field could not begin meaningfully in the absence of a Western proposal on the matter. The delay was mainly due to unresolved differences between France and the United States, and reaching a compromise took considerable time. Needless to say, the Eastern delegations blamed the West for the delay. In fact, on human rights and Basket III there was, throughout 1987, an 'absence of the political will necessary for meaningful progress'[29] on all sides. The reigning uncertainty in East–West relations made the situation in Vienna 'highly unpredictable' and more conducive to a 'wait and see' approach. Under such circumstances the prevailing negotiating strategy was the tough stance spearheaded by the United States, Canada, the United Kingdom and the Netherlands, which were the main speakers on the Western side once the meeting switched to 'informal mode'.

The Eastern delegations tried to inject second generation rights, the 'right of entry', and various well-known safety clauses into the debate, but were less effective than in previous CSCE meetings owing to their internal division and lack of cohesion. They were divided into two or perhaps even three groups. The intransigent group was comprised of Czechoslovakia, the GDR, Bulgaria and, above all, Romania. The moderates were Hungary and Poland. The Soviet delegation was initially with the hard-liners but, as time went by, they appeared to be somewhere between the two extremes.

In Vienna compromise took a considerable time to evolve for a variety of reasons, making the negotiations and the drafting seem on more than one occasion almost as fitful and acrimonious as those of Madrid, with the usual spate of angry outbursts and clashes, notably in Basket III. One of the reasons for this state of affairs, which frustrated Western as well as the like-minded NNA delegates in 1987 and the first part of 1988, was that the Soviet delegation gave a distinct impression that it was unclear as to how far it would be permitted to 'give' on the human dimension, and how much it would be willing to 'pay' for the convening of a Moscow meeting and other *desiderata*. In general, there was a noticeable contrast between the boldness of the Moscow proposal and the negotiating stance of the Soviet delegation in Vienna.

On the Moscow proposal itself, a hint was given by a top Soviet foreign ministry official in 1988: in trying to justify their far from forceful position on the Moscow Conference he said that several members in the Soviet delegation in Vienna represented the 'old thinking'.[30] Presumably this would have been even more the case in the Kremlin and in the Soviet foreign ministry with the ongoing differences between reformists and conservatives. Even when the

Shevardnadze line had prevailed, it then had to trickle down through the policy hierarchy, probably losing much of its thrust along the way since, after all, it was far too revolutionary for the majority of diplomats to even comprehend, let alone champion.

The Western group was committed to cohesion, almost as in Madrid, with the hard-liners 'calling the shots'. Of course, Western cohesion had a price, the most obvious one being that important proposals, as well as reasonable compromises with the East, would be greatly delayed. This was particularly the case with the Western proposal on military security, finally submitted as late as 10 July 1987, and in the time taken by the West to streamline their position on WT.19 so as to be able to accommodate some of the valid Eastern exigencies.[31]

The NNA in their meeting at Limassol in June 1987 arranged to have Austria co-ordinate Basket I–principles, Finland Basket I–military aspects, Switzerland Basket II, Sweden Basket III, and Yugoslavia the Follow-up. Thus on the human dimension the main burden fell on Austrian ambassador Rudolf Torovsky and his deputy Stefan Lehne on Basket I–principles and on the Swedish diplomat Nils Eliasson on Basket III, who went about their task most effectively, despite the many, often unexpected difficulties they had to face, and the obvious fact that both co-ordinators were clearly committed to the Western approach on such matters.

Negotiations took place in two kinds of informal setting: the more formal 'informal groups', with the three groups on three sides of a long table, where introductory remarks were made on the proposals; and the contact groups in smaller, cramped rooms, where the bulk of the negotiations took place from autumn 1987 onwards. The standard in Basket III was set by a non-paper launched unexpectedly before the summer recess on 30 July 1987, which was not produced by the co-ordinator but by the Austrian and Swiss delegations. The 'Austro-Swiss paper', as it came to be known, was clearly inclined towards the West and set a high standard. This was a gamble, for little previous consultation had taken place (other than, one suspects, with some of the Western delegates). However, the Eastern delegations did not reject it, but accepted it as the basis for negotiations, though they pointed out that it was ill-balanced (favouring the Western side) and that several of its provisions were totally unacceptable to them.[32]

With the coming of the next session in autumn 1987, the Austrian co-ordinator in Basket I–principles presented various non-papers following the high standards and Western bias of the Austro-Swiss paper in Basket III. As Lehne (Torovsky's deputy) has pointed out, the final Vienna document actually resembles in many respects the non-papers of those days. Little progress was made in the contact groups. The situation was worse in Basket III, where the Soviet delegation assisted by the Eastern hard-liners appearing to be giving very little and trying to weaken the Austro-Swiss text considerably. Apparently, the aim was to prove that it was unworkable as a basis for negotiations. By Christmas only some four provisions had been accepted out of around fifty. Then the co-ordinator, with Eastern prompting, came up with a text of his own but, to Western relief, he made only minor adjustments, keeping to the thrust of the Austro–Swiss paper.[33]

The next year saw a hardening of the Eastern position with the submission of a large number of new amendments. To break the impasse the Basket III co-ordinator put together a package of pro-posals meant to be adopted immediately as 'ice-breaker operations', but more 'ice' was added than broken, and by the end of spring only one-third of Basket III had been completed.[34] In this state of affairs, the NNA as a whole took the initiative and, with the co-ordinators in the forefront, started preparing a draft Vienna concluding document which was completed in some five weeks. It was introduced by the NNA foreign ministers on 13 May 1988 and was positively received.

From then on, however, Romania emerged as the major problem, by introducing a great number of amendments and threatening non-acceptance of the text. The Soviet delegation was able to keep its other allies in line, presenting relatively few amendments. In this manner, the negotiations were spurred on and were moving towards a conclusion. It was not clear whether Romania was actually toying with the idea of blocking the document or was using the threat to water down the draft document to the greatest degree possible. Soviet officials advised the West to give in to marginal changes to meet some of the Romanian demands.[35]

The main outstanding problem was the fundamental CHD con-ference/mechanism intertwined with the Moscow proposal, which is discussed below. Outside the human dimension field there were also two unexpected difficulties, one a sudden review by the French of their position on the structure of the future military negotiations, which led to some adjustments of the NATO position, further stressing the link between CFE (Conventional Armed Forces in Europe) talks and the CSCE; the other was a Greek–Turkish difference on the exception in the zone of application of the future conventional arms reductions regarding the port of Mersin (which is situated opposite Cyprus and was actually used during the Turkish military intervention in Cyprus in 1974). This latter question seriously threatened delaying the adoption of the Vienna Concluding Document, but at the last moment a formula was found according to which the exclusion of Mersin was left open (note, however, that several Western states and the Soviet Union provided Turkey with written assurances that they would support it in the negotiations that were to follow).

TOWARDS THE CHD CONFERENCE AND MECHANISM

Soviet criticism of the Western CHD proposal can be summarized as follows: that it was too supranational in nature; that it created a bureaucratic mechanism that went well beyond the UN and the CSCE; that its patent goal was to change the socialist system of the Soviet Union; that it went counter to Principle I of the Final Act on sovereign equality; that it was too limited in scope, leaving out most of Basket III; that instead of being conducive to resolving humanitarian problems through mutual understanding and co-operation, it was more likely to lead to confrontation and impasse; that it implied conditions, something which placed the Soviet Union in a humiliating position as a sovereign independent state. More specifically, its main difficulties were with regard to individual petitions in point 1, point 4 on requests for meetings, and the fact that the date and place of the main conference (which it saw as a Moscow conference) was not to be decided in Vienna, but was left open and conditional. Among the secondary questions raised was that the conference should not take place simply at expert level. The Soviet Union's first modest step at furthering its own proposal and timidly trying to meet WT.19 was made on 24 July 1987 (in WT.2/Add.1). A second, more daring attempt came on 10 December of the same year in the form of a non-paper.[36]

The 24 July version, introduced in plenary by the Soviet head of delegation, Ambassador Kashlev, had few amendments, but was noteworthy in that it was the first time in an official CSCE document that the Soviet Union mentioned the concept of the 'human dimension'. The Conference was aimed at 'the broadening of humanitarian co-operation in the context of the *human dimension*' (emphasis added), and was to consider 'co-operation in promoting the effective exercises of civil, political, economic, social, cultural and other personal rights and freedoms', and 'co-operation in the sphere' of the various Basket III questions with special mention of 'contacts on the basis of family ties and of travel for personal and professional reasons'. An important addition, especially coming from the East at the time (which, however, could also be interpreted as a veiled safety clause) was that 'the discussion will be oriented towards a practical result and pursue the aim of improving conditions for the free and full development and spiritual enrichment of the human personality in all CSCE participating States'. The Soviet delegate explained that this was in line with Mikhail Gorbachev's policy goal of 'the need for "humanizing" international relations', with the human being becoming 'the objective, the means and the protagonist'. In reacting to 'conditions', it was accepted that plenary meetings would be 'open to representatives of the press and public'. The conference was to be opened at the political level.[37]

The West reacted coolly to the Soviet initiative and maintained its 'neither yes nor no' approach, Warren Zimmermann coming up with no less than ten conditions for a Moscow meeting, at the pinnacle of which was the insurmountable condition, that by the end of the Vienna Meeting the Soviet Union already had to have 'an exemplary record on human rights and humanitarian co-operation'.[38]

The Western countries were placed in an obvious dilemma: to insist on the purity of their proposal by, at the most, giving the Soviet Union a meeting in Moscow on something secondary, say on education; or to be ready for a greater level of compromise. As the former would clearly be unacceptable to the Soviet Union, the FRG and also the Netherlands and to some extent France and the United Kingdom started being more flexible from late autumn 1987, realizing that the Moscow Conference was their best negotiating lever. In the final analysis they could not reject a serious proposal without good reason. The United Kingdom still officially kept to its firm dismissal of Moscow as a venue (or one of the venues), but this was more of a negotiating stance, so as to strike the 'final bargain' at 'the last moment'.[39] Washington continued its 'neither yes nor no' policy and insistence on 'conditions', but at the State Department level (though apparently not yet in the US Commission of Congress) a softening was obvious, and there was a leaning towards the Bonn view that after all a Moscow conference would benefit the cause of human rights in the Soviet Union.[40] Austria, in trying to assess the reasons for lack of progress in Vienna, warned the '12' against the 'risk of overestimating the potential' of the Vienna Meeting, but added pointedly that the long delay was not unwelcome to the Soviet Union, which was reluctant as yet to enter into serious negotiations on the human dimension.[41]

The Western dilemma became more acute following a series of *démarches* and other contacts by the Soviet Union in Moscow and Western capitals explaining their position and indicating a level of flexibility, culminating in the Soviet non-paper of December 1987. To their contacts they went so far as to state that a Moscow conference would contribute to the democratization process under way in their country and to *glasnost* and *perestroika*; that the process would continue and that it was 'an internal necessity' and had nothing to do with meeting specific conditions (which were humiliating for a sovereign state); that the West must finally believe in the Soviet Union's 'good faith'; that they were prepared for far-reaching concessions in order to achieve a reasonable compromise, including a special mechanism as long as it was not supranational or obligatory, which, they added, could then be tested and improved in a Moscow conference (of course, not even Soviet diplomats could have been aware how prophetic the Soviets were on this). Then came the important Soviet non-paper of 10 December 1987, which was co-sponsored by Bulgaria, Czechoslovakia and, curiously enough, also by Romania. Point 1 of the Western CHD proposal was reformulated as 'exchange of information' between governments (foreign ministries or other agencies designated by the states); point 2, bilateral meeting, was qualified as 'on a voluntary basis'; a paragraph was added on becoming party to multilateral conventions; and, of course, there was the provision on the Moscow Conference. But the West kept up the pressure by rejecting the non-paper for not going far enough.[42]

At about the same time France and the United Kingdom, the main hard-liners among the '12', were toying with new versions of the CHD proposal. France and the FRG started thinking in terms of three conferences, each devoted to a different issue of the human dimension, and, together with Greece and some others, considered dropping the problematic point 4 (requests for special meetings at the level of thirty-five). The Netherlands, of course, was against such a move, for that was all that remained of its own proposal. The United Kingdom was inclined to keep it in for a while for negotiating purposes. As for the United States, it seemed relatively detached from the CHD affair at the time. Finally, on 9 December the United Kingdom came up within the '12' with a revised version of WT.19, which dropped individual requests from point 1, reformulating it instead in the context of governments requesting information 'on their own behalf or on behalf of private individuals or groups'. Furthermore, it provided for one conference comprised of three meetings, each devoted to a slightly different, though not completely distinct, subject within the human dimension.[43] However, at the time, and in the first months of the next year, no common '12' position was forged so as not to give the message of having accepted Moscow as a venue.[44]

In the following year (which had not commenced very encouragingly in the overall negotiations), the momentum on CHD was lost, with the West maintaining its hard line on the Moscow conference. A new idea, proposed by one EC member, of dropping point 4 and putting in its place two to four regular annual meetings was kept as a fall-back position.[45] As the NNA were formulating their draft (which was to be submitted on 13 May), the Soviet head of delegation pointed out in plenary (on 29 April) that there was an emerging agreement on the human dimension mechanism, except for the following: the 'automatism' whereby any single state was given 'the automatic right to convene *ad hoc* meetings of 35 countries', which would be 'in violation of the consensus rule and the principle of sovereignty'; the automaticity of bilateral meetings; and the narrow definition of the human dimension excluding most of Basket III.

The NNA draft concluding document presented a fortnight later went a long way towards meeting the opposing views on CHD, and its text is very nearly the final compromise reached. The Netherlands' point 4 was omitted and the 'human dimension' definition which was almost the same as the final compromise, was cleverly drafted so that it was broadened to include all of Basket III, yet the main emphasis was placed on human rights and human contacts (the word 'all' was placed in front of 'human' to satisfy Eastern delegations, not to limit it only to civil and political rights). Point 3 was split into two parts, which in the final text were to be points 3 and 4. The conference was to comprise three meetings. The positions of East and West appeared to converge, but the issue of Moscow was still unresolved.[46]

At that point the West received conflicting messages. Kashlev in an interview for *Izvestia* said that the third meeting of the conference could take place in Moscow or Geneva,[47] and some Soviet officials gave a distinct impression to their Western contacts that they were wavering.[48] Shevardnadze, on the other hand, stressed to his Western colleagues in New York in September 1988 that the Soviet Union was firmly behind the Moscow candidacy, without which it would not accept the mechanism or the two other meetings (to be held in Paris and Copenhagen).[49]

The final compromise took some time to materialize, from October to December 1988, and negotiations were mainly centred on accepting Moscow as the venue. France agreed to it, while the United Kingdom, in the words of Prime Minister Margaret Thatcher, stated (in late October 1988) that there should be no conference on human rights in Moscow 'unless there are human rights in Moscow'.[50] Chancellor Helmut Kohl accepted a Moscow meeting, but also referred to conditions. The United States, mainly concerned with the feelings of

Congress and the powerful pressure groups on such matters, presented a list of conditions in November, which apart from reiterating guarantees for openness and so on, set out three requirements to be met before the end of the Vienna meeting: the release of all political and religious prisoners, permission for all long-term *refuseniks* to emigrate, and a satisfactory solution to the outstanding human rights issues under debate in Vienna. To these were added further conditions for the next year (1989): a continued increase in the rate of emigration, elimination of jamming of foreign radio broadcasts, abolition or amendment of the 'political' and 'religious' articles of the criminal code, and effective legislation on press freedom, emigration, freedom of religion and judicial reform. It concluded with a threat that should 'there be a major disruption in East–West relations' they 'would reconsider any decision made in today's context'.[51] This line, which took most other Western delegations aback, was supported by the United Kingdom, which pointed out that only under such conditions would it finally agree to go to Moscow. The United States posture was puzzling, given the warmer relations and an emerging *rapport* between Washington and Moscow. However, in view of the strong pressure by the United States and United Kingdom, their allies agreed by mid-November, albeit reluctantly, to a common tough stance on this issue.[52]

As one would have expected, at that point Soviet reaction was to stop insisting on the Moscow meeting. Thatcher and Mitterrand stated in a joint press conference that the Vienna Meeting could be concluded without a decision on a Moscow meeting. The matter was finally resolved after a series of bilateral contacts between the United States and the Soviet Union, with the latter doing its utmost to meet as many conditions as possible despite the limited time available, an unimaginable situation a few months earlier. Of course, not all the conditions could be met, but under the circumstances, which clearly indicated how genuine the new frame of mind of the Soviet leadership was, the United States could hardly insist on every minute detail in its catalogue. Yet even when the final compromise was achieved, the United States and the United Kingdom made their actual participation in the Moscow Meeting in September 1991 conditional on continued improvement of the human rights situation in the Soviet Union. (Interestingly, this proviso was found helpful when, following the coup in August 1991, the West decided not to go to Moscow.)

Thus, regarding CHD, there was now only the question of Romania's stance. Ceauşescu, at a New Year's reception, said that 'Romania would not sign a document which in some areas takes mankind back 500 years into the era of the Inquisition', adding that respect for human rights could not mean a return to 'bigotry, reaction and slavery, but to advance on the basis of scientific and cultural progress'.[53] On 5 January the Romanian delegation in Vienna informed the NNA that if their seventeen points were not met, a situation 'could' arise whereby Romania would veto the document.[54] Finally, however, Romania gave in, but after the formal adoption of the Vienna Concluding Document it tabled a lengthy 'declaration' under paragraph 79 of the Rules of Procedure (comprising no less than four pages, probably the longest paragraph-79 statement ever), which was curiously qualified as 'an interpretative statement of reservations'. In fact, Romania rejected the CSCE human dimension without actually naming CHD. It stated that the Vienna Document contained elements which clearly violated the fundamental CSCE principle of non-interference in internal affairs, and, among other matters, criticized the text on Basket II as too weak, and the text on Principle VII as ignoring economic, social and cultural rights.[55]

The Canadian delegate rejected the statement on the basis of the consensus principle, which implies that 'all provisions are equally binding on all participating states'. The Austrian delegation associated itself with this view, and several delegations referred to the Romanian stance in the same spirit in their concluding speeches, while no one came to its support.[56]

THE VIENNA CONCLUDING DOCUMENT: ENTER THE HUMAN DIMENSION

The pivotal Vienna Concluding Document was adopted on 15 January 1989. Apart from the Romanian statement of reservations and the reactions to it, the other Paragraph-79 statements were largely concerned with CSBMs and military security, Turkey, apparently prompted by the United States example *vis-à-vis* the Moscow Meeting, stated that if the situation of the Turkish Muslim minority in Bulgaria did not improve it would 'face a strong opposition at home' to taking part in the Sofia Meeting on the Protection of the Environment and that the Turkish government could not ignore 'such an opposition'. Bulgaria retorted with its familiar argument of the non-existence of a 'Turkish national minority' (which, of course, was not true, as Bulgaria itself was to admit a year later), and correctly pointed out that the decision on the meeting in question had been taken by consensus in Vienna.[57]

The document's main achievement is without doubt to be found in the human dimension. The CHD conference/mechanism, as well as the new normative commitments under human rights and Basket III, constituted a qualitative step forward, much greater than that between the Final Act and the Madrid Concluding Document, further strengthening 'the interdependence of human rights and peace'.[58] On the whole, the document exceeded the most optimistic expectations, not only those held before the convocation of the meeting, but also those of a few months before its conclusion.[59]

The CHD (Conference on the Human Dimension) or human dimension mechanism was placed in a chapter of its own entitled 'Human Dimension of the CSCE'. Thus, human rights and humanitarian issues, which had been kept apart so far in the CSCE (the two-pronged approach), were brought together, opening the way for their complete integration in following CSCE documents.

The human dimension of the CSCE is defined in the first preambular paragraph of this chapter as 'human rights and fundamental freedoms, human contacts and other issues of a related humanitarian character'.[60] The precise wording is slightly ambiguous, but it certainly does not exclude the rest of Basket III, even though it places greater emphasis on human contacts by mentioning them by name. This was the result of a compromise between the original Western concept of the human dimension spearheaded by Denmark, consisting only of human rights (Principle VII) and human contacts, and the Eastern view which evolved in Vienna and came to accept the human dimension as comprising human rights and the whole of Basket III. Indeed the way information, culture and education were treated in the Vienna Document, with substantial guidelines and practical suggestions, meant they could be seen as integral parts of the operational dimension of human rights.

The human dimension, or CHD mechanism, was comprised of four 'points' or 'paragraphs', and not stages or steps as many states have loosely called them, for that would imply a sequence, which in fact has not been generally accepted:[61]

1. 'to exchange information and to respond to requests for information and to representations made to them by other participating States on questions relating to the human dimension of the CSCE. Such communications may be forwarded through diplomatic channels or be addressed to any agency designated for these purposes';
2. 'to hold bilateral meetings with other participating States that so request, in order to examine questions relating to the human dimension of the CSCE, including situations and specific cases,

with a view to resolving them. The date and place of such meetings will be arranged by mutual agreement through diplomatic channels';
3. bringing 'situations and cases', including those 'raised at bilateral meetings ... to the attention of other participating States through diplomatic channels';
4. providing any relevant information on the above if deemed necessary to the meetings of the Conference on the Human Dimension (CHD) as well as at the main CSCE follow-up meetings.

As can be seen, the first, second and third points were taken from WT.19, from which point 4 of Dutch origin was dropped. In its place was put the almost superfluous point 4, which would have been useful in the 1970s when implementation had not been assured. (And note that it was also included as one of the main items of the agenda of the Conference.)

The Conference on the Human Dimension was to have three four-week meetings, the first to be held in Paris in June 1989, the second in Copenhagen in June 1990 and the third in Moscow starting on 10 September 1991. The agendas for all three were the same and were set in detail in Vienna, as was the case with all the other intercessional meetings, so as to leave preparatory meetings only for main follow-ups. The main agenda was threefold: to review development in the human dimension, including implementation of commitments; to evaluate the functioning of the procedures described in paragraphs 1 to 4 (meaning the mechanism); and to 'consider practical proposals for new measures aimed at improving the implementation of the commitments' and 'enhancing the effectiveness of the procedures' (the mechanism).[62]

Apart from CHD, the various normative commitments building upon the Final Act and the Madrid Concluding Document made the Vienna Concluding Document, as Warren Zimmermann put it a few days after its adoption, 'the most comprehensive statement of human rights commitments that has ever existed in the East–West framework'.[63] Of special interest were the provisions on human rights activists, on freedom of movement, on religious freedom and on national minorities, the various provisions linked with personal freedom, human dignity and legal remedies, as well as the host of practical measures in Basket III, particularly under human contacts and information. Elements of the 'human dimension' appeared also in Basket II, in no less than five paragraphs on the 'human dimension' of migrant workers, based on initiatives by Yugoslavia and Turkey.

Provisions on human rights form more than two-thirds of the section on principles, and, in contrast to the Helsinki and Madrid texts, are mentioned in the preamble of Basket I. Of the other seven principles which are reiterated or very slightly expanded (sovereign equality, territorial integrity, peaceful settlement of disputes, non-intervention, self-determination, co-operation, and fulfilment of obligations under international law), at least two now had a human dimension element in them.

Reference to the Final Act proviso on the positive role of 'institutions, organizations and persons' in the co-operation principle amounted, in effect, not only to an acceptance of Helsinki monitors, but also facilitated their activities, access to information and free expression of their views (paragraph 26). The brief reference to the element of sovereign equality (Principle I), regarding each participating state's rights freely to choose and develop its political and other systems, was qualified by a proviso, taken from Principle X (on obligations under international law), that 'in exercising these rights, they will ensure that their laws, regulations, practices and policies conform with their obligations under international law and are brought into harmony with the provisions of the Declaration on Principles and other CSCE commitments' (paragraph 3). Note also that non-intervention, the traditional bogey of Principle VII, was not even mentioned in the principles section of the Vienna Document, and there is only reference to combating terrorism (which some countries have at times wrongly tended to associate with human rights, not only in CSCE meetings), which in the Final Act was included under Principle VI. The Eastern countries obtained little satisfaction in their attempt to include second generation human rights. As for safety clauses, they were limited to a minimum, and balanced by adding international law standards.[64]

The role of human rights activists was one of the major difficulties between East and West, for it was correctly perceived the Eastern delegations 'as an assault on basic tenets of their system of government'.[65] They tried to have such NGOs state-sponsored and their activities carried out 'in accordance with national legislation', and wanted this provision to appear in the more 'neutral' environment of Principle IX (on co-operation). The West gave in only to the last request, but not fully, for the monitoring concept is mentioned not only in the aforementioned co-operation paragraph (paragraph 26 in Principles), but also in another short paragraph (paragraph 13.5) as 'the right of their citizens to contribute actively, individually or in association with others, to the promotion and protection of human rights'.[66]

The freedom of movement, which had not previously been mentioned in CSCE documents, was another source of difficulty. Eastern delegations accepted the idea fairly quickly but tried to inject it with the various exceptions mentioned in Article 12 of the UN Covenant on Civil and Political Rights, which give ample room for abuse. The West and the Neutrals insisted that CSCE documents, being non-legal in nature, but political texts setting standards, should follow the line of the relevant article of the Universal Declaration on Human Rights. The NNA compromise was first to state respect for the right of everyone to 'freedom of movement and residence within the borders of each State' and 'to leave any country, including his own, and to return to his country'(paragraph 20), and then in the next paragraph (paragraph 21) to indicate that this right would be subject only to those restrictions 'which are provided by law and are consistent with their obligations under international law', mentioning both the Covenant and the Universal Declaration and adding that 'these restrictions have the character of exceptions' and 'will ensure that these restrictions are not abused and are not applied in an arbitrary manner, but in such a way that the effective exercise of these rights is ensured'.[67]

The freedom of religion in the Vienna Document ended by being one of the most comprehensive texts regarding human rights. It appears in paragraph 16 (with no less than eleven sub-paragraphs, 16.1–16.11) which is complemented by various paragraphs in Basket III. Religious freedom was spearheaded by the Holy See, Austria and the West, with Bulgaria, Czechoslovakia and initially the Soviet Union trying to dilute it with the inclusion of rights of non-believers, religious exclusivity and enmity resulting from religious beliefs. When this line was unsuccessful they tried to place as many restrictive clauses as possible, derived from the relevant article in the UN Covenant on Civil and Political Rights (Article 18), insisting mainly on the existing internal legislation clause in the Helsinki and Madrid Documents. The final compromise (to be found in paragraph 17) was similar to that on freedom of movement, that is 'limitations as are provided by law and consistent with their obligations under international law and with their international commitments'.[68]

The Soviet Union's internal liberalization on religion was reflected in its gradual greater flexibility in Vienna, and the end result was that almost all of the elements of the original extended proposals were included, the main omission being the Austrian provision on conscientious objection, with which not only the Eastern delegations had problems. A measure of how extensive the text on religious freedom was is the fact that even a text on religious education in the language of one's choice was included in unrestricted form, despite 'prolonged resistance' from Eastern delegations.[69]

On national minorities, the most ambitious provisions, spearheaded by Yugoslavia and actively supported by Hungary, were injected with the collective aspect of these rights, including self-definition as national minorities. The FRG, Norway, the Netherlands, Austria and, above all, Canada were also supportive of proposals on national minorities, but were more middle of the road, stressing the 'individual' character of human rights, thus providing the elements of a compromise. The group of states which were happy with as little commitment as possible on this question and with safety clauses had dwindled by comparison with Helsinki/Geneva to only three or four, chiefly Greece from the West (France kept silent) and Bulgaria and, in particular, Romania from the East.[70]

In the Principles section a compromise wording suggested by the Austrian co-ordinator was to include the collective aspect but otherwise have the rights of minorities at the 'individual' level of 'persons belonging to' as in the UN and previous CSCE documents. This was done very astutely by indicating the collective identity aspect of national minorities, 'the ethnic, cultural, linguistic and religious identity of national minorities'.[71] Most difficult to finalize were not so much the provisions in the Principles section, but the one under 'Human Contacts', which in its original version (in the Canadian proposal and Austro-Swiss non-paper) followed the wording of the draft document of the West in Bern, where the crucial phrase which caused difficulties was 'close affinities'. Greece pointed out that members of national minorities should not be seen as a separate group with regard to human contacts, which should be promoted for all citizens. Furthermore, no single group should be singled out for preferential treatment in this respect. After extensive talks, not least within the '12' and '16' setting, the final compromise was to put this provision on a non-discrimination basis ('the status of persons belonging to national minorities ... is equal to that of other citizens with regard to human contacts'), to mention the Final Act, to add the wording 'on their territories', and to limit somewhat the context of application. In place of 'close affinities' or other suggestions (such as 'common background' and a whole list of alternatives proposed over a long period of time by, in particular, the Basket III experts of Canada, the United Kingdom and the FRG), the compromise wording was 'with whom they share a common national origin or cultural heritage'.

The end result was a total of six paragraphs on national minorities, two in the Principles section, and one apiece in each of the four sub-chapters of Basket III, which though not particularly far-reaching by today's standards were important in paving the way for the great step forward that was to take place in this area within the CSCE framework in 1990.

Among the other achievements of the Vienna Concluding Document were various minimum standards of application of human rights, such as effective legal remedies, non-discrimination, personal freedoms, rights of persons in confinement, and others linked with the concept of rule of law, which though not very revolutionary, were important at the time and prepared the way for what was to come in the three human dimension meetings. In Basket III, all the provisions on human contacts and information, which had caused so much anguish in the contact group, were adopted.

Apart from the human dimension, the Vienna Meeting also owes its importance to the mandate for new talks on CSBMs (to be held in Vienna) and, in particular, to the inclusion of the CFE (Conventional Armed Forces in Europe) talks.

Eduard Shevardnadze, looking back at the Vienna Follow-up, concluded that it was 'a watershed', 'a major step in the development of the common European process', 'a turning point' in East–West relations, rendering the Helsinki process 'central' to these relations.[72]

8

BETWEEN VIENNA AND COPENHAGEN: THE CSCE IN THE TWILIGHT ZONE

THE TWILIGHT ZONE

Following the conclusion of the Vienna Follow-up the pace of events was relentless: from the distinct thaw in the Cold War in the first part of 1989, to the steady irrelevance of the East–West polarity by the second part of that year, and finally to the emergence of 'one Europe' by the next year. This was reflected in the CSCE, the venue of East–West conflict and attempts at co-operation, as in no other inter-governmental forum. The CSCE as such also played a far from negligible role in consolidating the changes and 'new thinking', and in spurring it on further to the point of no return.

For the CSCE the period from the end of the Vienna Meeting until the Paris Summit, some twenty-two months, was a twilight zone. One obstacle after another gave way from one intercessional CSCE meeting to the next, starting with the first post-Vienna meeting, the London Information Forum (which began in mid-April 1989) and the Paris First Meeting of the Conference on the Human Dimension (held in June 1989), and culminating in the Bonn Economic Conference, in early spring 1990, and, above all, in the Copenhagen Second CHD Meeting of June 1990. After that the new post-bipolar Europe was a reality and only needed its formal announcement, which was to come later in the year at the Paris Summit which adopted the Charter of Paris for a New Europe. A barometer of the changes was the frequency of use of the CHD mechanism, which was employed profusely in 1989, particularly in the first six months, but very rarely in the next year.

It was during this twilight period that the 'human', 'individual' dimension that had threatened to play havoc with the original, fragile CSCE-I now came to be acknowledged as one of the CSCE's major achievements because of its contribution to the collapse of man-made 'walls' between societies and peoples.

107

THE LONDON INFORMATION FORUM:
DIALOGUE AT LAST

The refreshing new breeze was already very much in evidence in the first post-Vienna intercessional meeting, which was appropriately a meeting of independent individuals dedicated to the free flow of information. And free flow of information it was, more than ever before in a CSCE meeting, as the various journalists and other media personalities dominated the discussions.

Arrangements were made so as to have most discussions in informal mode, by placing the delegations in the three working groups to allow for more open exchanges. The outcome was a true dialogue as never before seen in the CSCE context, stimulated on the Eastern side by Soviet delegates in particular, in one of the delegations most dominated and controlled by journalists and media personalities. Speakers even directly criticized their own government from the seat of their delegation, and not only those from the West (notably in the case of the United Kingdom), but, in at least one instance, also those from the East (with an eminent Hungarian journalist being gracefully tolerated by the official Hungarian delegation).

Several journalists censured the practices of other governments in ways that official delegates could not, notably British, Swedish, Swiss and other journalists speaking on the prevailing situation in Turkey for freedom of information and the Kurds (to which the Turkish delegation reacted by having Turkish journalists take the floor rather than officials). The familiar Turkish–Bulgarian clash on the Muslim/Turkish minority in Bulgaria continued, with the Bulgarian delegation probably making its best defence ever in the CSCE. In London another dispute was to make its entry into the CSCE halls, the first intra-Eastern clash in the human dimension sphere – between Hungary and Romania on the plight of the Hungarian minority, which was a sign of things to come (Hungary was later to use the human dimension mechanism against Romania).

The negotiating setting was also beginning to look different, though the *modus operandi* was still technically the same, with the East on one side and the West on the other, and the NNA as prospective bridge-builders in between. However, this traditional scheme could not work its old magic any more since there was no longer a balance between the two sides. The NNA delegations were less active than usual and appeared unable to organize themselves, with Austria, followed by Switzerland, doing most of the job, while Sweden was distancing itself from both of them, being more inclined towards the '12'. As for

Yugoslavia, it seemed virtually non-existent. However, it was chiefly the shape that the East was finding for itself that made the biggest difference, rendering the traditional negotiating setting increasingly irrelevant. The Eastern side was clearly evaporating as a distinct group. Apparently there had been very few meetings of the Eastern caucus, and the Eastern delegations were split, far more than in Vienna, between the 'reformists', which this time included the Soviet Union (headed by a distinguished journalist and editor), Hungary and Poland, and the conservative 'non-reformists', consisting of the GDR, Bulgaria, Czechoslovakia and, of course, Romania. In London and in the subsequent CSCE meetings throughout 1989 Romania was the *bête noire* of the Helsinki process, to the extent of facing virtual ostracism. The only traditional group worthy of the name was the Western group. The West looked rock-hard on the surface, but it sheltered an increasingly assertive EC. Indeed, the non-European Community members of the '16' were on uneasy terms with the '12', a situation at times reminiscent of the worst moments in Community–NATO consensus-building in the CSCE.

Given the anaemic condition of the East, the '12', in an obvious attempt to reassert itself as in past CSCE days (particularly the 1970s), submitted a '12' omnibus proposal, but the outcome was friction with Canada and the United States. The North American rationale was roughly along the lines of the arguments used in January 1987 at the Vienna Meeting with regard to the '12' proposal on a human dimension conference and mechanism.[1] After some difficult moments in the '16', ably handled on the EC side by established CSCE hands,[2] the '12' proposal (LIF.59) was submitted by seventeen Western delegations. Similarly, the Austrian and Swiss delegations submitted another omnibus-type proposal (LIF.67), co-sponsored by the FRG, Italy and Liechtenstein, but also by Hungary and Poland, which indicated how far the traditional blocs were receding into the background. Overall, there was an avalanche of almost seventy proposals, as well as many unofficial ones distributed by the journalists.

The disappearance of the traditional blocs in CSCE, the fact that the meeting was held only three months after the close of the Vienna Meeting (with its numerous commitments under 'Information') and, above all, the Romanian stance did not permit, as had been predicted, the emergence of a document with new commitments. Instead, there appeared three versions of a brief, two-page resumé, by the West, the East and Austria. There was also the alternative of simply forwarding the proposals to the Helsinki Follow-up while the Nordics suggested a follow-up to the Forum. As for Romania, it would not accept a text that included an undertaking to implement fully the relevant CSCE provisions. In view of the impasse, an informal working group was formed from the three traditional groups to prepare a brief chairman's statement forwarding the proposals to Helsinki-II, the importance of which would be mainly symbolic – of the ability to arrive at such a statement. But even that could not be achieved owing to Romania. In Vienna, the Western delegations, cognizant of such an eventuality, had provided a further option: if the Forum could not reach 'any agreed conclusions', the host country would forward proposals and projects to the next follow-up meeting, and this was what happened. Thus the meeting ended. It was hardly a disappointment for, in contrast to those intercessional meetings between Madrid and Vienna where the Western goal was to 'put a foot in the door' with a substantial text, now the door was ajar, and the visitor – radical democratic change – was welcomed by more than one Eastern state.

THE PARIS CHD MEETING: THE PRELUDE

The First CHD Meeting in Paris (30 May–23 June 1989) was characterized by a good atmosphere, similar to the one in London, with very limited conflict along East–West lines. Romania's intransigence, the fact that the meeting was taking place only a few months after Vienna and, to some extent, the Turkish–Bulgarian clash, which reached a high point, would not permit a document, not even a short communiqué. But, as in London, this had been expected and, since the meeting was part of a wider conference, the various proposals would not be lost, but would *eo ipso* remain proposals of the Conference on the Human Dimension.[3]

Western fears that Romania might try to boycott the meeting or delay its proceedings by using procedural tactics did not materialize. The meeting opened impressively enough at the Sorbonne with a statement by President François Mitterrand, and opening statements by no fewer than twenty-two foreign ministers (including Shevardnadze, but not his United States and United Kingdom counterparts), a clear indication of the upgrading for the human dimension achieved in Vienna. The meeting was then conducted in the Centre Kléber, where the Paris Summit Meeting was to take place a year and a half later. Hungary and Poland, and, to a lesser extent, the Soviet Union, were praised for their important steps towards democratization. The brunt of the condemnation of the West and the Neutrals was borne by Romania, particularly with regard to its systematization programme and other Ceauşescu 'concepts', then by Bulgaria and, to a lesser

110

degree, by Czechoslovakia and the GDR. The Soviet Union was criticized primarily by Canada and, in a less pronounced manner, by the United States and the United Kingdom, mainly in the vein that much still remained to be done. The Soviet reaction to such criticism was relatively calm, admitting its still existing shortcomings, but adding that the West's record was not as perfect as it was thought to be, and that, in the final analysis, 'human rights must be a two-way street'.[4]

The limited East–West conflict along such lines contributed to a rise in inter-state differences, even among members of the same alliance. The main clash was between Turkey and Bulgaria, at a time when the situation of the Turkish/Muslim minority had reached a peak with the mass exodus of several thousand Turkish speakers to Turkey. A new conflict, already evident in London, that between Hungary and Romania regarding the Hungarian minority, came out far more openly and was duly picked up by the international press at the time. Turkey's behaviour on human rights was raised by Bulgaria and Cyprus, and also at one point by Sweden. Cyprus's predicament was put forward in a highly emotional opening speech by Foreign Minister George Iacovou, to which Turkey chose not to react. In the course of the plenary Cyprus returned to the fray, and was supported in one instance by Greece, with regard to altering the demographic composition of the island, which, however, did not lead to a Turkish–Greek clash.[5]

Romania participated throughout the meeting and reacted to criticism with various far-fetched arguments, but quite ably given the circumstances. Its delegate upheld the systematization programme as a perfectly legitimate move aimed at greater justice and progress which was conceived to prevent the creation of 'artificial restrictions' which would lead to situations akin to the policy of apartheid and the Bantustans. It was claimed that Romania's Hungarian national minority and the other *nationalités cohabitantes* – as they were called in Romania – were treated on a basis of equality with other Romanian citizens. Also characteristic of Romania's opting for 'playing ball' was the submission of an official (that is within the CHD, which it did not accept) proposal entitled 'Implementation of Fundamental Human Rights' (CHDP.23), which referred, among other things, to the well-known Romanian argument of a 'brain drain'. It was the longest proposal introduced in Paris (no less than three pages), and was revoked in the course of the Second CHD Meeting in Copenhagen.

Another indication that Romania was keen not to be left out completely was its 'four conditions for co-operation' in the human rights field, which it made known to the other participants before the Paris Meeting. These were: (1) an exchange of views and opinions on how best to implement commitments 'in a spirit of *rapprochement* and not of confrontation'; (2) an in-depth exchange of views at the bilateral and round table levels only on 'general questions, principles, and not on specific cases'; (3) humanitarian cases, such as family reunification, to be studied on a case by case basis; and (4) the three above to necessarily go hand in hand with 'an extension and diversification [*sic*]' of economic and scientific co-operation.[6] Needless to say the West and the other participants would have none of this and Romania remained isolated as never before in the CSCE.

Even though a substantial concluding document was almost inconceivable, the various delegations 'went through the motions',[7] introducing proposals and so on, while the main emphasis was placed on reviewing implementation and discussing the functioning of the human dimension mechanism. This last question led to interesting, if somewhat technical, debates on how best to ameliorate the mechanism. Four months' experience with it indicated that all the participating states against which the mechanism had been invoked had accepted it, with the exception of Romania which had alluded to its reservations. Bulgaria was accused by Turkey of avoiding point 2 by suggesting an examination of the Kurdish question and the situation on human rights in Turkey as well. The most telling Bulgarian counter-argument was that Turkey had abused the mechanism by using it a dozen times within a month. The dominant feeling, expressed by the United Kingdom in Paris, was that the mechanism was 'delicate' by nature and had to be used 'sparingly' and 'as a last resort'. (The mechanism will be examined in greater detail in the following chapter.)

Some thirty-six proposals were submitted in Paris, evenly distributed between Eastern and Western delegations. One-sixth of them were co-sponsored by delegations of both East and West, which in half the cases was due to Hungarian participation as co-sponsor with the West. However, the truly common initiative by both East and West was the Soviet–French proposal on a comparative analysis of legislation, regulations and jurisprudence, the 'long-term objective' being 'the creation of a common legal area based on a Europe of States in which the rule of law prevails'. It was derived from Shevardnadze's idea of a 'common European legal space', launched in his opening speech of the meeting. Among the other worthwhile proposals were two on the rule of law, one by France and one by the United Kingdom (which were destined to be merged at the Copenhagen Meeting); two '12' proposals on freedom of expression and the right of peaceful assembly and association; a proposal by the United States and the United Kingdom on free elections, regarded by the West, in those days, as utopian;[8]

on trade union freedoms, by Austria and Greece; on conscientious objection, by the Benelux countries; on NGOs; on aspects of the mechanism (two proposals); on observers in trials, by Switzerland (including among its co-sponsors Hungary); on freedom of movement, by Canada; and on national minorities, by Hungary (co-sponsored by Austria and Norway, but interestingly not by Yugoslavia, which presented no proposal in this meeting). Also worth mentioning was the Turkish proposal on 'massive population movement', obviously prompted by the exodus of ethnic Turks from Bulgaria. The various proposals from the non-reformist Eastern countries of the time – the GDR, Bulgaria and Czechoslovakia – which now seemed somewhat outdated, were for the most part presented by individual delegations, and most were to be dropped in the course of the Second CHD Meeting.

The Warsaw Pact kept only a façade of unity for what was destined to be its last appearance in the CSCE, as Poland and, in particular, Hungary acted more as members of the West than the East. The NNA could not play their traditional role as bridge-builders, despite the attempts of the Austrian delegate in particular. The '12' were active and were able to carry with them, though with difficulty, the Canadian and United States delegations, which were headed by two well-known Cold War 'warriors', who clearly had problems with reconciling themselves to the demise of the East–West conflict.[9]

Taking Romania's rejection of a document for granted, the other participating delegations did not attempt to produce a substantial document. Thus no informal contact group was set up. On French initiative a short, factual communiqué was drafted in the last days of the meeting, within the '12' and then the NATO group. The Canadian and United States delegates were against this approach since, given Romania's stance, no strongly worded clauses would go through, but they were finally convinced to go ahead with drafting by the experienced delegates of the United Kingdom, Belgium, the FRG and Spain (the '12' presidency).[10] It was clear that the Soviet Union and the other Eastern delegations as well as the Neutrals would go along, even though they were unhappy that the West was taking over their coveted role as drafters of the final text.

The drafting exercise was finalized in the NATO caucus at expert level under Greek chairmanship by 21 June, three days before the end of the Paris meeting. Its most important passage was the one which 'welcomed considerable developments' in several countries and expressed 'concern at serious deficiencies in the implementation of agreed commitments on the part of certain countries'. But as the text was about to be agreed at the level of the Western heads of delegation (then to be handed to the NNA to go about their traditional task) and it was clear that the Soviet Union and its allies, apart from Romania, could accept it, the Turkish delegate unexpectedly objected. It was stated that Turkey could agree to the text only if there was an explicit phrase condemning the Bulgarian policy regarding the ethnic Turks of Bulgaria. This was not normally done in those days in a CSCE text, least of all in a short, factual communiqué. The Turkish delegation was under pressure from its allies, but was 'saved' by Canada with the argument that a process should not be launched that would isolate an ally. Thus, the exercise for a concluding document stopped there.

There were no hard feelings about the lack of a text, even though an opportunity had been missed to put the blame on Romania for rejecting even a factual communiqué. The First CHD Meeting was generally regarded as useful and as a kind of pre-conference for the next CHD meeting. Indeed with the benefit of hindsight it can be seen as a prelude to what was to follow in Copenhagen.[11]

Before going on to the Copenhagen Meeting, I will examine the application of the Vienna Human Dimension Mechanism, for it was mainly used and had its maximum impact in 1989, that is in the period under the general sway of the First Paris Meeting.

THE VIENNA HUMAN DIMENSION MECHANISM AND ITS APPLICATION

Looked at closely, the Vienna human dimension or CHD mechanism does not amount to very much, in the sense that it is not a comprehensive mechanism, does not imply sanctions, and so on. It could well be argued that such a diplomatic, confidential approach was already established practice, as can be seen from the numerous presentations of the '12' and other Western countries to Eastern countries regarding human rights abuses before the adoption of the mechanism, and until today for that matter. Such issues were being raised in the course of various CSCE meetings and in UN forums (notably in the UN Commission on Human Rights and the Third Committee of the UN General Assembly). However, in the UN setting no rapporteur mission could easily be established for an Eastern European country, nor could such a country be put on the so-called 'black list' of the UN Commission on Human Rights (based on the procedure of ECOSOC Resolution 1503) for it was seldom possible to muster enough votes. Perhaps the most innovative feature of the human dimension mechanism in CSCE terms lay in the fact that, in spite of the consensus principle, any participating state could in effect 'raise any human rights issue with any other country at any time'.[12]

As pointed out above, the use of the mechanism was not meant to be sequential. However, several states have supported the idea of a sequence, notably Italy and Belgium. Although the United Kingdom, the United States and others have consistently been against this line and advocated maximum flexibility, the actual practice inclines towards a sequential approach. Thus it seems that point 2 has been used only after the use of point 1 on any specific issue. Point 3 has never been used on its own, but has been used following the use of point 1, or the use of both points 1 and 2. As for point 4 – the superfluous point – there is no need for a previous point to be used for a subject to be raised in a conference, as was recognized by several delegations in the course of the Paris and Copenhagen meetings, with no dissenting voice. However, before the First CHD Meeting in Paris there were fears that some Eastern states could create procedural difficulties by inaccurately arguing that the points were sequential, and that if something was not put forward under the previous points it could not be raised in a CHD meeting. No such difficulty has occurred, not even with Romania. However, at the time point 4 was not without importance, mainly symbolic, for it expressed unequivocally that such issues could legitimately be treated.

In the course of the first two CHD meetings, and notably during the Paris Meeting, attention was drawn to several shortcomings and difficulties in the mechanism and its use. It was pointed out that the mechanism should be used sparingly, as a last resort, and should not be made to appear as an unfriendly act. Such restrained use would maximize its impact and raise its stature as a diplomatic method. It was also pointed out that no state should regard itself as beyond reproach; that the mechanism should not be used as a tribunal or for domestic purposes, but should be aimed at resolving cases through co-operation; that the receiving state could not evade the application of point 2 by counteracting with extraneous elements, however justified they might be on their own (as with Bulgaria towards Turkey regarding the Kurds); and that there had to be a certain form and promptness in respect of points 1 and 2.[13]

These discussions led to the submission of two proposals in the Paris CHD Meeting, one by Denmark, then co-sponsored by France, which, among other things, stated that 'the procedure should be completed without being complicated by the establishment of linkage with other topics than those raised by the requesting participating State'.[14] The second was an Italian–Belgian proposal, co-sponsored by the Netherlands, Luxemburg, the FRG and Portugal, according to which responses to point 1 had to take place within four weeks in written form, bilateral meetings would take place within three weeks of the request, and subjects discussed under point 2 had first to be discussed under point 1.[15] (There was also a Belgian non-paper at the Paris CHD Meeting regarding recourse by persons and private groups which in the event was not officially submitted.) The two official proposals were adopted in the Document of Copenhagen of June 1990 (in its paragraphs 42.1–42.3), with the exception of the last item because of objections by Switzerland, Ireland and others which supported the United Kingdom/United States line of maximum flexibility. In the Moscow Document (October 1991) the four weeks in point 1 went down to only ten days, and the time allowed for convening a bilateral meeting was reduced from three weeks to one week.

In Copenhagen, and at the Geneva Meeting of Experts on National Minorities, several other proposals were submitted as attempts at 'enhancing the procedures' of the mechanism as set by the Vienna Concluding Document. Most were so elaborate, when compared with the original Vienna mechanism, as to constitute a new mechanism in their own right. As a result, a procedure along such lines was not adopted until the Third CHD Meeting held in Moscow in the autumn of 1991.

Now let us look at the application of the Vienna CHD mechanism.[16] It was principally evoked during the year 1989, mainly under its first point, in few instances under its second point, and only very rarely under its third and fourth points, basically during the Paris CHD Meeting. It must be noted that uses of point 4 are difficult to track down. A state may mention another state and criticize its record, but this is not *per se* a use of point 4, if the state in question does not say so at the time or does not later indicate that it was a use of point 4.

The first to make use of the mechanism was the Netherlands, barely a fortnight after the adoption of the Vienna Concluding Document, with regard to Czechoslovakia on arrests made during demonstrations on the commemoration of the self-immolation of Jan Palach. Point 2 was also used first by the Netherlands, in mid-March 1989, with regard to Vaclav Havel and other interned dissidents. Point 3 was used first in mid-April 1989 by the '12' under Spanish presidency, with regard to Dona Cornea and twenty-two other signatories of a letter against 'systematization' in Romania. This was with reference to the use of point 1 in the previous month, to which Romania had reacted by rejecting the *note verbale* but after having listened to the oral presentation.

One cannot be completely certain, but it appears that until the end of 1991, some twenty-seven of the participating states made use of the mechanism at least once. Greece, in contrast to its other EC partners, has not made use of the mechanism on its own but only as the '12'. The other states which have not made use of it up to the time of writing are Yugoslavia, Cyprus, Malta, the Holy See, Poland, Romania, Liechtenstein and Monaco. The '12' within the newly reinforced and institutionalized European Political Co-operation (EPC) – with its specific emphasis on cohesion – has made it a point to make use of the mechanism *à Douze* as much as possible.

Throughout 1989 invoking the mechanism was used as a form of pressure against the East. Eastern countries singled out in 1989 were: Czechoslovakia, about thirty times by seventeen states and by the '12' (mainly with regard to the fate of dissidents such as Havel, Hajek and Dubcek); Bulgaria, some thirty times, of which no fewer than thirteen were by Turkey (mainly with regard to the Turkish minority) but only one by the '12' (for the case of Trentchev – the inability to proceed *à Douze* on this subject was due to Greece's reaction, particularly in June 1989); Romania, some twenty times by seven states and by the '12' (mainly with regard to systematization, the activity against critics of the regime, such as Cornea, Mazilu and Pastor Toekes, and various other violations of the CSCE human dimension provisions); the GDR, some six times, mainly by the '12' and once by the FRG and Switzerland (regarding incidents on the Berlin Wall and others); the Soviet Union in 1989 for individual cases, which were later resolved (those of Plotnikov, Samoilovich, and Kuznetsov), on point 1, by Belgium, the United Kingdom, France, the '12', Canada and the United States.

In 1990 and 1991 the mechanism was used by the '12' and others mainly against Yugoslavia (about Kosovo and other questions), and in rare instances against the Soviet Union with regard to the Baltic states and events in the Caucasus region.

Czechoslovakia, in particular, tended to react with detailed answers, the Soviet Union tended to 'resolve' individual cases, and all Eastern countries agreed to answer to requests made by other participating states, with the exception of Romania which denied to answer on the basis of its original reservations. After the fall of Ceauşescu, Romania accepted the CHD and the other human dimension commitments.

The '12' used the mechanism against five out of the seven countries of the Warsaw Pact, the exceptions being Poland and Hungary, and later with regard to Yugoslavia; the United Kingdom used it against Bulgaria, Czechoslovakia, Romania and the Soviet Union; the FRG against the GDR, Bulgaria and Czechoslovakia; France against

Bulgaria, Czechoslovakia and the Soviet Union; the Netherlands, Italy, Spain, Denmark, Ireland, Luxembourg, Norway, Iceland, Sweden and San Marino against Czechoslovakia; Belgium against Bulgaria, Czechoslovakia and the Soviet Union; Portugal against Bulgaria and Czechoslovakia; the United States and Canada against Bulgaria, Romania, Czechoslovakia and the Soviet Union; Austria against Bulgaria, Romania and Czechoslovakia; Finland against Bulgaria; and Switzerland against Bulgaria, Romania and the GDR. On the Eastern side (as it existed in 1989) there has been minimal use of the mechanism, notably by: Czechoslovakia, once with regard to Austria and the Netherlands; the Soviet Union, once with regard to the United States (on a ban on the right to strike); the GDR, towards the United States regarding two entry visa cases, and twice by Bulgaria on the Kurds in Turkey. Until today there has been only one instance of the use of the mechanism by members of the same alliance – Hungary against Romania, not concerning the Hungarian minority, but with regard to Pastor Toekes.

Most prone to use the mechanism have been the '12' as '12' (some twenty-five times, eighteen of them in 1989), followed by Turkey (thirteen times, all against Bulgaria), the United States and Canada (around ten times), and then the United Kingdom, France, Belgium and Austria (about half a dozen times each), followed closely by the Netherlands. The greatest number of uses of the mechanism by one single state is that of Turkey – thirteen times – which also holds the record for time of activation of the mechanism within one month – twelve in the month of May 1989.

Soon after the end of the Sofia Meeting on the Protection of the Environment at the beginning of November 1989, with the fall of Jivkov there was only one anachronism left, the abominable regime of Ceauşescu in Romania. Within the CSCE, the first break with the past came in April 1990 at the Bonn Economic Conference, whose document endorsed the market economy and emphasized its link with pluralistic democracy and full respect for human rights. However, the most impressive break with the past came a little later, at the Second CHD Meeting held in Copenhagen, on the very subject, the human dimension, that had previously been the source of so much dissension.

COPENHAGEN: EUROPE UNITED ON THE HUMAN DIMENSION

THE COPENHAGEN CHD MEETING

The Second CHD Meeting in Copenhagen was in many respects unique, almost unbelievable for anyone who had followed the progress of the CSCE human dimension until then. From the start the atmosphere was unprecedented. The opening statements were made at foreign minister level, to underline the dramatic changes but also for the practical reason of convening a special meeting to launch the preparatory committee which was to prepare a CSCE Summit Meeting in Paris. The historic changes could not have been illustrated more vividly than by the fact that Vaclav Havel, the playwright/dissident for whom the mechanism had been invoked so many times, and whose name had been repeatedly mentioned in the First CHD Meeting, was now president of Czechoslovakia, while one leading figure of Czechoslovakia's 1968 'Spring' (also the subject of the mechanism in 1989), Alexander Dubcek, was now president of his country's parliament, and another, the then foreign minister and well-known activist, Professor Yiri Hajek, was heading the Czechoslovak delegation in Copenhagen. Equally, several foreign ministers from the Eastern European states who came to deliver opening statements were former dissidents and celebrated human rights activists. And when the initiative to start working on a document in Copenhagen came from Hajek, the magic of Copenhagen became tangible.

In many respects the Copenhagen Meeting was a new beginning for the CSCE, indeed a move into uncharted territory for the CSCE, for four reasons: (1) it was the end of bloc-to-bloc politics; (2) the implementation debate receded in importance; (3) the negotiation terrain was drastically different and in many respects more difficult; and (4) it opened up an era in the human dimension where a substantial concluding document was regarded as a 'must'.

There was hardly any implementation debate, for that was not

deemed necessary given the giant steps taken by all Eastern states.[1]
One could hardly condemn them for their past, or for their still-
existing shortcomings, when they were genuinely in the business of
reconstructing a democratic society. Thus as far as implementation
was concerned, there was largely praise for the achievements of the
Soviet Union and other Eastern countries. Only Romania came
momentarily under sustained criticism for the disturbances that had
recently occurred there, but it reacted positively, often providing
explanations uninvited. The situation in the Baltic republics was also
touched upon by several speakers, but in a mild manner, urging a
negotiated solution to the conflict.

On the other hand, there was the appearance of a new inter-state
clash as a result of the unprecedented attack made by the Yugoslav
delegate on Greece and Bulgaria regarding the 'plight of the
Macedonian minority' residing in these two countries.[2] The Bulgarian
delegate[3] took the floor in a hard-hitting right of reply, arguing, among
other things, that the time had come to open up this obscure chapter of
Balkan history and ask what had become of the more than one million
Bulgarians in the part of Yugoslavia known as Macedonia who had
been violently subjected to a process of relinquishing their Bulgarian
identity. In the next plenary Greece presented a comprehensive and
matter-of-fact exposé dealing with the 'Macedonian question'.[4]

At Copenhagen, Albania was admitted to participate as an observer
for the first time in CSCE history. The way Albania's candidacy was
handled by the Danish Foreign Minister raised several eyebrows and
was a source of embarrassment to the foreign ministers there present.[5]
The case of the Baltic states' candidacy was treated more 'by the book',
and there was general agreement that they could not become observers
since they were not yet independent states.[6]

Copenhagen was intriguing from the negotiation point of view. It
was to a large extent a 'free for all' situation. One of the three traditional
blocs, the East, no longer existed as a group, and the NNA played their
traditional role but more as individual delegations rather than as a
group. In fact out of four co-ordinators chosen, one was not even an
NNA representative but was the delegate from Hungary. The '12'
were assertive and cohesive in most fields, with the exception of
national minorities, and this time they were on good terms with the
other NATO delegations, notably with the United States contingent,
probably because the latter was headed by Madrid veteran Max
Kampelman, known for working closely and smoothly with his NATO
counterparts. Particularly assertive was a new grouping of participants,
the Pentagonale, which was characteristic of how things had changed

in the CSCE and in Europe in general. This group comprised one Neutral state, Austria, one Non-Aligned state, Yugoslavia, one Western and EC state, Italy, and two former Eastern bloc states, Hungary and Czechoslovakia. The Pentagonale, which was a source of some uneasiness particularly to the '12', given Italy's dual role, was to be the *enfant terrible* of the Helsinki process for a little over a year (from Copenhagen until Geneva, its high point probably being the Cracow Symposium of 1991).

As far as proposals were concerned, the most prominent group was the EC, with four lengthy submissions, including the most fundamental proposal of all, the rule of law, which was to be the greatest achievement of the concluding document. The main difficulty in formulating a common EC stance was on national minorities, owing to the reservations of France and Greece. The Pentagonale in its first appearance as a group in the CSCE presented a lengthy and comprehensive proposal on national minorities, while the NNA grouped together for a proposal on a mechanism on observers, which was apparently of Swiss origin.

The co-sponsorship of proposals, as well as their content, was a clear indication of how things had changed. With the exception of certain proposals on convening special meetings or on the mechanism and a few somewhat 'idiosyncratic' proposals, the rest were sponsored by various combinations of Western, former Eastern, neutral and non-aligned states. Never before had human dimension proposals on the rule of law, on NGOs, on the promotion of human rights or on free elections received such widespread support.

The final co-sponsors for the '12' proposal on the rule of law (initiated by France and the United Kingdom) reached thirty-one; for free and fair elections (by the United States, Canada and the United Kingdom), twenty-three co-sponsors; for NGOs, twenty-four; the '12' proposal for the rights of the child, twenty-seven; the two proposals (one by Portugal, the other by the Nordics) on the abolition of the death penalty together had twenty-five co-sponsors; on racism and xenophobia, twenty-one; on a 'common European legal area' (a redrafting based on the French–Soviet proposal of the Paris CHD Meeting), fourteen; on the transfer of sentenced persons, eighteen; and various proposals on the rights of national minorities (by the Pentagonale, by the FRG and Canada, by Spain, and two by Romania) – together with two on the convening of a meeting – in all had over twenty co-sponsors.

Other proposals put forward were concerned with migrant workers (by Yugoslavia, Turkey and Poland); with the prohibition of torture, by

Bulgaria and several others; with the elimination of hate propaganda, by Canada, the Soviet Union, Italy and others (interestingly, this was a subject formerly regarded as a 'propaganda proposal' by Eastern states); on co-operation on democratic institutions, by Canada; on the right to leave one's country and return, by Canada and others; on the right to promote and protect human rights, by Canada and others; on easing entry policy, by Poland, the Soviet Union and Yugoslavia; on criminal proceedings, by Denmark and others; on visas (three proposals), by Czechoslovakia; on social security, by the GDR; and a few secondary 'textual/normative' proposals. There was also a proposal by the two German states against tyranny, totalitarianism, racial hatred, anti-semitism etc. There were also proposals concerned with additions to the mechanism, or rather new mechanisms, which were mainly sponsored by one delegation or by a few delegations (to be presented below). Others were concerned with specific meetings: a Swiss proposal with six co-sponsors on an 'extraordinary CSCE meeting on national minorities in 1991', with a vague agenda; a Greek proposal on an 'expert meeting' on national minorities, with a precise agenda aimed at examining 'the issue of national minorities' in all its aspects, historical, political, sociological and legal;[7] a Norwegian proposal on an 'expert meeting on democratic institutions'; and a Soviet proposal on a 'meeting of experts on consular matters'.

Given the obvious prospects for achieving something very substantial, negotiations started early on, in the middle of the second week (on Thursday 14 June, before the time scheduled for all proposals to be submitted), at the informal level, after the highly respected head of the Czechoslovak delegation, Yiri Hajek, had called an informal meeting of heads of delegation on Tuesday 13 June. Apparently, the initiative had been steered by the Pentagonale.[8] Four working groups were formed: on the rule of law and democracy, on national minorities, on the mechanism, and on human rights/contacts and other miscellaneous matters. Group I, rule of law and democracy, was headed by the deputy head of the Swiss delegation;[9] Group II, minorities, by Ambassador Helmut Tuerk of Austria, who also acted as chairman of the co-ordinators; Group III, mechanism, by one of the most experienced CSCE hands, Ambassador Andre Erdos of Hungary; and Group IV, human rights/contacts, by the Finnish delegation.

The work of the four informal groups lasted for one and a half weeks, ending on Saturday 23 June, with the first consolidated draft document appearing late next day. In the informal groups progress was initially slow, even under rule of law/democracy, which was the first one to make any advance, followed a little later by Group IV on human rights/contacts. This slow pace was largely caused by the fact that the exercise was not the traditional, more orderly one of the three groups negotiating through main speakers, but rather, in most instances, an 'each one for himself' exercise. Thus, although much of the success of the Copenhagen document must be attributed to the co-ordinators, it was also due to the level and mix of co-sponsors of proposals, and the fact that the wording of many of the texts had already been carefully worked out. Yet, even more important than this determination to produce a substantial, pace-setting document were the emergence of the 'new thinking', and the unfolding of a 'new Europe', making Ottawa, Bern, and even the Paris meeting of only a year earlier seem very far away.

The most arduous negotiations by far were in Group II on minorities, with the exception of the various proposals on racism, ethnic hatred and related questions which were examined in a small sub-group comprised of the main sponsors. The most ambitious 'pro-minority' delegations were those of Hungary, Yugoslavia, Italy, Finland, Sweden and Norway. In the pro-minority camp, but somewhat more conciliatory towards the delegations that had difficulties, were the FRG, Canada, Spain, the Netherlands, Denmark, the United States and Austria. The Soviet Union kept a low profile. The various counter-arguments against the development of detailed undertakings that would go beyond the level of non-discrimination were presented by the delegations of Greece, France, Bulgaria, Romania and Turkey. The discussions, even though strenuous, were usually of a high level, touching on substantial aspects of this difficult issue, the full complexity of which was not totally understood by several delegates. The main difficulties concerned the following questions:[10]

1. The old legal problem of whether minority rights are to be regarded as individual or group rights. This was resolved by a compromise that went further than the formula adopted in Vienna. Throughout the text adopted wherever rights are mentioned it is with regard to 'persons belonging to national minorities' (this on the insistence of several delegations, including France, Turkey, Bulgaria and Greece, overcoming the objections of Hungary, Yugoslavia, Switzerland and others). The group aspect is seen in the form of the 'ethnic' and other identities of a minority and its culture, but also, on Hungarian insistence, in a provision whereby minority rights are to be enjoyed 'individually as well as in community with other members of their group'. This was a formula previously existing in CSCE texts with regard to religious communities. Related to the

group aspect was the suggestion made by the Greek expert to add a ban on assimilation against a group's will.

2. The question of how far to go on the road from non-discrimination and protection to some level of positive discrimination, without at the same time creating inequality and preferential treatment that would be resented by the majority. The compromise was a formula suggested by the Yugoslav expert, taken from the UN convention on racial discrimination, which spoke in terms of 'special measures' aimed at 'full equality', thus not reaching the level of positive discrimination.

3. The problem of recognition or self-definition of minorities, which brought to the fore the perennial problem of the definition of national minorities and the inadequacy of the very term 'national' minority. This ended with the compromise formula suggested by the United States expert, which placed the emphasis at the individual level, as 'a matter of a person's individual choice'. To this was added that 'no disadvantage must arise from the exercise of such choice'. The Greek delegate, referring to integration and voluntary assimilation, added that, equally, no disadvantage may arise from not wanting to belong to a minority, an idea finally included somewhat obscurely, as 'no disadvantage' arising 'on account of the exercise or non-exercise' of minority rights.

4. The scope of application of the provisions, that is whether they would also apply to 'ethnic' minorities and groups, or 'new' minorities, such as migrant workers (a Turkish request, which the FRG in particular strenuously resisted, but which ended up in another chapter of the document) or ethnic groups from former colonies or even 'nationalities', as Spain wanted. Needless to say, this difficult question (which, incidentally, was one of the tasks set by the Greek proposal for an experts' meeting) could not be resolved.

5. The extent of teaching of a minority language and its use by public authorities. This raised the question of the damage done to legitimate attempts at integration aimed at not marginalizing members of minorities within a wider society, which worried several delegations including the two celebrated 'melting pots', the United States and Canada. The teaching aspect ended up with several clauses, notably the need also to learn the official language (or languages) of the state wherein they live (stressed in particular by Romania and supported by Greece and France), to 'have adequate opportunities for instruction' (not 'education') '*of* their mother tongue or *in* their mother tongue' (emphasis added), meaning that a state had a choice

and did not have to have the whole school curriculum in the minority language. As for the provision on the use of the minority language before public authorities, it was fairly weak, for good reasons, with several safety clauses ('wherever possible' and 'in conformity with applicable national legislation').

6. The funding aspect regarding schools, minority organizations, etc. This worried many delegations, including those of rich and powerful states not prepared to accept public funding.

7. The issue of autonomy, or 'autonomous administrations' as it was finally worded. This was championed by several delegations, notably by the Pentagonale and most of all by Italy, with the main opposed delegation being that of Greece.

On mechanism there was little move forward, and on this the Hungarian delegate was careful to follow the more traditional approach of the lowest common denominator, ending by taking on board only a slight elaboration on the existing mechanism based on parts of the two proposals from the Paris CHD Meeting (see previous chapter). At the suggestion of the Greek delegate, the various proposals examined were placed into three categories: secondary additions to render the existing four-point human mechanism more efficient; new additional mechanisms; and suggested intercessional meetings. The sequence idea was not adopted, not even between points 1 and 2 or 1 and 3 of the existing mechanism, because of the call for maximum flexibility supported by the United Kingdom, Ireland, Switzerland, Czechoslovakia and others. The United States, Canada and the Soviet Union felt that three weeks was too short a time-span for a reply under point 1, and that four weeks would be more realistic for 'some sort of reply', though not necessarily a comprehensive one. A Cypriot proposal on forwarding communications on point 1 of the mechanism through the host country of the preceding CHD meeting, was not adopted owing to the strenuous resistance of Turkey.

The proposals on new mechanisms consisted of the following: observers, by the NNA (to be added to the four existing points and to be activated on the initiative of only one state); rapporteurs, by Canada (again fairly automatic upon the initiative of one state); the longest proposal of all (comprising eight pages), by Denmark, on a complicated procedure consisting of a seven-person Committee on the Human Dimension which would make inquiries and submit a report on the basis of requests by participating states (after having used points 1 and 2 of the human dimension mechanism), and also by individuals having exhausted available domestic remedies; the Benelux proposal (largely a

Netherlands initiative) on the right of individuals and organizations to send details of their grievances to the CHD, where a designated committee would review them with the aim of establishing whether there existed a pattern of such violations; and on representatives of minorities, by Sweden.

Most delegations avoided expressing their views on these proposals, and few supported any proposal on mechanism other than their own, which they tried to push as far as possible by indicating the short-comings of the competing proposals. This was the case with Canada, the Netherlands and Denmark. Particularly vocal in their scepticism were the delegates of the United States, Greece, France, the United Kingdom and Romania, which, among other things, pointed out the dangers of duplication, institutionalization for its own sake, and undue bureaucratization.

It was obvious that the time for a more elaborate mechanism than that of Vienna had not yet come, especially when – before the Paris Summit – CSCE institutionalization itself was still an unresolved question. Also, with the exception of the NNA proposal on observers, none of the proposals had gained consensus even in their own group. However, discussion took place on the merits of each proposal as a result of a last-minute presentation of a United States proposal on mediation on a voluntary basis, but again there was no agreement. Several devices were tried to overcome this impasse. The Soviet Union recommended commenting on the various suggestions in a favourable light in the document but without indicating which was more suitable. Canada and Austria tried to distinguish between those that were simpler and could be adopted fairly quickly and those for the longer term, which needed more careful study. According to the Austrian delegate, it might be that the Copenhagen Meeting was a 'window of opportunity' which must not be missed. The final compromise, arrived at with some difficulty, indicated that the proposals had been examined and that they would continue to be studied together with other suggestions, the aim being to strengthen the human dimension mechanism. However, not all the suggestions were actually mentioned. The United States and the Swedish proposed mechanisms were not included.

Late on Sunday 24 June, the co-ordinators presented a first draft of a consolidated document, which was an attempt to reach the highest common denominator possible. France, Greece, Bulgaria and Romania circulated detailed amendments mainly, but not exclusively, on the minorities chapter. The United States also had problems with a number of provisions. Turkey, curiously enough, appeared to be less concerned with national minorities and more with the provisions on conscientious objection to military service. There followed bilateral meetings between the chairman of the co-ordinators and the interested delegations. Several of the considerations were met, particularly those of the United States and, to a certain extent, those presented on minorities by France, Greece, Bulgaria and Romania, which largely coincided. The main concern of France was the formulation of the paragraph on the teaching of minority languages, which as a result became attenuated, while Greece was concerned with the paragraph on autonomous administration and with including a strongly worded paragraph on the other principles, notably territorial integrity. There followed three other versions of the draft document. The United States and Turkey seemed satisfied with the changes made, and even Romania, though unhappy with several of the minority provisions, avoided being obstructive.

By Wednesday 27 June it was clear that the chairman of the co-ordinators could not water down the texts any further without losing the consensus of the other delegations, particularly on the chapter on minorities. This left France, Greece and Bulgaria in an unpleasant dilemma. Could they possibly *à trois* withhold consensus to such a document or riddle it with reservations and interpretative statements? After briefly meeting with each other, they sought instructions, all three suggesting to their capitals that they accept the document. They pointed, among other things, to their isolation, to the fact that several of their views had been taken on board one way or another and, above all, that this was sure to be a historic document. The last two delegations to receive the green light were Bulgaria and Greece, delaying the adoption of the document by some four hours. The last outstanding problems for Athens had been the autonomy clause in the minorities chapter and the chairman's statement on access to NGOs.[11] It was the Italian delegation in particular (apparently on the insistence of their foreign minister) which had been adamant on having something on autonomous administration. Greece only accepted the autonomy clause with great reluctance.[12]

The chairman of the co-ordinators introduced the document (CHDC.43) on 28 June on behalf of the delegations of Austria, Finland, Hungary and Switzerland, in a carefully worded intervention, stressing that it had been the outcome of 'difficult and protracted negotiations on some highly controversial issues'. The document was described as 'a milestone' and the results as 'truly revolutionary'. He ended by giving two interpretations, both very much wanted by some delegations: that the rights of persons belonging to national minorities 'have to be seen as an inseparable element of universally recognized human rights'; and, with regard to establishing autonomous administrations, that 'this reflects the actual situation in certain European countries and is not meant to imply any commitment for any participating State to follow such a course of action'.[13]

After the adoption of the document Greece and Bulgaria made interpretative statements under paragraph 79, both with reference to the chapter on national minorities.[14] Of the other three in the 'anti-minority' camp, France and Romania did not make paragraph-79 statements, but Turkey did, though not in the generally accepted manner, which cast doubts as to the validity of the statement. Procedure apart, the content of the Turkish interpretative statement made it more like a reservation regarding the whole of Chapter IV on national minorities, and as such would normally have led to it being questioned by several delegations.[15]

THE COPENHAGEN DOCUMENT: RULE OF LAW, DEMOCRACY AND MINORITY RIGHTS

The document of the Second CHD Meeting was admittedly the most far-reaching CSCE document on human rights ever, a true, international landmark for the areas it covers. Coming out of the meeting with a substantial document has been a realistic prospect in the wake of the amazing changes of the previous year, but most delegations had not expected it to achieve so much. Some commentators have complained that the document could have gone further, notably with regard to the difficult issue of national minorities, had it not been for the stance of certain delegations.[16] However, the true measure of how comprehensive and far-reaching the document was became obvious the following year, when meetings had great difficulty in producing something worthwhile and substantial to add to the Copenhagen Document, including the question of national minorities.

The Copenhagen Document (the official title is 'Document of the Copenhagen Meeting of the Conference on the Human Dimension of the CSCE'), adopted on 29 June 1990, consists of a short preamble and five chapters designated with roman numerals and no titles (so as to avoid long debates about titles). Chapter I deals with democracy and the rule of law, Chapter II with human rights and fundamental freedoms, Chapter III with co-operation on democratic institutions, Chapter IV with national minorities and with the related issues of racism, ethnic hatred, xenophobia etc., and Chapter V with the mechanism.

As pointed out by international lawyers, the first three chapters of the Copenhagen Document are far from a mere enumeration or recasting of already existing traditional legal provisions on civil and political rights taken from UN texts and the Council of Europe. They go well beyond these, particularly in the area of the rule of law and pluralistic democracy, covering the principles of the wider political system. With the Copenhagen Document, as Thomas Buergenthal has pointed out, 'a new pan-European public order' was proclaimed, and there was henceforth a 'consensus within the CSCE' as to which political system was to be adopted.[17]

The first two chapters are interlinked and based on the proposals on the rule of law and on free elections. Chapter I sets out the basis of the rule of law and democracy in some detail. It starts with four provisions on the existing relations between the rule of law, pluralistic democracy and human rights, then comes a catalogue of twenty-one principles of justice 'essential to the full expression of the inherent dignity and of the equal and unalienable rights of all human beings' (paragraphs 5, 5.1–5.21). The principle on free elections is elaborated on the basis of nine characteristics (paragraphs 7.1–7.9), declaring that 'the will of the people, freely and fairly expressed through periodic and genuine elections, is the basis of the authority and legitimacy of all government' (paragraph 6). In addition there is a condemnation of terrorism (paragraph 6) and an explicit declaration of the state's responsibility to defend and protect their human rights obligations and the democratic order 'against the activities of persons, groups or organizations that engage in or refuse to renounce terrorism or violence aimed at the overthrow of that order or of that of another participating State'. This chapter ends with a recommendation which in its original form caused some difficulty, hence it was modified to: states 'consider that the presence of observers, both foreign and domestic, can enhance the electoral process for States in which elections take place' and 'therefore invite observers from any other CSCE participating States and any appropriate private institutions and organizations who may wish to do so to observe the course of their national election proceedings, to the extent permitted by law'. This would also apply to elections below the national level.[18]

Chapter II, which should be viewed as a *corpus* with the previous chapter, comprises a long and very comprehensive catalogue of human rights, including human contacts. Among these rights several had not been contained in previous CSCE documents, such as the right to peaceful demonstration, the right to association, the rights of the child, and rights on conscientious objection to compulsory military service (by considering the introduction of some alternative service). Included also are the right to free expression, thought, conscience, or belief and the right to free movement. Furthermore, the state is to respect NGO activity, take measures on the banning of torture, and address the rights of migrant workers. There was a reference to abolition of the death penalty but it was so watered down (after objections from the United Kingdom and the United States) that it would have been better had it not been included.

Chapter II also contains two pace-setting clauses, one on the conditions for the admissibility of restrictions, and the other on the conditions of public emergency. The first (in paragraph 24) states that the exercise of human rights 'will not be subject to any restrictions except those which are provided by law and are consistent with their obligations under international law', that '[t]hese restrictions have the character of exceptions', and 'are not abused and are not applied in an arbitrary manner, but in such a way that the effective exercise of these rights is ensured'. The second states that restriction in a state of public emergency 'must remain strictly within the limits provided by international law' and sets out four basic conditions for the application of a state of public emergency.

Chapter III is short and is largely based on proposals by Canada, Norway, the Soviet Union and the GDR on co-operation on democratic institutions by way of contacts, and co-operation at various levels. Some specific areas are mentioned, including the establishment of independent national institutions in the field of human rights and the rule of law, and the encouragement of contacts between parliamentarians. There is also reference to the role of the Council of Europe. This chapter closes by considering the idea of convening a 'meeting or seminar of experts to review and discuss co-operative measures designated to promote and sustain democratic institutions' (paragraph 29).

Chapter IV on national minorities and the eradication of ethnic/racial hatred is one of the major achievements of the whole document. It is particularly innovative in this sphere, going well beyond the Vienna Concluding Document. In a little above two pages one finds a list *par excellence* of existing minorities.[19]

The first paragraph of Chapter IV (paragraph 30) starts by asserting that 'questions relating to national minorities can only be satisfactorily resolved in a democratic political framework based on the rule of law, with a functioning independent judiciary', which is the framework within which full respect for human rights can be guaranteed. A second sub-paragraph refers to the role of NGOs and other organizations, including political parties and even trade unions, in 'the promotion of tolerance, cultural diversity and the resolution of questions relating to national minorities'. Noteworthy is the last sub-paragraph, which states that 'respect for the rights of persons belonging to national minorities as part of universally recognized human rights is an essential factor for peace, justice, stability and democracy in the participating States'.

The second paragraph (paragraph 31) is the non-discrimination paragraph based on the UN text on non-discrimination. The third paragraph (paragraph 32) is the longest in Chapter IV, including several sub-paragraphs. It starts with the famous compromise on a person's individual choice, formulated as: to 'belong to a national minority is a matter of a person's individual choice and no disadvantage may arise from the exercise of such choice'. What was left open, however, and has confused discussions to develop this clause ever since, is whether someone could choose to belong to a non-recognized national minority. In addition, one is still faced with the old problem of who is to say when a minority exists in the first place. In the same paragraph there is also the fundamental provision on 'the right freely to express, preserve and develop their ethnic, cultural, linguistic or religious identity, and to maintain and develop their culture in all its aspects', ending with the Greek clause formulated as 'free of any attempts at assimilation against their will'.

Paragraph 32 leads on to six sub-paragraphs which consist of a list of rights of persons belonging to national minorities as follows: to use freely their mother tongue; to establish and maintain educational and other institutions; to profess and practise their religion; to establish and maintain unimpeded contacts within and across frontiers with those with whom they share a common ethnic or national origin, culture or religion; to disseminate and exchange information; to establish associations or organizations and participate in international NGOs. Most of these were previously part of Basket III, and were not 'rights' as such – for instance, human contacts or even education. This list leads on to an important paragraph (not numbered) which states that these rights can be exercised and enjoyed 'individually as well as in community with other members of their group', and ends by affirming that 'no disadvantage may arise' for such a person 'on account of the *exercise* or *non-exercise* of any such rights' (emphasis added).

Paragraph 33 details the active measures to be taken by the state so as to protect and promote the identity of minorities, taking into consideration the views of the minorities on decisions which concern them, 'after due consultations, including contacts with organizations or associations of such minorities', and ends with what was to be a new, more modern-sounding safety clause in the CSCE annals – 'in accordance with the decision-making procedures of each State'.

Paragraph 34 is concerned with the mother tongue of minorities in teaching and before public authorities (see above). The next paragraph (paragraph 35) is concerned with 'effective participation in public affairs', which adds '*including* participation in the affairs relating to the protection and promotion of the identity of such minorities' (emphasis added). Thus, participation is not only limited to matters of their own identity, as some delegations had hoped. There follows the paragraph on autonomous administration, which is clearly intended as a factual, noncommittal statement:

> The participating States *note* the efforts undertaken to protect and create conditions for the promotion of the ethnic, cultural, linguistic and religious identity of *certain* national minorities by establishing, *as one of the possible means* to achieve these aims, *appropriate* local or autonomous administrations *corresponding to the specific historical* and *territorial circumstances* of such minorities and *in accordance with the policies* of the State concerned. (emphasis placed on the attenuating clauses)

Paragraph 36 is concerned with the international dimension, of 'increasing constructive co-operation among themselves on questions relating to national minorities'. This provision worried some states, for it could give rise to unwarranted external interference. For this reason the word 'constructive' was added and there followed a second sentence, which can be interpreted as a condition, that such co-operation 'seeks to promote mutual understanding and confidence, friendly and good-neighbourly relations, international peace, security and justice'.

Paragraph 37 is to be seen as the overall safety clause for the provisions on national minorities. It is a somewhat weakened version of a Greek suggestion (which was supported by several states, even by pro-minority delegations such as Italy). It states that

> [n]one of these commitments may be interpreted as implying any right to engage in activity or perform any action in contravention of the purposes and principles of the Charter of the United Nations, other obligations under international law or the provisions of the Final Act, including the principle of territorial integrity of States.

The next two paragraphs deal with adhering to international instruments, including those 'providing for a right of complaint by individuals', and with co-operating with competent international organizations, such as the UN and the Council of Europe. They end with a suggestion for a meeting of experts on national minorities, which of the three meetings proposed found the least favour, hence the attenuated wording running thus: 'They will consider convening a meeting of experts for a thorough discussion of the issue of national minorities', which was based mostly on the Greek proposal for a meeting (with the mention of 'thorough' and 'issue').

Chapter IV ends with the section on various measures condemning 'totalitarianism, racial and ethnic hatred, anti-semitism, xenophobia and discrimination against anyone as well as persecution on religious and ideological grounds', on which there were no major difficulties. More problematic was the phrase, 'they also recognize the particular problems of Roma [gypsies]'. The reason for the difficulty was that no specific ethnic or religious group had been named until then in CSCE texts, and whenever it had been requested it was not accepted, as in the case of the ethnic Turks of Bulgaria by Turkey in the First CHD Meeting in Paris. The Roma reference would open up this possibility and perhaps would even be a Pandora's Box.

THE COMING OF A NEW ERA OF NEGOTIATIONS: BLESSING OR NIGHTMARE?

The twilight zone between the Vienna Follow-up Meeting and the Copenhagen Meeting gradually altered the character of the negotiations, rendering the setting more unstructured and far less predictable than ever before in the CSCE on matters of the human rights dimension. By June 1990 in Copenhagen, a different and uncharted territory from the point of view of negotiations had presented itself and this situation has continued until the eve of Helsinki-II. It is worth identifying basic features in human dimension negotiations from 1989 onwards:

– Negotiations are no longer 'bloc-to-bloc', between the designated negotiators of the Eastern and Western delegations, with the NNA placed in between.
– The disappearance of the Eastern bloc has not been replaced by any form of co-ordination to rival the Western (NATO) caucus.
– Central and eastern European states have gradually appeared as protagonists in the human dimension, first and foremost Hungary, and then one by one the other states, even including the former Soviet Union.

- The neutrals, in view of the lack of a bridge-building role for them between East and West, insist on playing their traditional role in the new setting, but now individually, as bridge-builders between diametrically opposed delegations, something at which they have not been successful, with the exception of Austria (which had important successes in the Copenhagen and Moscow CHD meetings).
- Delegations other than the NNA have emerged as acceptable co-ordinators, for instance Hungary, Czechoslovakia, Poland, Norway and even the Soviet Union.
- The five states of the Pentagonale emerged for a time as an effective and well-coordinated group, rivalling even the cohesion and drive of the '12'.
- Solidarity and cohesion within the '16' (NATO) is more shaky than in the days between Madrid and Vienna (1980–88).
- The void resulting from the disappearance of the traditional blocs was filled for a time by the '12', which on some occasions has appeared to be taking over the role of the NNA, though in fact '12' solidarity and cohesion in practice is less apparent than real, particularly since 1991.
- The pressure for text-production has been relentless and drafting has rarely taken heed of the old principle of lowest common denominator (whereby a lack of consensus meant dropping a concept or phrase), but has striven for the highest possible denominator, given the tendency of the majority to support the more far-reaching commitments on the human dimension.
- The absence of an East–West clash has led to a somewhat greater emphasis on bilateral differences, which, however, continue to be seen by most delegations as an aberration and far from fruitful.

Thus, ironically, as negotiations have come nearer to the ideal set by the Helsinki 'Rules of Procedure', of each state acting individually outside alliances, the negotiator's ultimate nightmare of a 'one against all' situation has become a reality. There has often been a 'free for all'[20] from Copenhagen onwards. Contrary to the days up to the end of the Vienna Follow-up, there is an obvious advantage in favour of delegations putting forward or supporting bold proposals, owing to at least two interrelated factors. One is the incessant striving to produce a substantial document as the mark of a successful CSCE meeting. The second is the fact that most of the proposals made in this field are, to varying degrees, far-reaching. There exist no countervailing 'antithetical' proposals, as in the old days, stemming from a different philosophy, which could lead to a middle of the road compromise. Indeed, it has been the case, on more than one occasion, that even proposals supported by a minority of delegations and not gaining overwhelming support somehow succeed in getting through. Moreover, delegations opposing a proposal are less likely to see their views prevail, however sound their arguments may be. This latter situation has been experienced even by large states known for their effectiveness in the CSCE context, making the old implicit assumption of the CSCE, 'the diminishing influence of the strong',[21] far more real, particularly from 1990 onwards.

VIENNA AND PARIS: PROCLAIMING THE 'NEW EUROPE' AND THE NEW CSCE

A SUMMIT

The convening of a summit within the CSCE framework was another Gorbachev/Shevardnadze idea treated initially with caution by several Western governments, especially by the United States. It was inspired by the need to take stock of the dramatic changes in Europe during 1989 and, in doing so, also to deal with the question of German reunification. The idea of a summit in 1990 was launched by President Gorbachev on 30 November 1989 in Rome in the course of an unofficial visit, and the first to support the idea in the West were France and the FRG.[1]

Early the following year, on 20 January 1990, the foreign ministers of the '12' agreed in principle to the convening of a summit in the course of 1990, issuing a month later a declaration on the subject at their Ministerial Meeting in Dublin. The United States, which had regarded the idea of a summit as premature, finally accepted it, but on one basic condition, the conclusion of the round of talks on CFE in Vienna before the summit.[2] The '12' and other CSCE participating states hoped that the CSBM talks too would have reached a conclusion by the summit. The principle of a summit meeting was endorsed in the margins of the Open Skies Conference by the NATO and Warsaw Pact members, and by the NNA in their Valletta Meeting in early spring 1990. Austria and France offered to host the summit meeting in their respective capitals. It was finally decided to host the preparatory meeting in Vienna and the summit in Paris, a decision which was not unrelated to the weight of the '12', and NATO particularly, in the new CSCE. The decision for a preparatory committee in Vienna to start on 10 July 1990, which would lead to a summit meeting in Paris later in the year, was adopted at the Copenhagen CHD Meeting in a special meeting of Foreign Ministers convened by the Danish Foreign Minister.[3]

The Soviet Union had been the originator of the idea of a summit, but it was the '12', assisted by several other delegations, which was the main driving force, in part due to their early consultations and co-ordination. As early as March and April 1990 one can see in the consultations held within the framework of European Political Co-operation (EPC) of the EC, under able Irish presidency, the main elements of the CSCE future institutional framework: a CSCE consultative mechanism at the level of foreign ministers to meet annually, with additional meetings at the official level; CSCE main follow-ups every two years, with a fixed, shorter duration and a summit meeting each time; a small CSCE administrative secretariat (seen at the time as 'migrant'); a conflict or crisis management centre; conciliation machinery to include, among other things, issues relating to minorities; and several other ideas which were not pursued afterwards.

The Soviet Union indicated to the '12' that it approved of this approach, but seemed somewhat hesitant to go very far on the adoption of specific institutions. The United States and Canada, on the other hand, were thinking along lines similar to the '12', also adding a mechanism for monitoring elections and a CSCE parliamentary assembly. Thus, in the important 'London Declaration on a transformed North Atlantic Alliance' issued by the heads of state or government participating in the North Atlantic Council, a 'more prominent' role for the CSCE was endorsed, and a list of six institutional arrangements recommended for the CSCE. These were presented by the '16' in the course of the Vienna Preparatory Committee. The London Declaration included the United States condition for a CFE agreement to be signed at the Paris Summit. Of great symbolic importance for those days was a proposal to the member states of the Warsaw Treaty Organization for a joint declaration, to be adopted at the Paris Summit, whereby it would be solemnly pronounced that they were 'no longer adversaries', and to reaffirm their 'intention to refrain from the threat or use of force against the territorial or political independence of any state'.[4]

THE VIENNA TALKS:
THE MAKING OF THE SUMMIT DOCUMENT

The Vienna Preparatory Committee, the 'Prepcom' as it was commonly known, proceeded in two sessions, the first in July (10–27)

137

and the second from 9 September until mid-November. It was not an actual 'prepcom' in the usual sense of the word in the CSCE, of a preparatory meeting setting an agenda for a main meeting, but was itself a main meeting such as the one at Geneva in 1973–75. It prepared, in every detail, the document which was to be adopted at the Paris Summit.

On the whole the negotiation setting was similar to that of the Copenhagen Meeting, with the main protagonists being the '12', followed by the Pentagonale and the United States and Canada, with the NNA trying somewhat unsuccessfully to engage in their traditional mediating role. A related trend was the so-called 'friends phenomenon', whereby delegations from different groups would get together and promote certain texts. This was particularly prominent in the case of institutions.

The '12', under the able Italian presidency, were, even more than in the Vienna Follow-up and in Copenhagen, the main force propelling the meeting to its final conclusion, and this in spite of certain differences between its state-members on certain issues. Indeed, one could regard the '12' as having supplanted to some extent the role of the NNA, by producing the texts on which the co-ordinators relied for their own documents, both as regards institutions and textual/normative paragraphs. Relations with the other Western delegations, notably with the United States delegation led by Ambassador John J. Maresca, were not smooth and, in fact, deteriorated as time went by, with more than one clash, notably between the United States and the French delegation, even though the differences were really not of such magnitude as to warrant any awkward moments. As for the wider negotiations (at the level of all the delegations), they were on more than one occasion, as in Copenhagen, a 'free for all'.

An *ad hoc* group, set up under Austrian co-ordination,[5] concluded with a first draft and a revised version on 23 and 26 July respectively. There were seven main proposals submitted in the first session of the Prepcom, which had considerable overlap on institution-building.

Poland, the CSFR (the Czech and Slovak Federal Republic) and the GDR proposed a Council for Security and Co-operation in Europe at ministerial and at ambassadorial levels, to meet twice a year and once a month respectively, but also to convene extraordinary sessions if urgent cases arose; meetings of heads of state or government to be held every two years on a rotational basis; a small permanent secretariat; a centre for confidence-building, arms control and verification; and a centre for conflict prevention.[6]

The NNA presented the structure of one or more concluding

documents under three chapters, 'elements of a European peace order', 'efforts to strengthen security and co-operation in Europe', and 'development of the structures of the CSCE process'. The latter included periodic meetings of heads of state or government, regular follow-ups, a small secretariat, new structures in the field of security including conflict prevention, crisis management and implementation of agreements on military security, guidelines for a mechanism on the peaceful settlement of disputes, the creation of a parliamentary body for the CSCE, and relations with the other relevant institutions, in particular with the Council of Europe.[7]

The '16' proposal on institutions, submitted in the name of France, was in fact the list that had been adopted in the NATO London Declaration of 6 July.[8] It comprised six elements: consultations at ministerial level at least once a year and periodic meetings of officials; a schedule of CSCE review conferences once every two years; a small CSCE secretariat; a CSCE mechanism to monitor elections on the basis of the relevant provision of the Copenhagen Document; a centre for the prevention of conflict, which could serve as a forum for exchanges of military information and unusual military activities, as well as 'the conciliation of disputes involving CSCE member states'; and a parliamentary body, an 'assembly of Europe, to be based on the existing parliamentary assembly of the Council of Europe'. A non-paper of the United States contained themes on a 'political declaration on democracy and the role of the CSCE in a reunited Europe', 'CSCE activities since Vienna', and 'future directions for CSCE'.[9] A Canadian working-paper started with 'general principles and concepts' and was more traditional in that it provided for separate sub-chapters for each of the three Baskets (Baskets I, II and III), a structure not followed in the Vienna Prepcom.[10] France submitted a framework for the principal elements that could be included in the first part of the final document or documents, entitled 'L'Europe démocratique, pacifique et unie', with sub-chapters for each of these three themes, which became the beacons of the new Europe as expounded in the Charter of Paris.[11]

The most complete document, which telescoped the basic elements of what might be the final text of the summit, was that presented in the name of the European Community on 19 July, comprising five chapters: 'changes in Europe', 'achievements of the CSCE', 'guidelines for the future', 'institutional arrangements' and 'follow-up to the summit'.[12]

The first co-ordinator's non-paper was a short text of basic themes for one or more documents of the summit meeting, consisting of four chapters, the first three of which were to lead, in the next session of the Prepcom, to the formation of three drafting groups and to the final three chapters of the Charter of Paris. Its main point of reference was the document of the '12'. In its slightly amended redraft of 26 July this short text has the following sections: 'a democratic, peaceful and united Europe', with a separate sub-chapter on 'the role of the CSCE process', 'guidelines for the future', 'developments of the structures of the CSCE process' and 'follow-up to the summit'. Under the 'guidelines' chapter the first draft had included the Swiss/Greek concept from Copenhagen of 'an experts meeting on minorities', but this was removed at the insistence of the United States and Turkey, which did not see merit in convening such a meeting. The institutional arrangements taken on board the co-ordinator's non-paper by the close of this session were based more on the NNA than the '16' paper. Thus, only the Centre for the Prevention of Conflict was added to the NNA listing, while the mechanism to monitor elections was omitted.[13]

In the period between the first and second phase of the Prepcom, the '12' and '16' consultations continued in earnest, identifying points of agreement and disagreement. The United Kingdom and France presented a proposal on a 'conflict prevention centre' (CPC), which was to be the final name adopted for that institution, whose tasks were limited to matters linked with CSBMs. This was not to the liking of the FRG, which favoured an expanded mandate for the Centre with 'a political function' and actual 'conflict prevention' powers, while the United States was keen not to include verification of disarmament measures. The question of conciliation was extracted from the functions of the CPC and was to be examined separately, at the Valletta Meeting, to be held in January 1991, whose task was to examine the peaceful settlement of disputes, which, of course, includes conciliation. The FRG did not want the council to be limited to meetings of foreign ministers but favoured allowing for the possibility of meetings by defence ministers or even economic ministers, something which was unacceptable to the United States in particular. At this stage the first clouds appeared over the question of the CSCE assembly, with the United States, one of the initiators of the idea, backing down because of the reaction of US legislators. France wanted the non-aggression declaration by the members of the two alliances proposed in the London Declaration to be signed also by the NNA, but this found little favour among the Western states and the NNA themselves.[14] As a result, France produced a text for a section entitled 'friendly relations', many elements of which were to be included in a sub-chapter with a similar title in the Charter of Paris. This text, which became one of the most important elements of the summit document, was to provide a link with the joint declaration on non-aggression, to which the United States attached great importance.[15]

The second session of the Preparatory Committee started on 3 September 1990. Three drafting groups were formed. Drafting group 1, with the Swedish delegate as co-ordinator, was concerned with democracy, peace and unity, including friendly relations; drafting group 2, led by the Swiss delegate, was to deal with the guidelines; and drafting group 3, led by the Finnish delegate, was to deal with the new structures. It was decided to have one consolidated document, provisionally called the 'Document of the Paris CSCE Summit'. In spite of the general agreement on most issues the talks were unexpectedly difficult. This was partly because of the complexity of the institutional aspect, which was a new venture for the CSCE, but also because of the new negotiating framework, which, as in Copenhagen, was not conducive to swift results. Furthermore, among the Western delegations, there was the problem of relations between the United States delegation and the '12'. There was also the difficulty of ironing out the differences between members of the prime movers in the Prepcom, the '12', particularly between those which wanted to go far on both institutions and standard-setting, such as Germany and Italy, and those with a more cautious line, such as France and the United Kingdom.

The elaboration of the three parts of the summit document was largely the result of give-and-take between the non-papers of the co-ordinators and the non-papers emanating from the '12'. Thus on 10 September, the '12' produced a non-paper on the first part of the first chapter, and circulated its 'friendly relations' section four days later. A few days after this the Swedish co-ordinator produced a more extensive text, largely based on the '12' text for the preamble and a sub-chapter entitled 'democracy and the rule of law', on some elements from the '12' for a sub-chapter entitled 'unity and co-operation', on an NNA non-paper for a sub-chapter entitled 'peace and security' (which the '12' did not regard as a basis for discussion), and on a Soviet paper regarding 'the Outside World' ('friendly relations' were not included). On 19 October the '12' presented a more complete first chapter of the document, comprising a preamble followed by five sub-chapters entitled 'democracy, rule of law and human rights', 'friendly relations among participating states', 'security', 'Europe united', and 'the role of the CSCE process'. On the same day the United States circulated a similar text of its own because, owing to the reigning uneasy relations with the '12', no common text could be arrived at. The main addition made by the United States was a sub-chapter on 'economic liberty'. 'Friendly relations', the text of which corresponded to the undertaking of the Helsinki *décalogue* of principles, was a particular concern, not only to France and the '12', but also to other states, notably to the Soviet Union and Hungary, both of which circulated relevant non-papers.[16]

On 22 October the Swedish co-ordinator circulated a new version of the first chapter (Rev.3), and on 30 October another version (Rev.4) which was mostly based on the new text of the '12', though the titles of the sub-chapters differed. The text that proved most difficult to draft was that under 'friendly relations'.

The '12' non-paper for drafting group 2 on 'Guidelines for the Future' appeared on 26 September. The co-ordinator's first draft, which came out almost a month later (on 18 October), accepted the chapters as presented by the '12' but expanded their text further as follows: after a short preamble comes 'security' (almost two pages), then 'human dimension' (over two pages), 'economic co-operation' (almost two pages), 'environment' (one page), and, finally, a few lines on 'culture', 'non-governmental organizations' and the 'Mediterranean'. Discussion on this text started on 19 October with the main difficulties arising over the paragraph on national minorities and, in particular, the expansion of the human dimension mechanism.

On the national minorities paragraph, France, Spain, the United Kingdom, Greece and Bulgaria felt that it was drafted in a confusing manner, one reason being that it mentioned 'identity' on its own without any of the qualifying adjectives, such as 'ethnic', which are in the Vienna and Copenhagen documents. It was mainly Germany and Italy which wanted 'identity' on its own, apparently the aim being to broaden its meaning. France, Belgium and Bulgaria had difficulties with the beginning of the paragraph which stated that 'national minorities form an integral part of the life of our state', and Turkey wanted to delete the last part of the paragraph which referred to 'increased co-operation' for the protection of such minorities. The first issue was resolved only with difficulty, and finally the references to 'ethnic' etc. were included, largely on the insistence of Greece. 'Increased co-operation' was retained.[17]

Another troublesome issue was whether or not to convene an experts' meeting on national minorities. Least enthusiastic about convening such a meeting were the United States, Turkey, Romania, Bulgaria, France, Belgium, and also some countries traditionally very ambitious on the protection of minorities, such as the Netherlands. Once the convening of a meeting was agreed, its agenda then became a source of difficulty, and it ended by taking on board the more traditional Swiss elements rather than those presented by Greece in Copenhagen which would have made the meeting more useful and better geared to the new European situation. The *chapeau* of the mandate followed the Greek concept of examining the issue in all its aspects, while the three sub-paragraphs followed the Swiss line and did not actually correspond to the *chapeau*, being far narrower in scope.

The expansion of the human dimension mechanism in the forth-coming Moscow Meeting proved problematic, particularly with regard to two issues: the inclusion, or not, of individual petitions, and which mechanism(s) to select or highlight from those that had appeared in the Copenhagen Meeting. The problem caused major difficulties even within the '12'. Finally a formula was devised – known as the 'Belgian clause' – which suggested a possible area of expansion and referred to the involvement of individuals.[18]

On institutions (the task of drafting group 3) the '12' submitted an important non-paper which suggested the following: a 'council' consisting of ministers of foreign affairs to convene twice a year, as well as in urgent cases; a 'committee of senior officials' (CSO) to prepare the work of the council; a possibility for additional meetings by other ministers (a German idea); follow-up meetings of three months each, every two years as a rule; a secretariat; an assembly of Europe; a mechanism comprising a small unit to observe elections; a summit meeting every two years in the course of follow-ups; and a Centre for the Prevention of Conflict, with functions on agreed CSBMs, but this 'without any prejudice to any additional proposals concerning a procedure for the conciliation of disputes as well as broader talks relating to dispute settlement, with which the centre may be entrusted in the future', thus not excluding the broader German concept for a CPC. Emergency sessions for the CSO were also envisaged. On the request of a participating state, an extraordinary meeting could be convened in a 'situation of potential conflict or crisis' arising from a violation of any principle of the Final Act or other CSCE commitments, or UN principles, or from a breach of international law, if adequate grounds were provided by the requesting state including evidence of its urgency, and as long as other remedies in appropriate CSCE mechanisms had been exhausted or did not apply.[19]

As the Prepcom was entering its last phase in November, the main outstanding difficulties were in the sphere of institution-building, notably the difference between the United States and Germany (now called by its old name following reunification) as to the latter's wish to include the possibility for ministers of defence and other ministers to participate in the council; whether to have one or two meetings of the council (the United States supporting one meeting, the '12' two); the limited support for a mechanism or institution on free elections urged by the United States and opposed by France in particular; the CSO emergency mechanism suggested by the '12', which was opposed especially by Turkey, and whether consensus would be needed for the convening of such a meeting; and the question of the Assembly of Europe. The United States did not want it to be an appendage to the existing assembly of the Council of Europe, and wanted the arrangements and decisions to be taken by the parliamentarians themselves, as urged by the US Congress, a view contrary to that of the '12' which wanted such decisions to be taken by governments, as are other CSCE decisions. There were also difficulties with the prospect of future mechanisms, notably the peaceful settlement of disputes with reference to the forthcoming Valletta Meeting on the subject, and the precise wording of the human dimension mechanism to be entrusted to the Moscow CHD Meeting.[20]

With time running out, and in view of the difficulties with the institutions chapter, the Austrian delegation, supported by several other delegations, took the initiative and formed an *ad hoc* group, thus in effect taking the task away from the Finnish co-ordinator, who was moving far too slowly in his attempts to be as even-handed as possible. In this way, the remaining difficulties on institutions reached a conclusion. But even as late as 14 November, three days before the summit, there were still two texts to be finalised – the expansion of the human dimension mechanism and the section on the CSCE parliamentary assembly – not to mention the name of the summit document, which at the very last moment changed from 'Document of the Paris CSCE Summit' to the more ambitious, but not particularly elegant, 'Charter of Paris for a New Europe'. However, the fight against the clock regarding the summit document was child's play in comparison with the frenzy experienced by those negotiating the CFE and CSBM texts.[21]

At last, the 'Charter' and three other pivotal documents were ready on time for the Paris Summit.

THE CHARTER OF PARIS FOR A NEW EUROPE

The Paris Summit took place in the grand hall of Le Centre Kléber, between 19 and 21 November 1990, where four documents were signed by the heads of state or government. The 'Charter of Paris for a New Europe' and the 'Vienna Document on Confidence- and

Security-Building Measures' were signed by thirty-four states, while twenty-two states signed a legally binding text, the 'Treaty on Conventional Armed Forces in Europe' (CFE), which had been negotiated within the CSCE framework on the basis of the mandate included in the Vienna Concluding Document. There was also the 'Joint Declaration of Twenty-Two States', in which the members of NATO and the Warsaw Pact welcomed the historic changes in Europe and declared that they were no longer adversaries.

Thus came about the CSCE's long-awaited appointment with mainstream history, by solemnly declaring an end to East–West confrontation and Cold War and the opening up of a new era for Europe. As a result, the CSCE, the venue *par excellence* of the East–West divide, which had faced being made obsolete and irrelevant almost overnight in view of the passing of the Cold War, was instead upgraded, transformed, and became, in its own right, a diplomatic regime of the wider Europe.

The 'Charter of Paris for a New Europe' can be compared in status only with the Final Act itself. In substance, however, its main contribution is not, as in the Final Act, to be found in the normative commitments as such – most had already been set out by the Sofia, Bonn, Copenhagen and other previous documents – but in the institution-building role of the CSCE. In CSCE terms this amounted to a veritable revolution, as the CSCE, the institution without institutions, became institutionalized. On the normative side, the Charter's main contribution is less the substance and more the solemnity of the undertakings, notably on those that concern us here, human rights, democracy and the rule of law, which thus acquired a superordinate importance as the foundations of the new Europe. Europe had became one as to basic principles. It was to be founded on three main elements, democracy, peace and unity.[22] The Charter declared on its very first page that 'the era of confrontation and division of Europe has ended ... Europe is liberating itself from the legacy of the past', and that 'a new era of democracy, peace and unity in Europe' had opened.[23]

As we saw from negotiations in the Prepcom, the traditional CSCE approach of the three Baskets was not followed, hence the different outcome. According to Victor-Yves Ghebali, the three Baskets had now become seven themes, the seven sub-chapters existing under the second chapter on 'Guidelines for the Future'.[24] But this is only partly true, and not necessarily a blueprint for the future – for instance for Helsinki-II. The main problem is that the seven subjects are hardly of equal importance and many major themes that would warrant a chapter of their own are not included. The patchwork outcome was the result of working in haste and was not a reasoned decision to 'break' the three Baskets, as it were, into seven 'Baskets'.

The Charter is an idiosyncratic document, as seen from its three chapters (the first two of which overlap considerably): 'A New Era of Democracy, Peace and Unity', 'Guidelines for the Future' and 'New Structures and Institutions of the CSCE Process'. The main emphasis from the start is placed on the human dimension, on democracy, the rule of law and human rights, including the rights of persons belonging to national minorities. The document further confirms the conclusions of the intercessional meetings, which had taken place on the basis of the Vienna Concluding Document, and the new steps on CSBMs. It decided to convene two new intercessional meetings, the meeting of experts on national minorities, and the seminar on democratic institutions; and to establish five permanent bodies, providing for the creation in the future of a Parliamentary Assembly (the setting up of the 'Assembly of Europe' was later decided in the course of the First CSCE Council in Berlin in June 1991, following a Spanish initiative).

The five CSCE bodies are a Council (of foreign ministers), scheduled to meet at least once annually, a Committee of Senior Officials (CSO), and three other deceptively modest institutions: an administrative Secretariat based in Prague; a Conflict Prevention Centre (CPC) in Vienna, in the first instance to limit itself to assisting the implementation of CSBMs (but this 'without prejudice to any additional tasks ... which may be assigned to it in the future');[25] and an Office for Free Elections (OFE) in Warsaw. The Charter also stipulates that from now on CSCE follow-up meetings are to take place every two years, would include a summit session, and would normally last for three months; it suggests the development of an emergency mechanism (later adopted in the Berlin Council meeting of June 1991 and put into operation immediately regarding the Yugoslav crisis), and expanding the human rights mechanism, among other things.

With regard to the Moscow Meeting, the Charter states that in view of the usefulness of the CHD mechanism, it should be expanded, 'involving, *inter alia*, the services of experts or a roster of eminent persons experienced in human rights', as well as involving individuals. The Valletta Meeting on the peaceful settlement of disputes is given the task of examining 'new forms of co-operation' for 'a range of methods for the peaceful settlement of disputes, including mandatory third-party involvement'. As for the Cracow Symposium on the Cultural Heritage, the Charter signatories were looking forward 'to its consideration of guidelines for intensified co-operation in the field of culture'.[26]

On the whole, with the exception of the provisions on institutions in the Paris Document, the Charter of Paris is a less balanced, less complete document than the Helsinki Final Act, which, as a result, retains its seminal importance, particularly regarding the ten vital principles. The Charter of Paris refers to the Final Act, and particularly to the Principles therein, some of which are selectively reinforced, above all Principle VII. The Charter, a short, loosely-written document of only ten pages (the Final Act is almost sixty pages), does not purport to be replacing or supplanting the Final Act, but clearly had more limited goals in mind: mainly, to herald the end of the Cold War, to enshrine the principles of pluralistic democracy, the rule of law and the market economy (the 'open society', to use Karl Popper's well-known concept), and to create certain permanent institutions.[27]

Criticism apart, it is undeniable that the Paris Charter closed one chapter of the CSCE and opened a new one, one based on agreement on fundamentals regarding the norms of the polity, where it would function henceforth on the basis of permanent institutions.

BEYOND PARIS AND UNTIL THE EVE OF HELSINKI-II

CRACOW: CULTURAL HERITAGE

The Cracow Symposium on the Cultural Heritage, a meeting of the forum genre, was one of the concessions made to the Warsaw Pact Eastern countries at the Vienna Follow-up. Poland understandably had ambitions regarding the meeting, and before the meeting circulated a lengthy non-paper as a draft concluding document which aimed, among other things, to have the subject matter institutionalized as a permanent feature of CSCE activities, with Cracow as its centre. Given Poland's sensitivity and the symbolic value of this first meeting taking place in eastern Europe in the wake of such dramatic changes, the West could not but acquiesce.

France, in an attempt to take the initiative from Poland, came forward within the '12' about two weeks before the start of the Symposium with a lengthy forty-paragraph document, filled with commitments and principles of conduct in this field. Not all its EC partners were happy with this unusual move, pointing out that the '12' should be more subtle this time, not appear as a bloc but permit the central and eastern European states to become more involved and claim a little victory of their own within mainstream Europe. This was the view of Greece, the United Kingdom, the Netherlands and Ireland, while others seemed more favourable towards the French approach. Compromise came with an Italian suggestion to divide the French text in half and try to arrive at an EC paper on the more general first part, while leaving the rest of the paper open to be submitted by France and other interested parties, if they so wished.[1]

The Symposium started with the traditional opening statements, the main feature of which was the condemnation of 'communism', first and foremost by the Polish Prime Minister Bialecki, and then by Hungary and the CSFR. The only disconcerting note was to come from the Soviet Minister for Culture, Goubenko, who retorted angrily that

Cracow had been saved by the Soviet Army, expressing his indignation at the statement of the Polish Prime Minister, who 'with the easiness of a weightlifter danced a tap dance on the coffin of the socialist system'(*sic*), and stressing that, after all, it was the Soviet Union which had 'set in motion today's developments in Central and Eastern Europe'. Another issue which created uneasiness was the question of a Baltic presence. Poland had invited the Lithuanian delegate to participate in its own delegation, while Denmark had approached the Latvian delegate with a similar offer. Needless to say, the Soviet Culture Minister did not fail to criticize this as an attempt 'to influence the internal processes developing' in his country, but the matter was left at that.

The official meeting was left to the various independent experts from fields as diverse as marine archaeology, cultural anthropology, law and art. Meanwhile, officials in the delegations, in good CSCE tradition, started the task of hammering out a concluding document. The United States, the United Kingdom and, to some extent, Canada were in favour of a short text ('short and sweet' as the United States delegate was to say in jest), if need be with an annex comprised of contributions by the experts. Most delegations, however, were inclined towards a lengthy document and, on Canada's initiative, it was decided that the chairmen of the official working groups should try to summarize the discussions of the specialists. The veteran Maltese delegate, Evariste Saliba, was chosen to cope with this burden and to present the conclusions to the informal group. It was also decided that Poland would play co-ordinator in what was called the 'Friends of Cracow', that is, a group of friends rather than a more official contact group. Meanwhile, the '12' had consolidated the twenty paragraphs of the French text and presented it as an EC non-paper for one part of the concluding document, while France on its own circulated the rest of its text.

An initial, exploratory, open-ended group was formed to try to map out a course of action based on the following papers: a new version of the Polish paper – which was more down to earth then the previous one; the '12' paper; a short United States text (on the essential elements of a document); a paper from the Pentagonale; and a French paper (the remaining part of their original text). On the initiative of the Greek delegation, who was immediately supported by the delegations of France, Hungary and Austria, it was the '12' paper which became the main basis for the first part of the document, to be complemented, where necessary, by the Polish paper. Then began hectic negotiations within the 'Friends of Cracow', with the Polish co-ordinator, a CSCE novice, at first ill at ease but gradually learning his new role (assisted by the more experienced deputy Executive-Secretary of the meeting). Negotiations continued well into the night for several days. Many issues caused difficulty, but this was partly due to the great length of the text as it unfolded.

During the negotiations, the most co-ordinated group was the Pentagonale – the '12' and the NNA not appearing as groups. The most active delegations were: from the Pentagonale, Austria, Hungary and Italy (the latter giving the clear impression of speaking with a Pentagonale rather than a '12' voice); from the NNA, Finland, Sweden and Switzerland; from the West, France, the United Kingdom, Greece, the United States and Canada; and from the remainder, Bulgaria and, of course, Poland.

The text was finally ready, with the last session, in CSCE tradition, going on well into the early hours of the morning. One last difficulty was how to deal with the summary of the specialists' discussions that the Maltese delegate had undertaken. As no conclusions had come from the chairmen of the working groups, Canada, the United States and the United Kingdom were strongly in favour of a long annexe containing the various speeches, so that the real experts on cultural heritage would not be left out. But this would have meant a huge text which would then have to be translated into all six CSCE working-languages. The compromise reached was to have all the written contributions to the discussions transmitted to the CSCE Secretariat in Prague.

The final outcome of Cracow was far from negligible. Even if the wording was relatively noncommittal, the Document of the Cracow Symposium was one of the longest texts in the CSCE human dimension to be produced in such a brief period of time, ten pages in all, of which eight pages were on standards of behaviour.[2]

GENEVA: NATIONAL MINORITIES

As pointed out above, the Copenhagen Document was so far-reaching and such a high point in the human rights dimension that subsequent meetings found it very difficult to go further in adding more substance to normative commitments. This was particularly the case with the Geneva Meeting of Experts on National Minorities, and with the Second CHD Meeting held in Moscow.

The Geneva Meeting of Experts on National Minorities was a model experts' meeting of government officials, assisted in some cases by academics and other experts on minorities acting as normal members of delegations, along the lines of the Ottawa and Bern meetings of experts. But it was only on the surface that the meeting was normal. In other respects it was full of difficulties, twists and turns and surprises, even for a CSCE meeting, and finally had a most unorthodox outcome. Final agreement on the document was reached with the greatest of difficulty, the meeting facing the real prospect, almost to the last moment, of ending with no document at all (which would have made it the first meeting with such a result since the Sofia Meeting on the Environment, which came up against a Romanian veto, later dropped after the fall of Ceauşescu). The final document from Geneva was unique in that it was not a document negotiated at the level of the participating delegations but at the level of the NATO group, as could have been the case had there been a short communiqué at the end of the Paris CHD Meeting of June 1989. Also unusual was the fact that there were very few clashes between individual delegations in the official sessions, despite a subject matter that had been one of the main causes of controversy at most CSCE meetings. The relatively minor exchanges occurred between Turkey and Cyprus, Hungary and Romania, and, in particular, Albania and Yugoslavia.[3]

Some nineteen proposals were officially submitted for the final document. The Copenhagen pattern of mixed co-sponsorships was followed. The two most important omnibus-type proposals, containing comprehensive lists of commitments, were those of the Pentagonale plus Poland (the emerging Hexagonale), comprising some seven pages and the most ambitious of the all-embracing texts;[4] and the text of the '12', comprising eight and a half pages, which was more pragmatic in its attempt to meet the divergent views within its group.[5] There were also two other shorter proposals, one by Canada, focusing on the identity of national minorities, and the other by France and Hungary, two countries on opposite sides of the minority debate.[6] There were also three very restrained Romanian proposals, with elements from their two extended Copenhagen proposals, though less far-reaching.

In addition, eight proposals were submitted on specific issues: on autonomy, by Norway, co-sponsored by Austria, Denmark, Finland, Iceland, Poland, Sweden, Switzerland and Hungary; on transfrontier co-operation, by Austria, Liechtenstein, Poland, Spain and Switzerland; on migrant workers, by Poland, Turkey and Yugoslavia; on accepting financial contributions, by Germany, Denmark and Poland; on extending minority rights to ethnic, linguistic or religious minorities or groups, by Bulgaria; on the recognition of diplomas, by Austria and others; on the Roma, by Yugoslavia; and on the exchange of culture and information, by Austria, Switzerland, Poland and Liechtenstein as well as Bulgaria.

A third category of proposals was those on the mechanism for national minorities: by the NNA, on observers (like that in Copenhagen, but now limited to national minorities); on a CSCE rapporteur for human dimension issues, including those related to national minorities, by Austria, the CSFR, Hungary, Norway, Poland and Sweden; and a United States proposal similar to the one submitted in Copenhagen on mediation, now termed a 'CSCE panel', to address or resolve questions involving a state's national minorities, to be initiated by the state itself.

However, the main basis of the final document was to be the non-paper submitted by the head of the United States delegation, Max M. Kampelman, in the NATO group. The United States text laid greater emphasis on non-discrimination, and included anti-racism policies as well as their proposal on the CSCE panel. Thus it can be said that the attempt to arrive at a document took place at four distinct levels, at first at the level of the Pentagonale plus Poland and also within the '12', then in the informal drafting groups of '35' delegations and, almost simultaneously, within the '16', based on the United States text.

The role of co-ordinator was undertaken by the Swiss ambassador, Jean-Pierre Ritter, who began his task on the wrong foot by not consulting at the '35' level and by producing on Sunday 14 July (which was already very late) a huge text of one hundred and six paragraphs. This was basically a 'scissors and paste job' using bits of all the proposals. After an overwhelmingly negative reaction, the co-ordinator next day offered a revised version, which though frequently awkward in wording was at least more manageable, being half the size of the previous text. But the pace of the negotiations was slow, as several of the classic debates on this subject emerged yet again – the definition and self-definition of minorities, group rights or individual rights, and so on. The negotiations took place in the large hall of the conference, a setting which was hardly conducive to informal, speedy exchanges. A third draft was produced only one day before the day when the document was to be adopted. It was obvious by then that no agreement was possible, with France, Romania, Yugoslavia and some other delegations having basic sticking points. The Swiss co-ordinator then produced what he called a 'mini-solution', a document which was not a mere communiqué, but consisted of a few pages with basic commitments. However, most delegations could not accept such a meagre harvest and it was felt that the only solution now was to prepare a factual communiqué.

It was then that the United States came to the fore with a new '16' non-paper to save the meeting from the very real prospect of failure. But as the '35' delegations waited in the grand hall until midnight, with one coffee break after another, to catch a glimpse of this paper, no paper arrived, to the frustration of the co-ordinator and the Pentagonale (minus Italy) in particular. The reason for the delay, not known to most delegations, was that in a little room in the basement of the building where the text was being drafted another little CSCE drama was unfolding.

It is worth noting that the redrafting of the United States non-paper in a '16' experts group with a view to making it the concluding document was accepted with great reluctance by those of the '16' with greater ambitions, notably Italy, Germany and the Netherlands, which expressed their preference for the approach of the co-ordinator. Under such circumstances, there would probably have been an intra-Western clash, but this was avoided within the '16' largely because of the subtle approach of the United States chief delegate, assisted by his United Kingdom, French and Belgian counterparts, and the equal professionalism shown by the delegations of the ambitious camp, namely those of Italy, Germany and the Netherlands. The United States non-paper was reformulated and rendered a little stronger mainly by following the '12' omnibus text and by including those elements from the Pentagonale paper and the co-ordinator's four redrafts that appeared to be going through. At last, the text was distributed in the early hours of 18 July, the day that the text had to be adopted, as a non-paper, presented in the co-ordinator's group by Belgium (by reason of being alphabetically first on the list) as a text of seventeen delegations (Ireland was added, even though it had not participated in the drafting). The initial reaction was a sigh of relief, though several delegates, notably the co-ordinator and the delegate of Austria, could not hide their irritation at the method used, particularly as the paper was presented as 'take it or leave it'.

It was then that another twist of the affair occurred, reminiscent of the endgame of the 1986 Bern Meeting but with a switch of the roles of the protagonists. When the text was to be submitted officially by the seventeen delegations, the German delegate unexpectedly stated that Bonn could not give its consent to the document because it was too weak and a step backward from Copenhagen (more or less the United States line in Bern in May 1986). Germany was joined by Italy.

There followed several hours during which the conference was at a standstill, with the final document hanging from a thread, as the United States and other delegations urged Germany to suggest concrete amendments which could be taken on board. Finally, the German delegation proposed some amendments. Contrary to what had been expected – a list so long and ambitious that it would have been unacceptable – the amendments were minor and the German delegate was even accommodating to suggested alterations to the amendments in the '16' caucus. It is not clear what had happened, whether there had been a misunderstanding or an internal disagreement in Bonn, or direct contact at a higher level between the foreign ministers of the United States and Germany, as had been the case in the final hours of the 1986 Bern Meeting. (According to one source the United States tried to make contact at a high level but could not reach Foreign Minister Genscher.)

Thus the text (REMN.20) was submitted, but its final adoption was the cause of one last agony well into the night, as the position of Romania was not assured and, among those who had worked hard for an ambitious text, neither was that of Austria or Hungary. Yet, in the end, it was Yugoslavia, the traditional champion of minority rights in the CSCE and other forums, which seemed to have the greatest difficulty because there was no mention that minorities do not have a right to self-determination (a clause it had stressed in the course of the co-ordinator's informal meetings of the '35'). Finally, Yugoslavia settled for making an interpretative statement to this effect.

The final outcome, the Geneva Report as it is generally known, consists of a descriptive preamble and eight parts. It can hardly be considered as a radically new step forward, but it does contain several additions or expansions in some areas covered by Chapter IV of the Document of Copenhagen and by the relevant provision of the Charter of Paris.[7] Worth mentioning are the various provisions against non-discrimination and measures to combat it: on effective participation in public life; on economic activities and on active involvement in society, with the taking of special measures; on dialogue with minorities so as to address issues which concern them; on increased contacts and information, as well as on transboundary co-operation (a new CSCE concept first launched in Cracow); and additional provisions against ethnic hatred, including laws against hate-related crimes.

Among the other commitments of the Report, special mention should be made of an explicit statement to the effect that such non-discrimination matters are of 'legitimate international concern and consequently do not constitute exclusively an internal affair of the respective state'. There is also a clause on the protection of the rights of members of the majority or of other minorities residing in regions largely inhabited by persons belonging to a national minority. There is also a so-called 'shopping list' of some fourteen particularly useful approaches in dealing with minorities in a democratic manner, placed as a suggested, non-exhaustive list (with *inter alia* at the beginning). Among them are local or autonomous administrations (championed in particular by Italy; decentralized or local forms of government (suggested by Greece); and self-administration 'where autonomy on a territorial basis does not apply'. This list was suggested by the United Kingdom at the '12' experts level and advocated by Greece as to its merits.

There was nothing on mechanism since two valid arguments prevailed: that this was to be the task of the Moscow CHD Meeting, whose main contribution was certain to be the expansion of the mechanism; and that one could hardly create a mechanism on just one aspect of the human dimension and then hope that it would be extended to the rest. Thus it was simply recommended to the Third CHD Meeting that they 'consider expanding the Human Dimension Mechanism' and that 'they will promote the involvement of individuals in the protection of these rights, including the rights of persons belonging to national minorities'.

Upon the adoption of the Report a number of interpretative statements were made. They included, apart from the above-mentioned Yugoslavian statement, the following: Albania, stating that the document applied only to national minorities and not to the Albanians of Kosovo and elsewhere in Yugoslavia, who being so numerous could not be regarded merely as a minority; and Poland, on behalf of Austria, the CSFR, Hungary, Norway, Sweden and Yugoslavia, stating that the provision which read that 'not all ethnic, cultural, linguistic or religious differences necessarily lead to the creation of national minorities' (an obscurely written one included, after considerable debate, because of the insistence of Switzerland, given its own model of cultural pluralism) did not prejudice the right of any individual to choose to belong or not to belong to a national minority. In their closing speeches several delegations pointed out that the document did not meet their ambitions but that it was acceptable as a compromise on such a difficult matter, and they referred to various elements dear to their hearts which were not included, and which they intended to raise in Moscow, such as financial support from abroad (Germany), migrant workers (Turkey) and the mechanism (the United States, Sweden, Austria). Yugoslavia reiterated that minorities did not have the right to self-determination, which is a right reserved only to peoples, and Turkey stated that as far as it was concerned national minorities were only those that are recognized by an international treaty.

Apart from the 'Copenhagen effect' (the high standards set by the Copenhagen Document), the lack of a major move forward in Geneva was also due to the great complexity of the issue, particularly as it appeared in 1991, at the end of the Cold War and in the light of ethnic tension in Eastern Europe, the Soviet Union and, above all, Yugoslavia. However, at the root of the difficulty was a fundamental philosophical difference – the clash between two dominant, equally respectable, approaches on the rights of minorities. The more traditional school of thought, the non-discrimination/equality/individual rights approach, was spearheaded in Geneva by France, the United States, the United Kingdom, Greece, Belgium, Canada, Bulgaria, Romania and some others. The other, the ambitious radical school of positive measures/ heightened participation/self-rule group rights, was championed by Hungary, Germany, Austria, Italy, the Nordic countries and Yugoslavia (though less so in Geneva, given its predicament at the time). The differences between the two are such that bridging them is an art in itself, which of course does not imply that the Geneva Report is a work of art.

THE MOSCOW CHD MEETING AND THE MOSCOW DOCUMENT

Given the high level of the Copenhagen Document, the additions made in the Charter of Paris and the Cracow and Geneva documents, it was generally believed that Moscow could not go much farther on normative commitments, that its main lasting contribution to the CSCE would be on the mechanism. Yet even that was not assured, as seen from the lukewarm attitude to such ideas of many states, including several Western ones, formerly the 'engine' of any developments in the human dimension. However, the unexpected turn of events with the abortive *coup d'état* in the Soviet Union at the beginning of August 1991, a month before the meeting was due to commence, spurred not only the adoption of an ambitious new mechanism but also additional normative commitments.

What was particularly striking in the Third CHD Meeting was that the CSCE world, as known until then in the human dimension, had been turned the other way round, with the former Warsaw Pact states being at the forefront of advances in normative commitments as well as in an implementation mechanism. The Soviet Union – totally transformed from the 'fetters of the past', and also from its former stupor in

CSCE meetings – came out, in what was to be its last major appearance in the Helsinki process as a state, in support of the most far-reaching and ambitious proposals on a variety of issues, ranging from the implementation mechanism to the rule of law and democracy, leaving several Western states well behind. Also noteworthy was the smooth end to the Baltic issue, with the formal acceptance of Lithuania, Estonia and Latvia as CSCE participating states following a brief meeting of foreign ministers in Moscow convened by Foreign Minister Genscher as Chairman-in-Office of the CSCE Council, before the start of the CHD Meeting.

The *coup d'état* was a clear sign that the *acquis* of the new Europe need not be taken for granted. At the same time its lack of success was an indication that the CSCE human rights principles had taken root and that turning back was near to impossible. With the onset of the coup the majority of CSCE states, including the '12' and the United States, stated that, under the circumstances, they were not prepared to go to Moscow. When the coup failed, the convening of the meeting was still to be finalized. The Soviet Union, and in particular the Russian Federation under Boris Yeltsin, were not enthusiastic about having such a meeting there and then, and informed the participating states accordingly, asking for their views. Given the obvious organizational and other problems the Soviet Union would be facing, the other states were prepared to allow for a postponement, so as not to place the host state in a difficult position, despite the tight CSCE agenda. Finally, a few days before the day scheduled for the meeting, the Soviet Union, apparently with the agreement of Russia, gave the green light for the meeting to start as planned.[8]

The meeting began impressively with an important speech by President Gorbachev and with another architect of the human dimension in the 'New Europe' among the guests in the audience, former Foreign Minister Shevardnadze (who had resigned in December 1990, prophetically alluding to a military coup which would fail). Despite the Soviet Union's problems, the atmosphere was conducive to achieving something worthwhile in Moscow. The venue of the meeting was the eighteenth-century Hall of Columns of Dom Soyuz (the House of the Union), the very hall where Stalin had held his sham trials in the 1930s.[9] This reminder of a grim past was one more incentive to come up with something rewarding in Moscow.

After the foreign ministers had delivered their opening speeches (this time with two rights of reply, one by Yugoslavia and the other by Greece) and left, the implementation debate followed by and large the businesslike exchanges known from Copenhagen onwards, though not this time without a few vicious clashes. The main issue, apart from the Yugoslav crisis, which raised the temperature of the meeting on more than one occasion, was that of national minorities. Most notable were the clashes between Yugoslavia and the following: Albania (on the Albanians of Kosovo), Austria, Hungary, Czechoslovakia, and Greece (on Macedonia). There were also clashes between Turkey and Greece (on the Muslim minority in Greece, an issue that appeared for the first time in a CSCE context), and Albania and Greece (mainly with regard to the ethnic Greeks in Albania). On the whole these exchanges, which brought to the CSCE the fissiparous Balkan dimension, were regarded by most participants as unfruitful exercises.[10]

In the Moscow Meeting the spectre of the abortive coup was visible in the speeches delivered as well as in the proposals submitted, forty-eight in all. The Soviet delegation initiated or co-sponsored almost half of the proposals, and in general the most far-reaching ones. A similar approach was followed by the other Eastern states, with the exception of Romania. Only one Soviet proposal was reminiscent of 'old thinking', though now it seemed fairly harmless, a proposal on demilitarizing and reducing armaments in the CSCE region as an element in the strengthening of democracy and human rights.

The various proposals submitted in Moscow can be placed under four headings: implementation/mechanism, rule of law with related issues, human rights and humanitarian issues, and institutions/follow-up. The first category, which was by far the most important, included the following: a United States proposal on a voluntary three-person panel for good offices aimed at facilitating agreement in an internal conflict of the state inviting the panel; a Netherlands proposal (later co-sponsored by seven other EC members – Belgium, Ireland, Germany, Greece, Luxembourg, Italy and Denmark), on a fact-finding mission of three rapporteurs to visit after the use of point 2 of the human dimension mechanism and on the basis of a request by one state, co-sponsored by three others; a '12' proposal on assistance to a CSCE mission of experts to assess the facts and provide advisory services; a Norwegian proposal co-sponsored by no less than twenty-one countries (including Albania and all the former Warsaw Pact states with the exception of Romania, as well as three EC states) on inviting a CSCE expert to establish the facts, or three experts to establish the facts and facilitate dialogue and agreement internally, and on a mandatory mechanism whereby a state, having put into effect the human dimension mechanism in its first two steps, could appoint a CSCE rapporteur ('appointee') to establish the facts, with the possibility of making recommendations; and a Soviet proposal (not officially submitted) whereby each state would appoint three experts to monitor compliance of their own state, the results of which could be communicated to other states or to the Conference on the Human Dimension. To this list should be added a proposal for compliance with the human dimension mechanism on the part of the non-central authorities of state, submitted by Germany and others.

The rule of law ensemble included two proposals on public emergency, one by the Soviet Union and the other by Netherlands; on the consolidation of the rule of law and democracy, by the Soviet Union and Poland; on freedom of movement, by Austria, the Soviet Union and others; on restraints on law enforcement agents by Greece and others; on the independence of the judiciary, by France; on the rights of persons in detention or imprisonment, by the Soviet Union; on the rule of law, by the United States; on civilian control over military and security forces, by Hungary and the United States; on a comparative study of legislation, by France and others; and on the abolition of the death penalty, by Portugal and Sweden and twenty-one co-sponsors. Under this umbrella was an important German proposal (co-sponsored by Austria, Bulgaria, Hungary, Ireland, the Netherlands, the Soviet Union, Luxembourg and Italy) on international measures to be taken individually or collectively to induce compliance in cases of serious human rights violations (which was somewhat awkwardly worded as to 'reduce relations' with an unlawful regime 'to a minimum'). A more subtle version of this idea was presented by the United Kingdom.

The ensemble of human rights and humanitarian issues included three proposals on national minorities: by Yugoslavia on regular reviews of implementation; by Austria, Hungary, Italy and the CSFR, as well as the Netherlands, Luxembourg, Switzerland and the Soviet Union on the rights of national minorities; and by Germany and the United Kingdom on peaceful solutions to problems of national minorities. Proposals on related issues were: on indigenous peoples, by the Nordic countries (the main sponsor being Denmark), as well as Canada, the Soviet Union and Greece; on the rights of the Roma (gypsies), by Romania and Yugoslavia; and on migrant workers, by Turkey and others. There were also proposals on equality between men and women, by Canada and others; on averting mass exodus of population, by Greece, as well as the Netherlands and the United Kingdom; three submissions on NGOs, one by Austria and others, the second by Denmark and others, and the third by the Soviet Union on a consultative status for NGOs (and a similar non-paper by Poland); on human rights education, by Poland and others; on the freedom of information and the rights of journalists during a state of public emergency, by the Soviet Union, and on the protection of journalists by the same sponsor; on independent media by the United States; on humanitarian relief operations, by Norway and others; on the protection of private and family life by Bulgaria and others; on the freedom of artistic creation, by Poland and others; and on the rights of the disabled, by the Soviet Union.

There were also several proposals on intercessional meetings of one kind or another, such as on cultural heritage, predictably by Poland; on a seminar on the comparative study of legislation, by the Soviet Union; on CSCE terminology in the human dimension, by Austria, the CSFR and Hungary; on a meeting of ombudsmen and related officials, by Poland and others; on a seminar on Roma problems, by the CSFR, as well as Romania and Yugoslavia.

It is of interest to note that the idea of recommending a follow-up to the Conference on the Human Dimension, which would have been reasonable at the conclusion of a successful conference (it had been suggested by the Netherlands within the '12' setting in EPC), had been put on one side, due, in particular, to the reaction of Italy, which saw this as being linked to the old CSCE of the Cold War days, whose main instrument had been the implementation debate. Italy's attitude was not unrelated to its initiative on expanding the mandate of the Office of Free Elections to render it an Office for Democratic Institutions. Such an expansion was proposed by about a dozen delegations: Austria, Canada, the CSFR, Germany, Hungary, Italy, Luxembourg, Norway, Poland, Sweden, Turkey and the United States, to which Albania was also added. This proposal, whose prime movers at the time appeared to be Poland, Italy and the United States, did not go into the specifics of the new mandate of the expanded office (these came a little later in the course of the Oslo seminar).

On the whole, the United States, the United Kingdom and France, and to some extent countries such as Canada and Belgium, traditionally (until 1989) at the forefront of normative and implementation/mechanism proposals, were somewhat reserved on the issue of a very elaborate compulsory mechanism. The United States mechanism was on a voluntary basis, while the United Kingdom did not permit consensus to evolve within the '12', which would have led to a substantial proposal on the mechanism. The United Kingdom, but also at least two or three other delegations within the '12', had serious difficulties with the ideas formulated by the Netherlands (with the support mainly of Germany, Italy, Denmark and Ireland), particularly regarding any reduction in the figure of five co-sponsors for a request

160

to send a rapporteur mission. It was finally decided that the Netherlands would submit the proposal on a national basis, and one aspect of it, that on assistance, would be extracted and submitted as a '12' proposal (this at the suggestion of the United Kingdom).

On the initiative of the Soviet and CSFR delegations, an informal group was summoned which decided on the formation of three drafting groups, one on the mechanism under the co-ordination of Austria, the second on the rule of law under Norwegian co-ordination, and the third on human rights (including national minorities and NGOs) under the co-ordination of the Soviet Union. It was by coincidence that the three co-ordinators came from the three former traditional groups of the CSCE – the NNA, the West and the East.

The most difficult negotiations were in the first and in the third drafting groups, the latter mainly because of the issue of national minorities and related questions such as indigenous peoples and migrant workers. Regarding national minorities, in particular, few states were prepared to accept new commitments only two months after the Geneva Meeting. Most adamant against any new substantial undertakings in this field were Turkey, Greece, France and Romania, but several other delegations also realized that it was not yet possible to pick up the missing elements from the Pentagonale or German proposals in Geneva, despite the insistence of Italy, Germany and Hungary, especially the latter.

Discussions in the drafting group on the mechanism, under Austrian ambassador Helmut Tuerk, were equally acrimonious, but were orderly and of a high level owing to the skills and legal expertise of the co-ordinator (the very opposite was the case with drafting group III, which often presented a very sorry sight), and the presence of other qualified legal experts from various delegations. The United Kingdom for its part together with some other delegations, which had certain difficulties, showed flexibility. The result, as we shall see, was a highly complex procedure. In view of the lack of enthusiasm for a far-reaching mechanism in the period between the Paris Summit and the Moscow Meeting, it was probably, above all, the spectre of the abortive coup that spurred things on, injecting the CSCE-human dimension with a new sense of mission.

The group on rule of law was ably co-ordinated by the Norwegian delegate, rarely running into trouble. One of its difficult issues was the German proposal on international measures to be taken individually or collectively to induce compliance in cases of serious human rights violations. The main difficulty with this useful proposal was that it was considered as going perhaps too far along the road of defying the consensus principle. However, even a less extreme version suggested by the United Kingdom and Greek delegates, to the effect that governments would 'not endorse' such a regime and that it would not 'enjoy a normal relationship with them', was unable to move ahead either. Another difficult issue was the proposal on expanding the mandate of the Office for Free Elections to render it an office for democratic institutions, which France could not accept, but which went through at the end in attenunated form.

After more than a week of drafting, the delegations, from Austria, Norway and the Soviet Union presented a first draft document. This was changed slightly in the course of bilateral discussion by the Austrian delegate (chairman of the co-ordinators, as in Copenhagen) and after a final informal group session in the large Hall of Columns. Drafting suggestions were made on national minorities, on NGOs, on reducing the length of some proposals, such as the one on the rights of women, and on not including some other proposals, such as the one on indigenous peoples. After some slight redrafts to the officially submitted proposal of a document, the Moscow Document (CHDM.49/ Rev.1) was adopted on 3 October 1991.

On adoption of the document, as in Geneva, a number of interpretative statements were made. This was a sign of how things had changed from the days before Copenhagen when paragraph-79 statements had been frowned upon. Germany, which had differences with Turkey on the wording on migrant workers, stated that it interpreted the relevant provision (paragraph 38 of the Moscow Document) as meaning 'migrant workers and their families lawfully residing in the participating States'. Belgium produced a human rights interpretation of the paragraph on national minorities, adding that 'whatever designation' persons claim for their community, it would have to comply with the state's international commitments 'regarding the rights of the human person, including the collective exercise of these rights'. France, with reference to the paragraph on expanding the Office of Free Elections, stated that 'institutional problems as a whole are a matter for the main Helsinki-II Follow-up Meeting', and that the provision adopted 'does not prejudice its position in this regard'. Spain expressed its satisfaction with a reference in the document to its offer to host a meeting of ombudsmen. Hungary made a most unusual paragraph-79 statement, which consisted of some five paragraphs based on amendments it had tried to introduce regarding national minorities. There were also two interpretative statements on the mechanism, one by the United Kingdom, and the other by Belgium together with France, Spain and the United Kingdom (to be discussed below).[11]

In Moscow negotiations continued in the non-traditional manner that had first appeared in Copenhagen. The NNA were hardly visible as a group, and even less so were the Pentagonale (which was in fact a Hexagonale turned into a Pentagonale, as Yugoslavia was out as a result of the clash with Austria and Hungary over the Croatia/Slovenia issue). On the other hand, neither the '12' nor the '16' could agree on a common stance on several questions. Thus, the '12' could not play its traditional role as pace-setter, despite the early consultations on the mechanism undertaken in July under the able Netherlands presidency. What was vexing to the '12', and not least to the Netherlands which had succeeded in previous difficult situations (in Bern and recently in Geneva), was the fact that the final outcome of the Moscow Meeting on the mechanism was, by and large, at the level of the proposed EC text for which agreement had never been reached in the '12' caucus.[12]

The Moscow Document[13] was not without a certain value in the area of normative commitments building on previous provisions, but its main achievement is without doubt the impressive expansion of the mechanism on implementation.

In the preamble it is declared 'categorically and irrevocably' that commitments undertaken on the human dimension 'are matters of direct and legitimate concern to all participating States and do not belong exclusively to the internal affairs of the State concerned', and that they 'express their collective determination to further safeguard human rights ... and to consolidate democratic advances', recognizing 'a compelling need to increase the CSCE's effectiveness in addressing human rights concerns that arise in their territories at this time of profound change in Europe'. Then follow three chapters, the first on the expansion of the mechanism. As regards the original Vienna Human Dimension Mechanism, the time for response is further reduced from that adopted in Copenhagen – to only ten days of a written response to point 1 and, as a rule, within a week as to point 2.

The second chapter, devoted to aspects of the rule of law, further elaborates several provisions existing in the Copenhagen Document, with its most worthwhile addition being on the state of public emergency. The third chapter is the least important of the Moscow Document. It contains little of any real substance, referring to a variety of subjects already covered profusely in international legal documents (and in some instances in CSCE texts as well), such as the equality between men and women or the rights of the disabled, which, had they been suggested in previous CSCE meetings, would have been left out or included simply as part of the overall bargain to give some satisfaction to 'the other side'. What is disturbing is that they are expanded well beyond their importance because the various attempts at cutting this chapter down were shouted down by the sponsors of the relevant proposals.

The length of the third chapter was partly the result of having nothing substantial on national minorities or other worthwhile issues, such as indigenous peoples. On national minorities, there is a call for a 'full and early implementation' of existing CSCE commitments, in particular those of the Copenhagen and Geneva Documents, and it states the obvious, that the expanded CSCE mechanisms will contribute to further protection and promotion. On NGOs, given the tough reaction of one or two delegations,[14] what is included, though lengthy, is for the most part a codification of existing practice from the Copenhagen Meeting onwards.

As far as CSCE standard-setting is concerned, the Moscow Meeting clearly indicated that new commitments on the human dimension had reached a limit beyond which it was very difficult or perhaps even pointless to go forward. Commitments on secondary issues already amply covered by other IGOs should be avoided in future if the CSCE wants to retain its political thrust and not appear as an attempt simply to rewrite in 'soft law' existing commitments of 'hard law'. This pressure for additional commitments is a legacy from the past, the Cold War, where few commitments on the human dimension existed, and new ones were aimed 'at the other side'. It is also due to the fact that the CSCE was first conceived as a process, and hence it was potentially a unidirectional one in the sense of standard-setting. Obviously now is the time to adjust to the new realities, and to ensure the scrupulous implementation of the existing high standards, which are in abundance, if need be with the assistance of the human dimension mechanisms, old and new. This was the implicit but clear message of the Moscow Meeting.

THE HUMAN DIMENSION EXPERTS/RAPPORTEURS MECHANISM OF MOSCOW

The Human Dimension Experts/Rapporteurs Mechanism of the Moscow Document is partly linked with the Vienna Human Dimension Mechanism, but for the most part it is independent, cleverly integrating the four main proposals submitted, those of the Netherlands, Norway, the '12' and the United States. The main structure is based on the Norwegian proposal, co-sponsored by two-thirds of the CSCE participating states, while on the mission of experts the United

States and '12' proposals were the main source, with the Netherlands and Norwegian proposals being the basis of the rapporteur system.

The Moscow mechanism can be seen as comprising three procedures: (1) a voluntary procedure of a mission of experts; (2) a compulsory rapporteur(s) procedure linked to the Vienna mechanism; and (3) a compulsory rapporteur system not related to the Vienna mechanism, to be used for serious threats. The mechanism can be employed by three initiating actors – the inviting state, another state, or states, and the Committee of Senior Officials (CSO) – in the following ways: (1) by a state which invites a mission of up to three experts on its own; (2) by a state which invites such a mission on the suggestion of another state (or states) which has already put into effect point 1 or 2 of the human dimension mechanism regarding this state; (3) by another state (or states) which having already made use of point 1 or 2 of the Vienna Human Dimension Mechanism requests an invitation for such a mission by the state where the problem exists as a particular, clearly defined question on its territory; (4) by another state with the support of five other CSCE participating states to initiate the establishment of a rapporteur(s) mission (comprised of one rapporteur or of a mission of three rapporteurs) if the other state has not accepted the request to invite a mission of experts or if it judges that the issue in question has not been resolved by the mission of experts; (5) by another state with the support of nine states to initiate a rapporteur mission in the case of a particularly serious threat to the fulfilment of the provisions of the CSCE human dimension; (6) by the CSO, with regard to both a mission of experts and a mission of rapporteurs (whether for serious or less serious matters), whose decision is taken, by definition, on the basis of consensus.

Each state can submit to 'a body', to be designated by the CSCE Council, the names of up to three experts ('eminent persons, preferably experienced in the field of the human dimension, from whom an impartial performance of their functions may be expected') from which a resource list will be created from which the experts or rapporteurs will be chosen for each mission. The resource list would become operational when forty-five experts had been appointed. Any state may make reservations regarding two of the three experts appointed by another state. If the other state insists on keeping them in the list, then the expert in question cannot take part in any procedure with regard to the state without its 'express consent'. In the case of missions of experts the inviting state can select the experts it wants, provided they are not its own nationals or residents, or persons it has appointed to the list. This also applies in the case of a request by another state. In the case of rapporteur(s), one is chosen from the requesting state. The requested state, if it so wishes, can choose a second rapporteur. (Neither of the two designated rapporteurs can be nationals or residents of the two states, or appointed by them in the resource list.) In this case, a third rapporteur is selected by the two designated rapporteurs. If the two can reach no agreement on the third person, he or she is to be selected by the ranking official of the CSCE body designated by the council.[15]

The respective tasks of the mission of experts and rapporteur(s) were carefully worded after considerable debate. The expert mission has the more limited tasks, particularly in the sense that it is less intrusive in the internal affairs of the state, in comparison to the rapporteur mission. Its duties are of a facilitating nature, namely 'to facilitate resolution of a particular question or problem relating to the human dimension of the CSCE'. It 'may gather the information necessary for carrying out its task and, as appropriate, use its good offices and mediation services to promote dialogue and co-operation among interested parties'.[16] The terms of reference of the mission will be agreed with the state concerned, which may assign it further functions, among others 'fact-finding and advisory services, in order to suggest ways and means of facilitating the observance of CSCE commitments'.[17] The mission of experts will submit its observations to the inviting state, and the inviting state will transmit them, together with any action it has taken or intends to undertake in this regard, to the other participating states by way of the chosen body not later than three weeks after the submission of the observations.[18] These may be discussed in the CSO, which may consider 'any possible follow-up'. Note that the observations remain confidential until brought to the attention of the CSO.

The mission of rapporteur(s) has as its task 'to establish the facts, report on them and may give advice on possible solutions to the question raised'. Its report 'containing observations of facts, proposals or advice' will be submitted to the state or states concerned, and to the body designated by the CSCE Council, unless otherwise agreed by the CSCE participating states.[19] The requested state will submit observations on the report unless otherwise agreed by the participating states. The report and any observations by the requested state, as well as those by any other participating state, will be transmitted to all CSCE participants and may be placed on the agenda of the CSO, remaining confidential until after the CSO meeting in question.[20] The 'serious threat' procedure, which requires endorsement by ten CSCE states, follows the terms regarding the rapporteur procedure.[21] If the decision to send an expert or rapporteur mission is taken by the CSO then there is greater flexibility as to the appropriate procedure and mandate, obviously given the fact that CSO decisions are taken by consensus.[22]

No doubt the experts/rapporteurs mechanism is an ingenious construct in many respects. At the same time it is liable to abuse and different interpretations upon use in a specific situation, and it is certainly cumbersome, 'baroque' as one Western delegate put it in Moscow. Its application will show how workable and effective it can be.

OSLO: DEMOCRATIC INSTITUTIONS

The Oslo Seminar of Experts on Democratic Institutions (4–15 November 1991) was the last of the traditional meetings scheduled before Helsinki-II (that is, not including the meetings of the permanent organs of the CSCE). It was of the forum genre, with independent experts as the main protagonists. However, it was not possible to accommodate the differing aims of the participating states, particularly those of the 'new democracies', and the array of subjects presented by scholars from various fields could not be given their due consideration.

The meeting was an unusually smooth operation as regards the various sessions – some would say too smooth – a unique situation for a CSCE meeting in the human dimension even by post-Cold War standards. Even Yugoslavia was, by and large, spared, although several delegates expressed their grave concern. Albania intervened in an unusually restrained manner, expressing the hope that Kosovo would return to normal, that is to its previous autonomy. The Yugoslav reaction was that the reason for the turmoil in their country was the lack of functioning democratic institutions under the previous regime. The chairman of the US Commission, Steny H. Hoyer, castigated 'the government of Serbia and the Federal Army' in plenary for its 'folly' of opting 'for force instead of dialogue'.[23] There were also two outbursts of a kind not seen before in the history of the CSCE, a sign of things to come. One was an expression of anxiety by Estonia about its democratic future and independence given the presence of Soviet troops in the country, during which the Soviet delegate intervened with a 'point of order', stating that the Soviet government and that of Estonia were in fact negotiating the withdrawal of the troops. A few days before this episode, the Armenian delegate, speaking from the seats of the Soviet delegation (its delegate was listed as a member of that delegation), expressed his country's indignation at the situation in Nagorno-

Karabakh, vehemently accusing Azerbaijan, another non-member of the CSCE.

As usual, it was the final text of the meeting that caused unexpected difficulties, not sparing even this secondary meeting from the standard CSCE drama, with the delegates working well beyond midnight and the whole document in jeopardy.[24] The Norwegian delegate undertook to present a draft based only on bilateral consultations with other delegations.[25] With such a course the die was cast for a text that was bound to be the antithesis of the Cracow Document, being a *proces-verbal* and laying the emphasis on discussions by the independent experts. When it came to possible recommendations, there was only the transformation of the Office of Free Elections (OFE) to a broadly mandated Office of Democratic Institutions (ODI). Three non-papers appeared on this, one by Austria, the CSFR, Italy and Poland (later to be co-sponsored by Bulgaria, Romania and the Baltic states), a second by the United States and a third not by a participating state but, surprisingly, by none other than the OFE itself, which recommended its own expansion in good bureaucratic tradition. All three had a detailed new mandate for the expanded Warsaw Office.[26]

The Norwegian draft did not satisfy the Soviet Union and the other 'new democracies', which were eager to have a kind of ready-made recipe for how to go about their transition to democratic rule. It was also not to the liking of some Western delegations, notably those of the United States and Germany, which regarded the text as far too long and unwieldy (they suggested an annex instead). When it was finally agreed to settle for a long text – 'a summary of proceedings' – the main bone of contention was the possibility of transforming the Warsaw Office. Austria, Hungary, Poland and Italy vigorously supported this single recommendation of the whole document. It was France which was against the expansion, as in the Moscow meeting. The French ambassador, Dejean de la Batie, totally isolated, argued that Oslo was not the forum in which to make such a recommendation and thus prejudge an issue which had much broader ramifications; that this was a question to be dealt with thoroughly and comprehensively in 1992, in the Prague Council Meeting (of January 1992) or at Helsinki-II. The French delegate brought in a second issue, the role of the Council of Europe, suggesting possible overlaps and *double emploi* with an expanded Warsaw Office.

Finally, after twists and turns worthy of the most hectic CSCE exercises, with the main protagonists, apart from the Norwegian co-ordinator, being the delegates of France, Austria, Canada, Poland, Finland, Cyprus, Germany and, initially, Malta,[27] agreement was reached at four thirty in the morning of the closing date of the meeting. This accommodation, however, did not prevent France from making no less than five interpretative statements clarifying its position. The document was entitled Report of the Oslo Seminar of Experts on Democratic Institutions.[28]

On the whole, the Oslo exercise, though not totally useless as a starting point for increased contacts and exchanges at various levels, can hardly be regarded as a success. It did not meet the needs of the 'new democracies' in any practical way and yielded only a 'superficial summary of the work of the experts'.[29] Technically speaking, the lack of any specific recommendations was related to the fact that the meeting was treated as a true 'forum', in a conscious attempt to avoid the precedent of Cracow. Furthermore, the subject matter was fraught with the problems of the 'New Europe'. On the other hand, it offers one more illustration that in the area of the human dimension the CSCE is 'running out of words'.[30] It is clear that future mandates in the human dimension should at least be more precisely and narrowly focused.

THE PRAGUE GUIDELINES FOR HELSINKI-II

The second meeting of the CSCE Council which took place in Prague (30–31 January 1992) was of greater significance than had been expected a few months earlier, for not only did it set out fairly detailed 'guidelines' for Helsinki-II, but also made specific decisions regarding the expansion of existing institutions and took the revolutionary step of admitting ten new members.

Ten of the eleven republics of the former Soviet Union were admitted: Armenia, Azerbaijan, Belarus, Kazakhstan, Kirgistan, Moldova, Tajikistan, Turkmenistan, Ukraine and Uzbekistan. Georgia did not request participation at the time (it had previously requested observer status in the Moscow Meeting), but did so a month later, before the start of the Preparatory Committee of the Helsinki Follow-up. In the Prague Meeting the new states of Croatia and Slovenia were admitted as observers. No consensus was reached on applications by two other putative states, Macedonia and Bosnia–Herzegovina, mainly because of Yugoslavia's stance. Through these admissions, unimaginable only a few months earlier, the CSCE opened a 'new frontier' for itself. Despite the non-European character of several of the new participants, the argument that it was better 'to have them in' than out prevailed. The immediate future will show whether this radical decision was a wise one or a major mistake for the CSCE.[31]

As was the case with the participation of Albania, the ten states were admitted on condition that they formally accepted 'in their entirety all commitments and responsibilities' in all the CSCE documents, and declared a 'determination to act in accordance with their provisions'. They also undertook to apply all the provisions of the Vienna Document on CSBMs and, for those in the CFE area, to make prompt ratification of the CFE Treaty and assume 'all CFE obligations of the former Soviet Union'. In addition, they had to accept a rapporteur mission which would 'report to the participating States on the progress ... toward full implementation of CSCE commitments and provide assistance toward that objective'.[32] The missions to Armenia and Azerbaijan, which were to be the first to take place, also visited the troubled area of Nagorno-Karabakh and had the broader mandate to offer suggestions for a political solution to the crisis.[33]

The 'Summary of Conclusions' of the Prague Council states that Helsinki-II 'should be an important milestone in the development of the CSCE process and should provide a clear vision for its future course', and that the CSCE has a prominent role to play in the evolving architecture of Europe. As regards the general guidelines, it is clear that the human dimension, the main achievement of the CSCE, remains a key element, especially in the implementation of existing commitments. New standard-setting is not explicitly mentioned, but could no doubt be raised in the summit document of Helsinki-II. The implementation review is to continue to be an essential part of the CSCE, as in the past, particularly for the new participants. The overall CSCE philosophy on the human dimension in the 'New Europe' remains the same: that the 'root causes of tension' are in fact the result of lack of democracy, lack of functioning and effective democratic institutions, and, of course, disrespect for human rights, including minority rights. However, as far as national minorities are concerned, the scope is broadened. It is admitted that such questions can lead to tension and conflict and that there should be 'a peaceful solution' for any problems, 'including possibilities for "early warning"'. It is added that the CSCE should develop its capability for 'conflict prevention, crisis management and peaceful settlement of disputes'. Among other human dimension questions, special concern is expressed over the 'new signs of intolerance, aggressive nationalism, xenophobia and racism', and emphasis is put on the importance of non-discrimination.[34]

In the second document of the meeting, entitled 'Prague Document on Further Development of CSCE Institutions and Structures', known as the Prague Document, the foreign ministers reaffirm their commitment to 'further strengthen the CSCE institutions and structures' and offer 'certain guidelines' for Helsinki-II. Within the sphere of the human dimension, the Warsaw Office is finally to be expanded, to be henceforth named 'Office for Democratic Institutions and Human Rights'. For the expanded office, a non-exhaustive list of functions is set out, including organizing meetings of short duration to review implementation on the CSCE human dimension every year in which a follow-up does not take place, as well as other meetings and seminars; assisting the 'new democracies' in their institution-building; cooperating with the Council of Europe; and establishing contacts with NGOs active in the human rights field. It is also to be 'the CSCE institution charged with the tasks in connection with expert and rapporteur missions' as laid down in the Moscow Document, and a potentially revolutionary clause is added. The CSO as well as the Council are to follow closely such issues, recommending appropriate action, 'if necessary in the absence of the consent of the State concerned, in cases of clear, gross and uncorrected [*sic*] violations of relevant CSCE commitments'[35] – what came to be known as 'consensus minus one'.

With regard to other institutions and structures, the following, which have a bearing on the human dimension, are worth mentioning: the CSO (Committee of Senior Officials) is to be enhanced and to meet more regularly; the CPC (Conflict Prevention Centre) was to have additional tasks, serving as a forum for consultation and co-operation in conflict prevention and crisis management; crisis management and conflict prevention would be ameliorated by improving fact-finding, rapporteur and monitor missions, by counselling, conciliation and dispute settlement, and by examining a possible CSCE peacekeeping role; and relations between NGOs and the CSCE were also to be strengthened.[36]

As will be seen below (see 'Postscript'), the Helsinki Meeting, the fourth CSCE follow-up meeting, made most of the human dimension, more than one would have expected in the wake of the Moscow and Prague meetings.

12

CONCLUDING REMARKS

THE NATURE AND IMPACT OF THE CSCE HUMAN DIMENSION

Today, with the benefit of hindsight, we can say that the CSCE always had more to it than was apparent. Compared to other world bodies with superpower participation it was probably most effective in the period from 1975 until 1991. During the Cold War, in particular, the CSCE can be registered as a qualified success of the quiet approach, by which means it also played a role in bringing about the end of a world (the Eastern European world) 'Not with a bang', to use T.S. Eliot's words, 'but a whimper'.

The CSCE as a standing dialogue and ongoing process had to produce results in the form of substantial new undertakings. As such it became decidedly unidirectional, particularly in the human dimension. New texts had to move further than previous ones. In this sense, CSCE meetings were in the long run, as one participant has put it, 'condemned to succeed'.[1] One could argue that it was within the CSCE and its documents, replete with extended commitments on the human dimension, that the 'new Europe' was anticipated by instalments, on paper, by scissors and paste as it were, a most unlikely outcome for the deliberations of professional diplomats bent on scoring debating points. Thus, ultimately, it was the texts that had won through – 'the importance of words' as Max Kampelman has put it.[2] Contrary to the original belief of the Eastern states, commitments had to be implemented and lack of action placed governments in an untenable position at CSCE meetings and in world public opinion.

With regard to human rights and Basket III issues, the relatively small output in quantity during CSCE-I (or no document at all, notably in the intercessional meetings between follow-ups) was not simply because of the reigning spirit of confrontation between East and West or reasons proper to the functioning of the CSCE. These were not negotiations in mere words that would not be implemented anyway, as

172

hard-headed realists at the time would have it. In the 1970s and 1980s it was not always realized how much was involved when it came to human rights and Basket III issues, and what expectations and forces the CSCE commitments could unleash. From a 'wherever necessary', an 'exist', a 'legitimate', a *'mutatis mutandis'*, an *'inter alia'*, or even a comma, hung actual or perceived vital interests of the states concerned and significant future diplomatic openings. At stake was the legitimacy of the two opposite political and social systems, no less than the worth of the two world views.

Contrary to what was stated in no uncertain terms in the Final Act (notably in Principle I, entitled 'Sovereign equality, respect for the rights inherent in statehood'), there was no genuine respect between East and West towards each other's social and political systems. The intention came to be not to overcome Europe's ideological division by mutual respect and understanding, but rather to render Europe one by discarding one of the two dominant value systems. On this the East was fighting a losing battle. Of course, the industrialized West could be taken to task by pointing to the slums and the homeless, and use could be made in CSCE plenary meetings of the penetrating critique developed by radical thinkers on the *malaise* of modern post-industrial society. But the Helsinki conference was not a social science or philosophy conference, and anyway such lines of argument sounded hollow when voiced by communist states, which, whatever their accomplishments on education, social justice and equality, were manifestly more conspicuous in the business of coercion against their citizens, in the business of restricting freedom and the human dimension.

One question now worth addressing is whether the CSCE had an impact on the events that changed Europe. This is almost impossible to answer with any degree of accuracy. It has not even been possible to assess the results of the use of the CHD mechanism on specific cases with certainty, for it involved so many elusive and unpredictable parameters. However, few would claim that the CSCE undertaking played no role whatsoever, direct or indirect, in the changes towards pluralistic democracy and civil liberties in Europe.

In a tentative attempt to indicate that the CSCE did play a role as one of the contributing factors, it is worth noting the official definitions of the situation by the governments of the then thirty-five participating states, as seen by the statements at all levels during the CSCE meetings in 1990–91 where 'the events' were commented upon. It was invariably stated that the CSCE was indeed a contributing factor. This also happened to be the official view of the 'new democracies' themselves, as seen in the pronouncements of no lesser figures than Havel, Hajek, Dienstbier and others at CSCE meetings – the very individuals who had suffered for democracy and human rights in their countries and were inspired by the CSCE human rights undertakings. The Charter of Paris confirms this view by stating, on its first page, that 'the courage of men and women, the strength of the will of the peoples and the power of the ideas of the Helsinki Final Act have opened a new era of democracy, peace and unity in Europe'.[3] Of course, these assertions should be treated with caution, for they can be regarded, in part at least, as self-serving. Participants are expected to praise the CSCE in a CSCE meeting, and a CSCE document is bound to praise the process.

A more convincing indicator of the role of the Helsinki process is the fact that it was only after the signing of the Final Act in 1975 and the emergence of the CSCE that the various active human rights groups in Eastern Europe as well as in the West emerged (the latter, until recently, to lobby against Eastern violations). The Helsinki undertakings provided a rallying point. More often than not these human rights NGOs emphatically pointed out the CSCE human rights commitments, and, as is well known, many of them added the name 'Helsinki', and were known as Helsinki monitoring groups.[4]

According to Max Kampelman, the CSCE's role in history until now will be seen as that of a '"moral tuning fork" and one of the most important milestones on the path to peace'.[5] At the very least it would seem that the CSCE was one of the catalysts with regard to democratization and the overcoming of East–West confrontation. In being an ongoing semi-permanent diplomatic conference it was the forum where the changes in Europe were registered and where new ideas were aired. Lack of change was condemned, while changes towards democracy and the rule of law were praised at CSCE meetings, and, before they could falter in any way, the 'new thinking' was reflected in more advanced documents, thereby shepherding the process towards pluralistic democracy. The role of the Vienna Human Dimension Mechanism, particularly in 1989, was not without significance, as Eastern countries were pushed into a corner by the frequent use of the mechanism. Thus, in conclusion, it is only reasonable for the CSCE to take at least some of the credit as a contributor to the events.

Yet, whatever the precise role of the CSCE and particularly of the human rights dimension of the CSCE in giving a helping hand to the changes, without doubt it provided a framework on which to build a new pan-European regime when the time came in 1989–90. When the winds of change had won completely, the CSCE was there – had the merit of 'being there' – an already existing framework for a European forum, which included the United States and Canada, and could cover almost everything that mattered in Europe. Through the years the CSCE has also produced a number of important side-effects. It became the arena for the pluralization of bipolar politics. It is generally acknowledged that it was within the CSCE that the countries of the EC made their first lasting mark in international politics, as distinct from United States and NATO associations.[6] Equally, the NNA countries found an independent and pivotal role to play as bridge-builders, and it was in the CSCE that the tight Eastern bloc became increasingly less rigid.

ON TO HELSINKI-II: THE ROAD AHEAD FOR THE CSCE

The fourth CSCE Follow-up Meeting at Helsinki-II promised to be a historic one, of great significance for a CSCE now at a crossroads, midway between a process and a permanent institution. The Concluding Document of Helsinki-II might usher us into another CSCE, CSCE-III, which might be a fully-fledged inter-governmental organization, or one in all but name, encompassing Europe, North America and the former Asian Soviet Union. But then it might not. The Prague guidelines are not clear on this, owing to the differing approaches of the participants, and left the matter open. At the very least it is clear that the CSCE will be developed further and its institutions and mechanisms consolidated.

On the eve of Helsinki-II, the main champions of the CSCE becoming a regional inter-governmental organization were France and Germany. France, characteristically, had followed a legal line, suggesting a Pan-European Security Treaty and that the CSCE become 'a fully-fledged international institution having the requisite legal status of action'.[7] Germany had been more subtle, arguing that the CSCE already meets all the criteria for a regional inter-governmental organization set by Chapter VIII of the UN Charter, and as an organization will have greater influence, which it will need since it will be called upon to deal with increasing difficulties in its region.[8] The country most averse to such a development was the United States, which wanted as little further bureaucratization as possible. Among the other states which had voiced their views, the United Kingdom and the Netherlands followed, by and large, the United States assessment.[9]

Come what may, however, the CSCE will continue to be important at least for the immediate future; special focus will be given to the new democracies and particularly to the states of the 'new frontier'; as far as the human dimension is concerned it has an institution of its own, the Warsaw Office; and the CPC will be expanded and tasks it will almost certainly face will include violent ethnic conflicts.

In the human dimension sphere, a number of questions are left unanswered, such as whether the CSCE will continue with its role of standard-setting on human rights, and if so, how it can do so without entering the realm of the law, which would mean transforming itself into a more traditional IGO. The CSCE must also consider how to avoid unnecessary duplication with the Council of Europe, the UN and other governmental institutions.

The CSCE that emerges from Helsinki-II will find itself in a complex and difficult environment. For the CSCE and for Europe's future peace, security and co-operation much will depend on the effectiveness with which it addresses and copes with the new challenges in Europe, such as ethnic conflict[10] and resurgent expansionism, as well as economic and environmental issues. In the CSCE region the East–West conflict has been supplanted by no less than two equally effective barriers to unity, a poverty gap between East and West and, further to the east, a cultural divide between Europe and Islam. Human rights, democracy and the rule of law will continue to be relevant, particularly now that the CSCE has discovered a 'new frontier'. The challenges are so daunting that they call for an effective regional inter-governmental organization, if not in form at least in essence.

POSTSCRIPT: HELSINKI-II
AND ITS AFTERMATH

At Helsinki-II it was obvious that the human dimension was past its heyday. This was to be expected. It was generally understood that the main task of Helsinki-II was to be the refinement and strengthening of the institutions, structures and mechanisms of the CSCE so as to make it operational and effective in dealing with the region's fissiparous problems, as the overall agency for conflict prevention, crisis management and conflict resolution, and perhaps a new inter-governmental organization, if not *de jure* at least *de facto*. Furthermore, it was generally acknowledged that normative standard-setting on the human dimension was virtually completed. There was very little to add on normative commitments without running the risk of appearing far-fetched or even trivial. Basically it was the human dimension mechanism and the Warsaw Office that needed some fine-tuning and further specifications, though the basic decisions had already been taken in Moscow and Prague.[1]

It was for reasons such as the above that the '12' of the European Community (EC), and initially the majority of delegations at Helsinki-II, had sought to subsume the human dimension under the wider item of co-operation that would also include Basket II issues and the Mediterranean. But finally the United States view prevailed of having four working groups, one of which – Working Group 3 (WG3) – was to be devoted to the human dimension. However, even though the human dimension did indeed play a secondary role at Helsinki-II, it nevertheless cropped up in the Plenary of the meeting, in the working group dealing with institutions and structures – particularly with regard to the proposal for a High Commissioner on national minorities, the modalities of the new 'consensus minus one' procedure (created in the Prague Council) and greater NGO involvement – and even in the group dealing with economics, environment, technology, Mediterranean, under the human dimension aspects of the environment. And characteristically, the human dimension had at the end, when the time came for the negotiations, something of a little 'revenge' for being neglected. WG3 ended up with the greater number of proposals tabled, as in the old days, and it came to rival the prestigious Working

Group 1 (institutions and structures) as to the length and arduousness of the negotiations, and often to surpass it as to the depth and high quality of the debates, finally being the last of the four working groups to reach agreement in the nick of time before the Summit of heads of state or government which was to take place on 8–9 July 1992.

The human dimension working group covered the following items: human rights and fundamental freedoms, relations with NGOs, relations with international organizations, democratic institution building and the rule of law, free media and information, the role of the Office of Democratic Institutions and Human Rights (ODIHR), national minorities, migrant workers, migration, tolerance and non-discrimination and, lastly, culture and education and exchanges. By far the most worthwhile and substantial discussions in the official sessions of WG3 were those under the item of national minorities. In general, there were very few exchanges of a confrontational nature, contrary to what had happened even as recently as the Moscow Meeting of autumn 1991, though there was some criticism of shortcomings. Confrontation was mainly limited to the Baltic States' unflinching and recurring attacks on the Russian Federation (about the presence of the Soviet/Russian Army), to which the Russian Federation reacted with relative composure. Estonia justified its new alarming discriminatory law on citizenship (which relegates some 40 per cent of its population to being 'non-Estonians'), on legal arguments of Soviet/Russian occupation and on 'colonialism' akin to Rhodesia and the British Raj. Among the other human dimension concerns raised (in WG3 as well as in the Plenary) were the treatment of the Kurds in Turkey by several delegations – as in no previous CSCE meeting – to which Turkey responded by claiming that it was simply reacting to PKK (Kurdistan Workers' Party) terrorism; the issue of Kosovo; the complicated case of Nagorno-Karabakh; the grave situation in Bosnia and Herzegovina; the case of the Hungarians of Romania; some of the shortcomings, though in mild terms, of the new Asian participating states, this mainly by the United States; continuing problems in the Russian Federation, Poland and the Czech and Slovak Federal Republic (CSFR), to which there were constructive replies earning praise; conditions in Albania, to which Albania tended to over-react to the most minute criticism; and the continuing problems faced by the Roma (Gypsies) and the Jews, as well as the disturbing rise of incidents of intolerance and ethnic hatred, whose victims were mainly members of minorities, including racial minorities, and migrant workers.

Twenty-seven proposals were submitted in the human dimension, more than in any other working group. (In fact 28 were tabled, but one

178

was withdrawn and later re-submitted in substantially altered form.) They were distinguished into two categories: those concerned with normative commitments and those concerned with structures, mechanisms, institutions and seminars (those on seminars sometimes overlapped with normative proposals). Negotiations on the proposals started in mid-May and ended on 6 July, two days before the Summit Meeting. The talks were far more difficult than anticipated. They can be divided into three phases: the initial exploratory phase, the 'rolling-text' phase (where an omnibus text of the co-ordinator was the flexible basis of the discussions), and finally the re-negotiations phase at the end under one co-ordinator. The endgame was basically a tussle between the United States and the European Community, with most of the other active delegations siding with one or the other, depending on the subject discussed. The United States was generally against new normative commitments and favoured mainly what were called human dimension seminars. This posture was chiefly assailed by the delega-tions of Italy, France, Greece, the Netherlands, Canada, Austria, Poland, Hungary, Sweden and Norway. The United States delegation stood firm and finally gave in on some points, but only after further weakening the normative language and getting what it wanted on seminars and relative openness of the CSCE to NGOs.

In general, despite the difficulty of 'filling gaps' in the normative commitments – or 'gap-filling' as it was more popularly known during the meeting,[2] all the ideas somehow came through and a few gaps were indeed filled, certainly more than was expected at the start of the meeting. Of course, the normative texts did not go far, and in most instances they did not have to, the main disappointment probably being combating discrimination and intolerance, which had been singled out in the Prague Document of the CSCE Council (January 1992) as a perturbing present-day problem. In the 'Human Dimension' chapter of the seminal document adopted by the Summit Meeting, entitled 'CSCE Helsinki Document 1992. The Challenges of Change', there are some noteworthy elements under national minorities, migrant workers, non-discrimination, the right to citizenship and local demo-cracy. There are also references on humanitarian law, the benefits of having guidelines on implementing the human dimension and refugees/displaced persons, as well as a mention for the first time in a CSCE document of indigenous populations enjoying human rights without discrimination. On the structural side, the tasks of the Warsaw Office were further developed, the basic agenda of the human dimen-sion implementation meeting (foreseen in the Prague Document) was formulated, some slight changes were made on the Vienna Human

Dimension Mechanism to meet the new institutional setting of the CSCE, and it was decided to organize no less than six seminars – on migration, positive results regarding minority issues, tolerance, free media, migrant workers and local democracy. There is also the possibility of the new participating states asking for a specific seminar to take place, and it can take place on their territory. The human dimension and minorities also features in one of the main achievements of Helsinki-II, the institution of the High Commissioner on National Minorities as an instrument of 'early warning' regarding simmering conflict involving minorities. Particularly noteworthy also are the solemn statements on the human dimension in the first part of the Helsinki Document (the document is divided into two parts: 'Helsinki Summit Declaration' and the operative part, 'Helsinki Decisions') which are worth quoting in part:[3]

> Respect for human rights and fundamental freedoms, including the rights of persons belonging to national minorities, democracy, the rule of law, economic liberty, social justice and environmental responsibility are our common aims. They are immutable. Adherence to our commitments provides the basis for participation and co-operation in the CSCE and a cornerstone for further development of our societies ... We emphasize that the commitments undertaken in the field of the human dimension of the CSCE are matters of direct and legitimate concern to all participating States and do not belong exclusively to the internal affairs of the State concerned. The protection and promotion of human rights and fundamental freedoms and the strengthening of democratic institutions continue to be a vital basis for our comprehensive security.

In November 1992 the first seminar organized by ODIHR took place in Warsaw and was devoted to tolerance. Even though the subject was too broad and unwieldy, the deliberations were more interesting than had been expected because of the participation of specialists, including NGO representatives, who spoke in their own name and not as representatives of an official delegation (as in the forum type of CSCE meetings), the first time ever in a CSCE setting.

On 14 and 15 December 1992 the third regular Meeting of the CSCE Council (of Foreign Ministers) took place in Stockholm. The human dimension took up two whole pages in the 'Summary of Conclusions' under the title 'The CSCE as a Community of Values' and therein is an interesting blending between the human dimension and early warning. It is stated more clearly than ever that the human dimension plays an important role in 'longer-term conflict prevention' and that 'the human dimension mechanisms are being used increasingly as a major foundation for the CSCE's efforts at early warning and conflict prevention'.[4]

To conclude, from the above it would seem that for the CSCE it is the end of an era, at least as far as normative human dimension commitments are concerned. However, the traditional implementation debates will continue in the follow-ups (now designated review conferences) and also in implementation meetings on the human dimension (to take place every year that a follow-up is not taking place). These meetings will not produce a negotiated document, neither will the various seminars on topics of the human dimension. Of course, this does not necessarily mean that the human dimension normative commitments – the old glory of the CSCE – will disappear completely from the scene in the foreseeable future, but they will have a much harder time coming through. The emphasis now is on implementation in its triple sense: unilateral implementation by states, implementation reviews and the use of the mechanism of implementation. The reasoning behind this is the following basic, implicit CSCE axiom on the human dimension: that unreserved adherence to the human dimension commitments is a moral and normative imperative, but also a political imperative, which states can neglect at their own risk, for most of the root causes of tension and intra-state conflict are to be found in discrimination, state high-handedness and the abuse of the human dimension.

Thus, for the foreseeable future, the human dimension remains, as far as the CSCE is concerned, one of its main foundations and *raisons d'être*.

NOTES

Note on Primary Sources: Documents of a confidential character will be quoted with the designation DOC only and grouped into three categories: DOC/G – Greek documents; DOC/N – NATO documents; DOC/E – European Political Co-operation (EC-EPC) documents.

PREFACE

1. For the concept of regime see Stephen D. Krasner, 'Structural Causes and Regime Consequences: Regimes as Intervening Variables', *International Organization*, 36, No. 2 (Spring 1982), pp. 185–6. For the CSCE as a regime during the Cold War see, for example, Kalevi J. Holsti, 'Who Got What and How: The CSCE Negotiations in Retrospect', in Robert Spencer (ed.), *Canada and the Conference on Security and Co-operation in Europe* (Toronto: University of Toronto Press, 1984), p. 164; Kari Mottola (ed.), *Ten Years After Helsinki: The Making of the European Security Regime* (Boulder, CO: Westview Press, 1986). For the CSCE and the emerging post-Cold War European architecture see, among others: Robert E. Hunter, 'The Future of European Security', *The Washington Quarterly* (Autumn 1990), pp. 59–60; Volker Rittberger, 'International Regimes in the CSCE Region – From Anarchy to Governance, and Stable Peace', *Österreichische Zeitschrift für Politikwissenschaft*, 90/4 (1990); Volker Rittberger, Manfred Efinger and Martin Mendler, 'Toward an East–West Security Regime: The Case of Confidence- and Security-Building Measures', *Journal of Peace Research*, 27 (February 1990); Dieter Senghaas, 'Europe 2000: A Peace Plan', *Alternatives*, 15, No. 4 (Fall 1990), pp. 467–78; Victor-Yves Ghebali, 'Les fondements de l'ordre européen de l'après-guerre froide', *Politique Etrangère*, 1 (1991), pp. 59–69; Marylin Wyatt (ed.), *CSCE and the New Blueprint for Europe* (Washington, DC: Georgetown University, 1991); Samuel F. Wells, Jr. (ed.), *The Helsinki Process and the Future of Europe* (Washington, DC: The Wilson Center Press, 1990).
2. 'The Charter of Paris for a New Europe', November 1990; Flora Lewis, 'Europe: Collective Security is Taking Shape', *International Herald Tribune*, 21 June 1991, p. 4.

CHAPTER ONE: THE CONFERENCE ON SECURITY AND CO-OPERATION IN EUROPE

1. 'Final Recommendations of the Helsinki Consultations', 1973, Paragraph 54; Victor-Yves Ghebali, *La diplomatie de la détente: la CSCE d'Helsinki à Vienne (1973–1989)* (Brussels: Emile Bruylant, 1989), pp. 42–3.
2. The term human dimension was used somewhat loosely by Western countries for many years, particularly from the 1980s onward, and in at least one case, that of Belgium, as far back as 1975 (I am indebted for this information to Belgian Ambassador J. Laurent), to indicate human rights and the human contacts section of Basket III. It was officially introduced and adopted in the Vienna Follow-up

Meeting, to include not only human rights and human contacts, but also the rest of Basket III (information, culture, education).

3. Alexis Heraclides, 'Helsinki-I: From Cold War to "A New Europe". The Human Rights Phase of the Conference on Security and Co-operation in Europe, 1975–1990', Greek Institute for International and Strategic Studies, Occasional Paper No. 2 (August 1991).

4. Bennett Kovrig, 'European Security in East–West Relations: History of a Diplomatic Encounter', in Robert Spencer (ed.), *Canada and the Conference on Security and Co-operation in Europe* (Toronto: University of Toronto Press, 1984), pp. 3–19; Robert Spencer, 'Canada and the Origins of the CSCE', in Spencer (ed.), op. cit., pp. 22–84.

5. Kovrig, op. cit., pp. 14–17.

6. Victor-Yves Ghebali, 'Le thème des droits de l'homme dans le processus de la Conférence sur la Sécurité et la Co-opération en Europe', *Le 'noyau intangible' de la protection des droits de l'homme*, Actes du Colloque de Fribourg (Fribourg, 1991), pp. 174–5.

7. Kovrig, op. cit., pp. 3–19; Spencer, op. cit., pp. 21–34; Stephen J. Flanagan, 'The Road to Helsinki', in Vojtech Mastny, *Helsinki, Human Rights and European Security* (Durham: Duke University Press, 1986), pp. 43–6.

8. See, for example, Vernon Aspaturian, 'The Foreign Policy of the Soviet Union', in James N. Rosenau *et al.* (eds.), *World Politics: An Introduction* (New York: The Free Press, 1976), p. 87.

9. Harold S. Russell, 'The Helsinki Declaration: Brobdingnag or Lilliput?', *American Journal of International Law*, 70 (1976), pp. 244–5; Kovrig, op. cit., pp. 3–19; Spencer, op. cit., pp. 25–72; Ghebali, 1989, op. cit., pp. 5–6; Flanagan, op. cit., pp. 43–6; Ioannis Bourloyiannis-Tsangaridis, 'CSCE: The Multilateral Preparatory Talks (November 1972–June 1973)', *Nomos*, 8, No. b, Thessaloniki (in Greek), p. 808.

10. Quoted in Kovrig, op. cit., p. 16. See also more generally, Kalevi J. Holsti, 'Who Got What and How: The CSCE Negotiations in Retrospect', in Spencer (ed.), op. cit, p. 142; Flanagan, op. cit., p. 142; Peyton V. Lyon, 'Canada at Geneva, 1973–1975', in Spencer (ed.), op. cit., p. 120.

11. Flanagan, op. cit., pp. 43–7; Robert Legvold, 'The Soviet Union and Western Europe', in Mastny, op. cit., pp. 51–3; Kovrig, op. cit., pp. 3–19; Holsti, op. cit., pp. 135–7; Vojtech Mastny, 'Introduction', in Mastny, op. cit., pp. 3–6; Russell, op. cit., pp. 244–6; John J. Maresca, 'Inviolability of Frontiers', in Mastny, op. cit., pp. 74–5.

12. Robert Legvold, 'The Problem of European Security', *Problems of Communism*, No. 23 (January–February 1973), pp. 18, 26.

13. This Soviet approach is clearly in evidence, as seen by the comments and criticism made by Eduard Shevardnadze in his book, *The Future Belongs to Freedom* (London: Sinclair-Stevenson, 1991).

14. Kissinger quoted in Kovrig, op. cit., p. 4.

15. Ball quoted in Russell, op. cit., p. 242; Aron and Ionesco quoted in Ghebali, 1989, op. cit., pp. 11–13. See also on this point Max M. Kampelman, *Entering New Worlds. The Memoirs of a Private Man in Public Life* (New York: Harper Collins, 1991), pp. 218–19.

16. Ibid.; Ghebali, 1989, op. cit., p. 13.

17. Thomas Buergenthal, 'Copenhagen: A Democratic Manifesto', *World Affairs*, 153, No. 1 (Summer 1990), p. 5; Kampelman, op. cit., pp. 218–19; Mastny, 'Introduction', op. cit., pp. 1–33.

18. See in particular the classic critique of Realism by John W. Burton in his *International Relations: A General Theory* (Cambridge: Cambridge University Press, 1965); also J. W. Burton, A. J. R. Groom, C. R. Mitchell and A. V. S. de Reuck, 'The Study of World Society: A London Perspective', Occasional Paper No. 1, International Studies Association (1974).

CHAPTER TWO: THE HELSINKI TALKS AND THE CSCE PROCEDURAL RULES

1. Interview with Ambassador Nicos Karandreas, the Greek delegate at the Helsinki Consultations. Confirmed in DOC/G, 10 June 1973. Luigi Vittorio Ferraris, *Report on a Negotiation. Helsinki–Geneva–Helsinki 1972–1975* (Alphen aan den Rijn: Sijthoff & Noordhoff, 1979), pp. 9–40; Ioannis Bourloyiannis-Tsangaridis, 'CSCE: The Multilateral Preparatory Talks (November 1972–June 1973)', *Nomos*, 8, No. b, Thessaloniki (in Greek); Robert Spencer, 'Canada and the Origins of the 'CSCE', in Robert Spencer (ed.), *Canada and the Conference on Security and Co-operation in Europe* (Toronto: University of Toronto Press, 1984), pp. 84–8.
2. Ferraris, op. cit., p. 13.
3. Harold S. Russell, 'The Helsinki Declaration: Brobdingnag or Lilliput?', *American Journal of International Law*, 70 (1976), pp. 246–9.
4. The FRG delegate told his NATO colleagues that they intended to mention the issue in the opening phase of the main conference, which they did. DOC/G, 10 June 1973.
5. John J. Maresca, *To Helsinki: The Conference on Security and Co-operation in Europe, 1973–1975* (Durham: Duke University Press, 1985), p. 110; Spencer, op. cit., p. 90; Vojtech Mastny, *Helsinki, Human Rights and European Security* (Durham: Duke University Press, 1986), p. 9.
6. The compromise was between not mentioning the principles at all (or only mentioning the related principle, the one with respect to the human rights principle) and mentioning sovereign equality, non-intervention and internal legislation. See generally Jeanne Kirk Laux, 'Human Contacts, Information, Culture, and Education', in Spencer (ed.), op. cit., pp. 257–8; Spencer, op. cit., pp. 90–2. Among the Soviets there was the conviction that the matter could be kept within bounds and little added in the course of the negotiations.
7. Bourloyiannis-Tsangaridis, op. cit.; 'Final Recommendations of the Helsinki Consultations' (Helsinki, 1973) (henceforth FRHC), paragraphs 50 and 52.
8. Victor-Yves Ghebali, *La diplomatie de la détente: la CSCE d'Helsinki à Vienne (1973–1989)* (Brussels: Emile Bruylant, 1989), pp. 76–7.
9. Ljubivoje Acimovic, 'Follow-Up to the Conference', in Mastny, op. cit., p. 68. See for the reasons for the United States attitude on follow-up, Max M. Kampelman, *Entering New Worlds. The Memoirs of a Private Man in Public Life* (New York: Harper Collins, 1991), p. 237
10. FRHC, paragraph 53. Note the elusiveness of the wording:

   such measures as may be required to give effect to the decisions of the Conference and to further the process of improving security and developing co-operation in Europe. Having considered proposals to this effect, it shall make any recommendations which it deems necessary.

11. Spencer, op. cit., pp. 93–4.

12. Interview with Ambassador Karandreas. Also in Bourloyiannis-Tsangaridis, op. cit.; and DOC/G, 10 June 1973.
13. Erika B. Schlager, 'The Procedural Framework of the CSCE: From the Helsinki Consultations to the Paris Charter, 1972–1990', *Human Rights Law Journal*, 12, Nos. 6–7 (12 July 1991), pp.226–7. See also Alexis Heraclides, 'Helsinki-I: From Cold War to "A New Europe". The Human Rights Phase of the Conference on Security and Co-operation in Europe, 1975–1990', Greek Institute for International and Strategic Studies, Occasional Paper No. 2 (August 1991), pp. 17–19.
14. Schlager, op. cit., pp.226–7.
15. Ibid., p.227. According to one view, Albania had not in fact asked to be 'an observer' to the CSCE but rather 'to observe a given meeting', hence the need to repeat its petition with each new meeting.
16. 'Berlin Meeting of the CSCE Council, 19–20 June 1991. Summary of Conclusions', p.1 and Annex 1 in p.5; Prague Meeting of the CSCE Council, 30–31 January 1992, Summary of Conclusions; CSCE, Sixth Meeting of the Committee of Senior Officials, Prague 1992, Journal No. 1, Annexe 2 (27 January 1992).
17. 'Declaration on the "Guidelines on the Recognition of New States in Eastern Europe and in the Soviet Union"', Extraordinary EPC Ministerial Meeting, Brussels, 16 December 1991. Included are the following: respect for the provisions and commitments of the UN Charter, the Final Act of Helsinki and the Charter of Paris 'especially with regard to the rule of law, democracy and human rights'; 'guarantees for the rights of ethnic and national groups and minorities' on the basis of CSCE commitments; respect for the inviolability of frontiers 'which can be only be changed by peaceful means and by common agreement'; acceptance of relevant commitments on disarmament, nuclear non-proliferation, security and regional stability; commitment to peaceful settlement of disputes; and the non-recognition of entities which are the result of aggression.
18. James Crawford, *The Creation of States in International Law* (Oxford: Clarendon Press, 1979), pp. 16–25; J. E. S. Fawcett, *The Law of Nations* (Middlesex: Penguin, 1971, pp.49–55; Ian Brownlie, *Principles of Public International Law* (Oxford: Clarendon Press, 1973), pp.74–81, 89–95.
19. See, among others, Rupert Emerson, 'Self-Determination', *American Journal of International Law*, 65 (1971), pp. 459–75; A. Rigo Sureda, *The Evolution of the Right to Self-Determination* (Leiden: A. Sijthoff, 1973); Hector Gross Espiell, *The Right of Self-Determination: Implementation of United Nations Resolutions* (UNDOC E/CN. 4/Sub. 2/405 Rev. 1, 1980), pp. 8–11, 13–14.
20. Alexis Heraclides, *The Self-Determination of Minorities in International Politics* (London: Frank Cass, 1991), pp. 21–6; Crawford, op. cit., pp. 16–25.
21. Schlager, op. cit., p. 223; Ghebali, op. cit., pp. 13–17; Emmanuel Decaux, *La Conférence sur la Sécurité et la Co-opération en Europe (CSCE)* (Paris: Presses Universitaires de France, 1992), pp.56–7.
22. Ibid., p.15.
23. Schlager, op. cit., p.223.
24. This was also confirmed in the author's discussions with more than one Executive-Secretary of CSCE meetings.
25. Note for instance that in the Cracow Meeting on the Cultural Heritage the Council of Europe and UNESCO were allowed, following a consensus decision, to participate in the formal working groups and to take the floor, and a similar approach has been followed, *mutatis mutandis*, in other CSCE meetings.
26. Vienna Meeting 1986, Journal No.397, 162nd Plenary Meeting, 15 January 1989.

27. This is precisely the answer a delegation gets when it asks the Executive-Secretary of a meeting how it should go about 'duly registering' a paragraph-79 statement.
28. Vienna Meeting 1986, CSCE, Journal No.397, 162nd Plenary Meeting, 15 January 1989; CSCE/BM-P, Journal, 5 August 1977.
29. CSCE Conference on the Human Dimension, Copenhagen Meeting, CSCE/CHDC/Inf.7, Copenhagen, 28 June 1990.
30. Susan Bastid, 'The Special Significance of the Helsinki Final Act', in Thomas Buergenthal (ed.), *Human Rights, International Law and the Helsinki Accord* (Montclair, NJ: Allanheld, Osmun, 1977), p.12.

CHAPTER THREE: THE HELSINKI/GENEVA CONFERENCE AND
THE FINAL ACT

1. Kalevi J. Holsti, 'Who Got What and How: The CSCE Negotiations in Retrospect', in Robert Spencer (ed.), *Canada and the Conference on Security and Co-operation in Europe* (Toronto: University of Toronto Press, 1984), p. 237.
2. Victor-Yves Ghebali, *La diplomatie de la détente: la CSCE d'Helsinki à Vienne (1973–1989)* (Brussels: Emile Bruylant, 1989), p.10, n.2.
3. Holsti, op. cit., p. 152.
4. The participation of extra-European states was dealt with as follows: '... Ministers examined the manner in which the conference would acquaint itself with points of view expressed by non-participating States on the subject of various agenda items ... No consensus was reached for the time being.' 'Communiqué on the First Stage of the Conference on Security and Co-operation in Europe', embargo until 7 July 1973, 4.00p.m., p.2.
5. Holsti, op. cit., p. 142. See also Karl E. Birnbaum, 'East–West Diplomacy in the Era of Multilateral Negotiations: The Case of the Conference on Security and Co-operation in Europe (CSCE)', in Nils Andren and Karl E. Birnbaum (eds.), *Beyond Détente: Prospects for East–West Co-operation and Security in Europe* (Amsterdam: Sijthoff, 1976), p.142.
6. Note that the United States delegation submitted only one proposal throughout the conference. However, it reassured its allies that it remained 'vigilant' . See Ioannis Bourloyiannis-Tsangaridis, 'CSCE: The Multilateral Preparatory Talks (November 1972–June 1973)', *Nomos*, 8, No.b, Thessaloniki (in Greek), p.830.
7. Harold S. Russell, 'The Helsinki Declaration: Brobdingnag or Lilliput?', *American Journal of International Law*, 70 (1976), p.246.
8. Ibid., p.247; Max M. Kampelman, *Entering New Worlds. The Memoirs of a Private Man in Public Life* (New York: Harper Collins, 1991), pp.217–18.
9. Luigi Vittorio Ferraris, *Report on a Negotiation. Helsinki–Geneva–Helsinki 1972–1975* (Alphen aan den Rijn: Sijthoff & Noordhoff, 1979), p.101.
10. Russell, op. cit., p.263.
11. Ibid., p.263.
12. Ibid., p.264.
13. Ibid., p.264.
14. It was a curious formulation which ran as follows: 'No consideration may be invoked to serve to warrant resort to the threat or use of force in contravention of this principle.' Greece, in particular, was very satisfied with this outcome. DOC/G, 19 and 20 July 1975.
15. John J. Maresca, *To Helsinki: The Conference on Security and Co-operation in Europe, 1973–1975* (Durham: Duke University Press, 1985), p.110.

16. Russell, op. cit., p.249.
17. Ibid., p.249.
18. The initial German/French proposed draft on the inviolability of frontiers concluded thus: '... The participating States are of the opinion that their frontiers can be changed only in accordance with international law, through peaceful means and by agreement with due regard for the rights of peoples to self-determination.' Ferraris, op. cit., pp.103–4.
19. Russell, op. cit., p.252.
20. The provisional text ran as follows: 'The Participating States consider that their frontiers can be changed only in accordance with international law by peaceful means and by agreement.' See Russell, op. cit., p.252; Maresca, op. cit., pp.112–16.
21. Ibid., pp.115–16; Ferraris, op. cit., p.134.
22. Russell, op. cit., p.253.
23. Ibid., p..253.
24. Ferraris, op. cit., p.101.
25. Ibid., p.125.
26. Russell, op. cit., pp.365–6.
27. Ferraris, op. cit., pp.165–6; Russell, op. cit., pp.266–7. For the Athens and Valletta meetings see respectively: Antonis Bredimas, 'La co-opération politique Européenne à la Conférence sur la Sécurité et la Co-opération en Europe et au Conférence sur le règlement pacifique des différents', in Constantin Stephanou (ed.), *La Communauté Europeenne et ses états membres* (Paris: Presses Universitaires de France, 1985); and Ph. Dascalopoulou-Livada, 'The CSCE Valletta Meeting on Peaceful Settlement of Disputes. A Step Forward or an Opportunity Missed?', *Revue Hellénique de Droit International* (1992).
28. Ferraris, op. cit., pp.106, 128. Note that the Western fears on the use of Principle VI as against Principle VII were only partly justified and with no real far-reaching consequences, as we shall see.
29. Russell, op. cit., pp.270–1.
30. Ferraris, op. cit., p.164.
31. Ibid., pp.135, 139.
32. Ibid., pp.132, 135, 137.
33. Ibid., pp.135, 137.
34. Ibid., p.138.
35. Based on information from DOC/G, 21 March, 5 September, 29 November 1974, 8 January and 8 April 1975, and also on Ferraris, op. cit., pp.135–8.
36. The cryptic word 'exist' was a Greek initiative supported by France, which to the authors and to some others means much more than is immediately discernible, namely that these rights are not applicable should a national minority 'not exist', this of course on the basis of a state's definition, not the self-definition of the minority.
37. Antonio Cassese, 'The Helsinki Declaration and Self-Determination', in Thomas Buergenthal (ed.), *Human Rights, International Law and the Helsinki Accord* (Montclair, NJ: Allanheld, Osmun, 1977), pp.94–5; Ferraris, op. cit., pp.139–40.
38. DOC/G, 28 November 1974.
39. Ferraris, op. cit., p.139.
40. Cassese, op. cit., pp.95–6.
41. Ferraris, op. cit., pp.140–1.
42. Ibid., p.141; Cassese, op. cit., p.99.

43. Ferraris, op. cit., pp. 141–2.
44. DOC/G, 22 February 1975.
45. Cassese, op. cit., pp. 98–105; Russell, op. cit., pp. 269–70; Ferraris, op. cit., pp. 141–2.
46. Jeanne Kirk Laux, 'Human Contacts, Information, Culture, and Education', in Spencer (ed.), op. cit., p. 259; Ferraris, op. cit., pp. 299–305, 308–12, 321–7.
47. Laux, op. cit., p. 259; Ferraris, op. cit., p. 301.
48. Ibid., p. 302.
49. Ibid., pp. 299–305, 308–11; Laux, op. cit., pp. 259–60; Holsti, op. cit., pp. 143–5.
50. DOC/G, 19 December 1973.
51. Ibid.
52. Ibid; and DOC/G, 21 March and 8 April 1974.
53. Laux, op. cit., pp. 259–60.
54. Ferraris, op. cit., p. 325.
55. Ljubivoje Acimovic, 'Follow-Up to the Conference', in Vojtech Mastny, *Helsinki, Human Rights, and European Security* (Durham: Duke University Press, 1986), p. 68; also DOC/G, 8 April, 29 November 1974, 8 January, 11 February and 1 March 1975.
56. Acimovic, op. cit., pp. 68–71.
57. Ibid., p. 71.
58. Jean-François Prévost, 'Observations sur la nature juridique de l'Acte Final de la Conférence sur la Sécurité et la Co-opération en Europe', *Annuaire Français de Droit International*, 21 (1975), p. 137.
59. Susan Bastid, 'The Special Significance of the Helsinki Final Act', in Thomas Buergenthal (ed.), op. cit., pp. 12, 15.
60. J. E. S. Fawcett, 'The Helsinki Act and International Law', *Revue Belge de Droit International*, 8 (1977), p. 5.
61. Bastid, op. cit., p. 12.
62. Prévost, op. cit., pp. 5–153; Bastid, op. cit., pp. 11–19.
63. Prévost, op. cit., p. 137.
64. Thomas Buergenthal, 'International Human Rights Law and the Helsinki Final Act: Conclusions', in Buergenthal (ed.), op. cit., p. 6.
65. Oscar Schachter, 'The Twilight Existence of Nonbinding International Agreements', *American Journal of International Law*, 71 (1977), pp. 296, 300, 304. Also see Emmanuel Roucounas, *Engagements parallèles et contradictoires*, in *Receuil des Cours* (Hague Academy of International Law, IV (1987)) (Dordrecht: Martius Nijhoff, 1991), pp. 176–8.
66. Buergenthal, op. cit., p. 6.
67. Gerard Cohen Jonathan and Jean-Paul Jacqué, 'Obligations Assumed by the Helsinki Signatories', in Thomas Buergenthal (ed.), op. cit., pp. 53–4; Emmanuel Decaux, *La Conférence sur la Sécurité et la Co-opération en Europe (CSCE)* (Paris: Presses Universitaires de France, 1992), pp. 56–61. Also more generally see Roucounas, op. cit., pp. 176–8.
68. Hannes Tretter, 'Human Rights in the Concluding Document of the Vienna Follow-up Meeting of the Conference on Security and Co-operation in Europe of January 15, 1989', *Human Rights Law Journal*, 10 (1989), p. 260.
69. Prévost, op. cit., p. 153.
70. Jonathan and Jacqué, op. cit., p. 53.
71. Walter Tornopolsky, 'The Principles Guiding Relations between Participating States: Human Rights and Non-Intervention', in Robert Spencer (ed.), *Canada*

and the Conference on Security and Co-operation in Europe (Toronto: University of Toronto Press, 1984), pp.171–2; Jochen Abr. Frowein, 'The Interrelationship between the Helsinki Final Act, the International Covenants on Human Rights, and the European Convention on Human Rights', in Buergenthal, op. cit., p.72.

72. Buergenthal, op. cit., p.6.
73. Prévost, op. cit., p.142.
74. Buergenthal, op. cit., pp.6–7; Jonathan and Jacqué, op. cit., p.52.
75. There is very little on disarmament and non-military aspects of security in the sub-chapter entitled 'Document on Confidence-building measures and Certain Aspects of Security and Disarmament'.
76. Decaux, op. cit., p.73; 'Final Act', pp.78, 82 (English version).
77. For an attempt at normative standard-setting on this difficult question see Alexis Heraclides, 'Secession, Self-Determination and Non-Intervention: In Quest of a Normative Symbiosis', *Journal of International Affairs* (Winter 1992), pp.399–420.
78. Buergenthal, op. cit., p.4; Decaux, op. cit., pp.90–2.
79. Louis Henkin, 'Human Rights and "Domestic Jurisdiction"', in Buergenthal (ed.), op. cit., p.26.
80. Felix Ermacora quoted in Henkin, op. cit., p.27.
81. Henkin, op. cit., p.27.
82. Laux, op. cit., pp.257–61; Jonathan and Jacqué, op. cit., pp.43–5; Tornopolsky, op. cit., pp.170–9; Gaetano Arangio-Ruíz, 'Human Rights and Non Intervention in the Helsinki Final Act', *Recueil des Cours*, Hague Academy of International Law, IV (1977), pp.195–232; Schachter, op. cit., pp.296–304; Fawcett, op. cit., pp.5–9.
83. Buergenthal, op. cit., p.6.
84. Ibid., p.6.
85. Tornopolsky, op. cit., p.188.
86. Arangio-Ruíz, op. cit., p.286.
87. Frowein, op. cit., p.72.
88. This imbalance is not evident in United Nations legal instruments and declarations. However, it is worth noting that by their very nature, 'first generation rights' are more 'rights' in the legal sense of the word, among other things, because (a) they contain the abstention (*nec facere*) of the state, an element which is at the very heart of the original concept of human rights and fundamental freedom; (b) they are directly enforceable, providing for judicial remedies in case of their violation; (c) they are immediately realizable; and (d) they are by definition 'individual' human rights, whereas the others have a more obvious collective aspect to them.
89. Cassese, op. cit., p. 103.
90. Ibid.
91. Ibid.
92. G. Jonathan Greenwald, 'Vienna – A Challenge for the Western Alliance', *Aussenpolitik*, 38, No.4 (1987), p.161.
93. Ibid.
94. Buergenthal, op. cit., p.8.
95. Mastny, op. cit., pp.9–10; see also Kampelman, op. cit., pp.218–19.

CHAPTER FOUR: THE CSCE DURING THE COLD WAR (1975–86):
AN OVERVIEW

1. Herbert Marcuse, *One Dimensional Man* (Boston: Beacon Press, 1964), pp.94–7.
2. Jeanne Kirk Laux, 'Human Contacts, Information, Culture, and Education', in

Security and Co-operation in Europe

Robert Spencer (ed.), *Canada and the Conference on Security and Co-operation in Europe* (Toronto: University of Toronto Press, 1984), p.267.

3. 'Final Act', p. 76 (English version).
4. Kalevi J. Holsti, 'Who Got What and How: The CSCE Negotiations in Retrospect', in Robert Spencer (ed.), op. cit., p.164.
5. R.J. Vincent, *Human Rights and International Relations* (London: Cambridge University Press, 1986), pp.66–75.
6. Vojtech Mastny, *Helsinki, Human Rights, and European Security* (Durham: Duke University Press, 1986), p.2.
7. Thomas Kuhn, *The Structure of Scientific Revolutions* (Chicago: University of Chicago Press, 1962).
8. Ljubivoje Acimovic, 'Follow-up to the Conference', in Mastny, op. cit., pp.68–73; Berndt von Staden, 'From Madrid to Vienna: The CSCE Process', *Aussenpolitik*, 37, No.4 (1986), p.351; Geoffrey Edwards, 'Human Rights and Basket III Issues: Areas of Change and Continuity', *International Affairs*, 61 (Autumn 1985), p.641.
9. John J. Maresca, quoted in G. Jonathan Greenwald, 'Vienna – A Challenge for the Western Alliance', *Aussenpolitik*, 38, No.4 (1987), p.159.
10. Edwards, op. cit., pp.640–2; Laux, op. cit., pp.263, 267; Mastny, op. cit., p. 10; von Staden, op. cit., pp.359–60; Greenwald, op. cit., pp.157–61.
11. Lewis Coser, *The Functions of Social Conflict* (New York: The Free Press, 1954); for a very good review of the Simmel–Coser approach see C.R. Mitchell, 'Evaluating Conflict', *Journal of Peace Research*, 17 (1981), pp.61–75.
12. Harold S. Russell, 'The Helsinki Declaration: Brobdingnag or Lilliput?', *American Journal of International Law*, 70 (1976), pp.245–9; Holsti, op. cit., pp.151–2, 154–5, 164; Karl Birnbaum, 'East–West Diplomacy in the Era of Multilateral Negotiations: the Case of the Conference on Security and Co-operation in Europe (CSCE)', in Nils Andren and Karl E. Birnbaum (eds.), *Beyond Détente: Prospect for East–West Co-operation and Security in Europe* (Amsterdam: Sijthoff, 1976), p.151.
13. Holsti, op. cit., pp.144, 159–61; Peyton V. Lyon, 'Canada at Geneva, 1973–1975', in Spencer (ed.), op. cit., p.114.
14. C.R. Mitchell, *The Structure of International Conflict* (London: Macmillan, 1981), pp.218–20.
15. See, for example, *Le Monde* (29 September 1974). Greece seemed serious enough in its threat not to give its consent to the Final Act, but had to back down later, particularly as Cyprus gave in, apparently in exchange for securing Archbishop Makarios's presence at Helsinki for the final stage of the Conference. (Based on numerous DOC/G.) The presence of the President of Cyprus as representative of Cyprus had been put into question by Turkey, which formally tabled a reservation (the issue was also mentioned by Prime Minister Suleyman Demirel in his statement at Helsinki) to the effect that 'the State of Cyprus is not legitimately represented at the Conference'. See 'Formal Reservation by the Turkish Government relating to the decision to adopt the Final Act', CSCE/III/1, Helsinki, 31 July 1975. Cyprus made an interpretative statement based on paragraph 65 of the Blue Book (on participation 'as sovereign and independent States in conditions of full equality'), rejecting the Turkish reservation. See 'Interpretative Statement by the Government of the Republic of Cyprus relating to the Adoption of the Final Act', CSCE/III/2, Helsinki, 1 August 1975.
16. Birnbaum, op. cit., p.152; Hannibal Velliadis, 'The Madrid Conference and the Consensus-Building Process in Decision-Making', *Hellenic Review of International Relations*, 2, No.1 (1981), pp.191–8.

CHAPTER FIVE: BELGRADE AND MADRID

1. H. Gordon Skilling, 'The Belgrade Follow-up', in Robert Spencer (ed.), *Canada and the Conference on Security and Co-operation in Europe* (Toronto: University of Toronto Press, 1984), p.286.
2. Ibid., pp.291–2.
3. The Commission on Security and Co-operation is an independent agency created by Congress in June 1976. It is charged with 'monitoring and encouraging compliance' with the provisions of the Final Act and subsequent CSCE documents 'with particular regard to the provisions relating to Human Rights and Humanitarian Co-operation' (Section 2 of Public Law 94–304). The Commission is composed of twenty-one legislative and executive branch officials, nine from the House of Representatives and nine from the US Senate (known as 'commissioners'), and one each from the Departments of State, Defense and Commerce. The main expertise is provided by some fifteen permanent staff, headed previously by R. Spencer Oliver (as staff director) and now by Samuel Wise (who was previously the deputy). Permanent members of the Commission are usually active members of United States delegations at CSCE meetings (staff directors have acted as deputies of United States delegations, notably in the Madrid and Vienna Follow-ups), while commissioners pay a visit in the course of the meeting and their chairman delivers a speech.
4. In Vojtech Mastny, *Helsinki, Human Rights, and European Security* (Durham: Duke University Press, 1986), p. 161.
5. Mastny, op. cit., pp.16–17; DOC/G, 18 April 1978. Sherer, was initially designated to head the United States delegation, but had to submit to a last-minute Carter decision to appoint Goldberg. For details of this affair see Max M. Kampelman, *Entering New Worlds. The Memoirs of a Private Man in Public Life* (New York: Harper Collins, 1991), pp.220–1.
6. France later mellowing its position. The rumour was that new instructions had come from President Giscard d'Estaing who did not want to alienate leftist voters in the forthcoming French elections. DOC/G, 18 April 1978.
7. Skilling, op. cit., p.292.
8. Ibid., p.286.
9. Ibid., pp.287, 294–6.
10. Ibid., p.296.
11. Ibid., pp.295–6; Victor-Yves Ghebali, *La diplomatie de la détente: la CSCE d'Helsinki à Vienne (1973–1989)* (Brussels: Emile Bruylant, 1989), p.26.
12. Skilling, op. cit., pp.288–90.
13. Ibid., pp. 290. Note that one of the key phrases of the Concluding Document of the Belgrade Meeting refers to the participating states' 'resolve to continue the multilateral process initiated by the CSCE'.
14. Albert Sherer, 'Inevitable Disappointment' (taken from *Foreign Policy*), in Mastny, op. cit., p.185.
15. Adam D. Rotfeld, in H.Gordon Skilling, 'The Madrid Follow-up', in Spencer (ed.), op. cit., p.309.
16. Jerzy Nowak, 'An East-European Perspective', in Nils Andren and Karl E. Birnbaum (eds.), *Belgrade and Beyond: The CSCE in Perspective* (Alphen aan den Rijn: Sijthoff & Noordhoff, 1980), pp.42–3.
17. Karl E. Birnbaum, 'Lessons of the Past, Guidelines for the Future', in Andren and Birnbaum (eds.), op. cit., p.71.
18. In DOC/G, 6 August 1977.

191

19. Birnbaum, op. cit., p.71.
20. 'Report of the "Scientific Forum" of the Conference on Security and Co-operation in Europe', Hamburg, 1980, p.24 (in English version).
21. Nils Andren, 'Expectations and Disillusionment', in Andren and Birnbaum (eds.), op. cit., p.96.
22. Mastny, op. cit., p.19.
23. This point is also made by Max Kampelman in his autobiography. See Kampelman, op. cit., p.236.
24. Ibid., pp.26–3, 265; H. Gordon Skilling, 'The Madrid Follow-up', in Spencer (ed.), op. cit., p.310.
25. Ibid., pp.309–14, 342–43; Victor-Yves Ghebali, 'Les résultats de la Réunion de Madrid sur les suites de la CSCE', *Défense Nationale* (December 1983), p.126.
26. Skilling, op. cit., p.312. Commission on Security and Co-operation in Europe, 'The Madrid CSCE Review Meeting' (Washington, November 1983) (henceforth 'Commission'), p.1. Also DOC/G, 3 December 1980.
27. DOC/G, 3 December 1980.
28. Several reports by Roland Eggleston reprinted in Mastny, op. cit., pp.200–6.
29. Skilling, op. cit., pp.313–14. Also DOC/G, 3 December 1980.
30. Mastny, op. cit., p.20.
31. 'Commission', p.1.
32. Max M. Kampelman, 'Reflections on the Madrid CSCE Review Conference', in Leon Sloss and M.Scott Davis (eds.), *A Game for High Stakes: Lessons Learned in Negotiating with the Soviet Union* (Roosevelt Center for American Policy Studies, 1985), p.113. See also Kampelman's speeches in Max M. Kampelman, *Three Years at the East–West Divide* (New York: Freedom House, 1983).
33. Skilling, op. cit., p.321.
34. 'Commission', p.4.
35. Mastny, op. cit., p.23.
36. In Madrid the United States delegation referred to some 119 individuals, according to their report: 'Commission', pp.2, 22–8. As Kampelman points out, 'naming names' was not supported by several NATO states, notably by the FRG. So as not to split the allies on this issue, he likened NATO cohesion on this question to an orchestra, each one playing a different musical instrument, and in different ways, some loudly and others softly, but at the end producing music and harmony. See Kampelman, in Sloss and Davis (eds), op. cit., pp.109–10.
37. Which in communist jargon meant those affecting 'the wide masses of people', such as unemployment, racial discrimination and so on.
38. Skilling, op. cit., pp.321–4; Mastny, op. cit., p.23.
39. Jan Sizzoo and Rudolf Th. Jurrgens, *CSCE Decision-Making: The Madrid Experience* (The Hague: Martinus Nijhoff, 1984), p.91.
40. Ibid., pp.93–7.
41. Mastny, op. cit., p.22.
42. Sizzoo and Jurrgens, op. cit., p.89.
43. Mastny, op. cit., p.28.
44. Kampelman, 1991, op. cit., pp.258–9, 267.
45. Ibid., pp.244–5, 258–9, 267; Mastny, op. cit., p.28. Also DOC/G, 4, 5 March and 5 August 1981.
46. 'Annual Report of the Commission on Security and Co-operation in Europe for the Period Covering January 1 Through December 31, 1986', 99th Congress, 2nd Session (Washington, 1987), p.5.

47. Among others worth mentioning were encouraging meetings of young people by the EC, and on the same subject by Romania, and separately by Hungary and the Soviet Union; facilitating the dissemination of newspapers, by Austria and others; access to printed matter, by the European Community; a cultural forum, by France and separately by Yugoslavia; terminating the emissions of Radio Liberty and Radio Free Europe, by the Soviet Union; exchange of textbooks, by the GDR; teaching of less widely spoken languages, by Finland and Hungary; measures against war propaganda and fascism, by Romania.
48. Sizzoo and Jurrgens, op. cit., pp.91–106; Kampelman, 1991, op. cit., pp.244–5.
49. Kampelman regarded Allied solidarity as essential for a successful outcome of the meeting and took pains not to find himself in the position of his Belgrade predecessor. See Kampelman, 1991, op. cit., pp.236, 241–3; Kampelman, in Sloss and Davis (eds.), op. cit., pp.108–13, 212ff; Max M. Kampelman, 'Madrid Conference: How to Negotiate with the Soviets', *Standing Committee on Law and National Security*, American Bar Association (February 1985), pp. 4–5.
50. Kondrashev was generally considered to be a KGB general.
51. Sizzoo and Jurrgens, op. cit., pp.91–106.
52. Ibid.
53. Ibid.; and DOC/G, 13 January 1982.
54. Mastny, op. cit., p.25.
55. Ibid.; Eggleston's report in ibid., p.244.
56. DOC/G, 13 January 1982.
57. Ibid.
58. Ibid.; and DOC/G, 12 March 1982.
59. Greece did not join in condemning the military takeover in Poland, dissociating itself from the relevant part of the EC's presidency speech of Belgian Foreign Minister Leo Tindemans: DOC/G, 12 March 1982.
60. Kampelman, 1991, op. cit., p.261. 'Commission', op. cit., pp.41–5; Eggleston report in Mastny, op. cit., pp.246–7; Emmanuel Decaux, *La Conférence sur la Sécurité et la Co-opération en Europe (CSCE)* (Paris: Presses Universitaires de France, 1992), pp.51–2; Skilling, op. cit., p.334.
61. Kampelman, 1991, op. cit.
62. Eggleston's report in Mastny, op. cit., p.248.
63. Sizzoo and Jurrgens, op. cit., pp.203–8; Skilling, op. cit., pp.335–6.
64. Mastny, op. cit., p.25.
65. Kampelman, 1991, op. cit., pp.264–5; Skilling, op. cit., pp.335–7.
66. Ibid.
67. Kampelman, 1991, op. cit., pp.268–9.
68. Skilling, op. cit., pp.338–9.
69. Eggleston, in Mastny, op. cit., pp.266–7.
70. For details of this see Kampelman, 1991, op. cit., pp.266–7, 274.
71. Eggleston, in Mastny, op. cit., pp.266–7; Skilling, op. cit., pp.337–40.
72. Eggleston, in Mastny, op. cit., p.277; Maltese statement in Mastny, op. cit., p.275.
73. The full official title is 'Concluding Document of the Madrid Meeting 1980 of Representatives of the Participating States of the Conference on Security and Co-operation in Europe, Held on the Basis of the Provisions of the Final Act Relating to the Follow-up to the Conference'.
74. As Shultz reported to President Reagan, according to Kampelman. See Kampelman, 1991, op. cit., p.274.
75. Kampelman's final speech in Kampelman, 1983, op. cit., pp.121–5; 'Commission', p.7.

76. Note, however, that there is no mention of national minorities under Basket III. Remember that in the Final Act it is mentioned under the sub-chapters on education and culture.
77. One was achieved by extracting one element of the commitments under Principle IX (Co-operation), and repeating it *verbatim* amid the paragraphs on human rights ('they reaffirm that governments, institutions, organizations and persons have a positive role to play ...'). Another was an addition to the reaffirmation of 'the right of the individual to know and act upon his rights', saying that states 'take the necessary action ... to effectively ensure this right'.
78. 'Commission', op. cit., p.7.
79. Ghebali, op. cit., p.133.
80. Ibid., p.133; 'Commission', p.17.
81. Kampelman, 1991, op. cit., p. 279–80.

CHAPTER SIX: BETWEEN MADRID AND VIENNA

1. Three proposals for an agenda were presented, one by the West (EC/NATO), one by the East (without Romania), and a third by Romania which was an attempt to bridge the differences between the two proposals (with nothing on publicity but more time allotted to implementation).
2. The presentation of the Ottawa and Bern meetings is largely based on the notes of the author, a participant in them. Particularly useful also are the following two articles: Ekkehard Eickhoff (the FRG head of delegation) in an article written in *Europa-Archiv*, 19, 1985, 'Assessment of the Meeting of Experts', translated in Mastny, op. cit., pp.304–11; and Berndt von Staden, 'From Madrid to Vienna: The CSCE Process', *Aussenpolitik*, 37, No.4 (1986), pp.350–65.
3. DOC/N, 24 June 1985.
4. The Soviet delegation in Ottawa was under the control of Sergei Kondrashev (who was second in command) as in Madrid. The United States delegation was headed by Richard Shifter, later to become Assistant Secretary of State for human rights.
5. Vojtech Mastny, *Helsinki, Human Rights, and European Security* (Durham: Duke University Press, 1986), p.30.
6. The proposal on terrorism was not acceptable to Greece, Denmark, Norway, Belgium and Portugal on the grounds that terrorism is not a human rights matter for it does not involve a relationship between a state and the individual, and laws and other measures to counter terrorism, however acceptable they may be in a society, actually infringe upon individual human rights.
7. The Western document was drafted at the '16' experts level, under permanent Dutch presidency because of the experience of the Netherlands deputy head of delegation.
8. When OME 47 was drafted, Ambassador Ekrem Guvendiren of Turkey, an experienced CSCE hand, was able to include its mention in the text, after threatening not to co-sponsor the '16' draft document.
9. Eichhoff, op. cit., pp.308–10.
10. Ibid., pp.304–11; *The Economist*, 22 June 1985, pp.58–9; DOC/N, 24 June 1985.
11. Ibid.; Eickhoff, op.cit; DOC/N, 1 July 1985 (by the USA, Denmark, Belgium); DOC/N, 24 June 1985; and the '12' Italian Presidency assessment (undated).
12. See Eduard Shevardnadze, *The Future Belongs to Freedom* (London: Sinclair-Stevenson, 1991), p.70.

Notes: Chapter Seven

13. *Keesings*, December 1985, p.3438.
14. Nathan Glazer, 'The Budapest Cultural Forum', *Odds and Ends*, 1 (1986), pp.98–102; Adam Daniel Rotfeld, 'Introduction: The New Dimensions of the CSCE Process', in Halina Ognik and Adam D. Rotfeld (eds.), *Cultural Heritage and the CSCE Process* (Warsaw: Polish Institute of International Affairs, 1991), p.xii; Draft 'Statement of the Cultural Forum of the Conference on Security and Co-operation in Europe', in ibid., p.11.
15. The British and FRG heads of delegation were the same as in Ottawa. The Canadian delegate, Ambassador William Bauer, was to leave an imprint by his particular style in the Vienna Follow-up Meeting (see below).
16. Fortunately for the United States it had a capable second in command, Sol Polansky, a professional diplomat, who was able to bring the more contemplative United States image to the fore as well.
17. The Turkish–Cypriot procedural debate ended in favour of the Cypriot delegate, Christophoros Yiangou, who was supported by his Soviet and British counterparts.
18. DOC/G, 30 May 1986; DOC/E, 24 June 1986.
19. Ibid.
20. The Belgian delegation was headed by one of the oldest and most able CSCE hands, Ambassador J. Laurent.
21. According to some Western delegations, the Soviet was conveniently hiding behind Romania, which was probably the case only in part.
22. Paragraph 13, line 14 of the Western draft document BME.47.
23. *Financial Times*, 28 May 1986.
24. Ibid.; and also DOC/G, 30 May 1986 and DOC/E, 24 June 1986.
25. The author's distinct impression at the time was that it was highly conceivable that Romania would have withheld consensus, had the United States not done so. This is also partly indicated by Romania's closing statement, which hardly praised the NNA document.
26. *Keesings*, December 1986, p. 34839; *Financial Times*, 28 May 1986; *Journal de Genève*, 28 May 1986.
27. *Keesings*, ibid.
28. The 'amateurism of certain delegations' was the expression used by the indignant Swiss Secretary of State Edouard Brunner in his statement to the press. See *Journal de Genève*, 28 May 1986.
29. See also the US Commission's official stance in 'Annual Report of the Commission on Security and Co-operation in Europe for the Period Covering January 1 Through December 31, 1986', 99th Congress, 2nd Session (Washington, 1987), pp.5–6.
30. DOC/N, 5 August 1986.
31. Erika B. Schlager, 'The Procedural Framework of the CSCE: From the Helsinki Consultations to the Paris Charter, 1972–1990', *Human Rights Law Journal*, 12, Nos. 6–7 (12 July 1991), p.224.
32. DOC/N, 5 August 1986.
33. DOC/N (c. August 1986); DOC/E, 24 June 1986.

CHAPTER SEVEN: THE VIENNA FOLLOW-UP: THE ARDUOUS
BREAKTHROUGH

1. Stefan Lehne, *The Vienna Meeting of the Conference on Security and Co-operation in Europe, 1986–1989* (Boulder, CO: Westview Press, 1991); Victor-Yves Ghebali,

'Les résultats de la Réunion de Madrid sur les suites de la CSCE', *Défense Nationale* (December 1983).
2. DOC/N, 22 July 1986.
3. DOC/N, 25 August 1986.
4. Lehne, op. cit., pp.85–8.
5. DOC/E, 22 October 1986.
6. Lehne, op. cit., p.89.
7. Ibid., p.91.
8. 'Commission', p.1.
9. Or as Lehne puts it, 'no compliance, no deal'. Lehne, op. cit., p.69.
10. Vienna Meeting 1986, CSCE/WT.2, 10 December 1986.
11. DOC/N, 25 November 1986.
12. DOC/G, 10 November 1986; DOC/E, 8 December 1986.
13. DOC/G, 13 October 1987, 15 and 23 December 1987; DOC/E, 8 December 1986 and 7 July 1987.
14. DOC/E, 19 February 1988; DOC/G, 1 April 1987.
15. DOC/E, 5 December 1986; DOC/G, 10 November 1986.
16. DOC/E, 3 December 1986.
17. DOC/E, 15 October 1986. Also information from the Danish CSCE expert, Harris Nielsen, as well as from Ambassador George Alexandropoulos, who headed the Greek delegation in Vienna at the time.
18. DOC/E, 24 October 1986 and 10 December 1986; DOC/E, 21 November, 10 and 11 December 1986.
19. DOC/E, 2, 5, 8, 10 and 12 December 1986.
20. DOC/E, 24 November and 10 December 1986.
21. DOC/E, 12 December 1986.
22. DOC/E, 11 December 1986.
23. DOC/E, 3 and 19 December 1986.
24. DOC/E, 15 December 1986.
25. DOC/E, 13 and 20 January 1987.
26. DOC/N, 7 February 1987. One of the curiosities of the whole affair was that the sponsors are repeated at the beginning of the proposal, stressing the 'Member States of the European Community'.
27. Vienna Meeting 1986, CSCE/WT.19, 4 February 1987.
28. Lehne, op. cit., pp.100–1.
29. Ibid., p.111.
30. Mentioned in DOC/E, 29 June 1988.
31. A lesser-known reason for Western delay was the difficulty Greece faced with the minorities proposal under human contacts, spearheaded very forcefully by Canada, and strongly supported by the FRG, the Netherlands and Norway (and co-sponsored also by Turkey and some others).
32. Lehne, op. cit., p.114.
33. Ibid., pp.111–15.
34. Ibid., pp.114–15, 117–18.
35. DOC/E, 29 June 1988.
36. Based on discussions with Ambassador Kashlev and other Soviet delegates. Confirmed in DOC/E, 10, 17, 19 and 28 November 1987.
37. Ambassador Kashlev's speech on 24 July 1987.
38. Ambassador Zimmermann's speech on 24 July 1987.
39. DOC/E, 17 July 1987 (UK); DOC/G, 21 September and 13 October 1987.

40. DOC/G, 18 December 1987.
41. DOC/E, 7 October 1987.
42. DOC/E, 16 October, 10, 11, 17, 19, 28 November and 30 December 1987; DOC/G, 23 December 1987. Non-paper of the delegations of Bulgaria, Romania, the USSR and Czechoslovakia.
43. DOC/G, 9, 15 December and 17 February 1988.
44. DOC/E, 29 January 1988.
45. DOC/E, 17 March 1988.
46. Lehne, op. cit., p. 127.
47. Ibid., p. 128.
48. DOC/E, 29 June 1988.
49. Lehne, op. cit., p. 128.
50. Ibid.
51. DOC/G, 9 November 1988.
52. Lehne, op. cit., p. 128.
53. Ibid., pp. 131–2.
54. Ibid., p. 132.
55. CSCE/WT, Journal No. 397, 15 January 1989.
56. Ibid.
57. Ibid.
58. Hannes Tretter, 'Human Rights in the Concluding Document of the Vienna Follow-up Meeting of the Conference on Security and Co-operation in Europe of January 15, 1989', *Human Rights Law Journal*, 10 (1989), p. 261.
59. This is widely accepted and well documented.
60. 'Document of the Vienna Meeting 1986 ...', p. 30.
61. Ibid. See also Emmanuel Decaux, *La Conférence sur la Sécurité et la Co-opération en Europe (CSCE)* (Paris: Presses Universitaires de France, 1992), pp. 104–5.
62. 'Document of the Vienna Meeting 1986 ...', p. 30.
63. Warren Zimmermann's article in *International Herald Tribune*, 19 January 1989.
64. Lehne, op. cit., pp. 153–4.
65. Ibid., p. 155.
66. Ibid.
67. 'Document of the Vienna Meeting ...', p. 9.
68. Lehne, op. cit., pp. 157–9.
69. Ibid., pp. 157–8.
70. Based on notes by the author. Also Lehne, op. cit., p. 159.
71. This suggestion by Ambassador Torovski (in December 1987) was so justified theoretically and otherwise that it could not be persuasively counteracted at the negotiating table.
72. Eduard Shevardnadze, *The Future Belongs to Freedom* (London: Sinclair-Stevenson, 1991), p. 129.

CHAPTER EIGHT: BETWEEN VIENNA AND COPENHAGEN: THE CSCE IN THE TWILIGHT ZONE

1. The head of the Canadian delegation was William Bauer, the 'hawk' par excellence of CSCE meetings in the second part of the 1980s.
2. These were the '12' chairman, the late Ambassador Pan de Soreluce of Spain, the late Sir Anthony Williams of the United Kingdom, and the now retired Ambassador J. Laurent of Belgium.

3. Harm Hazewinkel, 'Paris, Copenhagen, and Moscow', in A. Bloed and P. van Dijk (eds.), *The Human Dimension of the Helsinki Process* (Dordrecht: Martinus Nijhoff, 1991), p. 132. Note that this was seen in practice in the following: the Executive-Secretary of the Second CHD meeting in Copenhagen circulated a volume of all the Paris proposals; several Eastern delegations saw fit in Copenhagen to withdraw officially their Paris proposals (particularly those which smacked of 'old thinking'); on more than one occasion, the inclusion of a theme in the Copenhagen Document was made on the basis of a proposal at the Paris Meeting, e.g. on the Vienna Human Dimension Mechanism and on trade union freedoms (the proposals were not re-submitted in Copenhagen).

4. *Keesings*, June 1989, pp. 36749–50. See also in the French press: *Le Monde, Le Figaro, L'Humanité, Libération,* 1 June 1989.

5. *International Herald Tribune,* 22 June 1989; *Keesings,* June 1989, p. 36750.

6. Romanian 'Non-Paper', June 1989.

7. Hazewinkel, op. cit., p. 132.

8. Emmanuel Decaux, 'La Réunion de Copenhague de la conférence sur la dimension humaine de la CSCE', *Revue générale de Droit International Public,* No. 4 (October–November 1990), p. 1025.

9. They were the well-known William Bauer and Morris Abraam, a Jewish-American human rights activist with UN/Commission on Human Rights experience.

10. The most telling argument for 'hawks' was probably the one of the late Sir Anthony Williams, when he said that the West should 'not run away' just because the Romanians 'said boo', and allow them to 'run the ship'.

11. This part is based mainly on notes by the author.

12. Zimmermann, in *International Herald Tribune,* 19 January 1989. More generally on the mechanism see Arie Bloed and Pieter van Dijk, 'Supervisory Mechanism for the Human Dimension of the CSCE', in Bloed and van Dijk, op. cit., pp. 74–108.

13. Based mainly on the author's notes.

14. Danish proposal on mechanism in Paris, which France later co-sponsored. CSCE/CDHP.7, Paris, 16 June 1989.

15. The Italian–Belgian proposal submitted by Italy and Belgium, the FRG, Luxembourg, the Netherlands and Portugal. CSCE/CDHP.20, Paris, 16 June 1989.

16. Note that no complete official list of all the instances exists, and the confidential lists that do exist among individual countries or the '12' are not necessarily complete. The '12' communicate a catalogue of their own use of the mechanism to the European Parliament once every year.

CHAPTER NINE: COPENHAGEN: EUROPE UNITED ON THE
HUMAN DIMENSION

1. Harm Hazewinkel, 'Paris, Copenhagen, and Moscow', in Bloed and van Dijk, op. cit., p. 132.

2. By Ambassador Yovanovic, who was to become a year later, during the Yugoslav crisis, foreign minister of Serbia. According to a good Yugoslav source, the speech had been prepared in Skopje, approved in Belgrade, and then sent to Copenhagen, where it was apparently rendered considerably tougher by the members of the Yugoslavian Macedonian NGOs.

3. Ambassador Garvalov, later to become first deputy foreign minister of Bulgaria.

4. For the text of the Greek delivered by Ambassador Constantin Tsamados, see

Notes: Chapter Nine

Yearbook 1990, Hellenic Foundation for Defence and Foreign Policy (ELIAMEP), pp. 353–60.

5. Particularly disturbed were Secretary of State Baker and Foreign Minister Genscher. Baker was contemplating saying no, but was advised not to do so. According to confidential information to the author, the Danish Foreign Minister did not take heed of the advice of the Executive-Secretary of the meeting.

6. The Baltic states, for their part, realizing the technical difficulty involved, were not insistent. Note that the United States delegation permitted the foreign ministers of the Baltic states to hold a press conference under their auspices, but were very careful about it.

7. The secret aim of the initiator of this proposal, the present author (who was the Greek negotiator on minorities and mechanism) was to have Greece finally break with its traditional negative approach on rights of minorities.

8. Hazewinkel, op. cit., p. 133.

9. The Swiss co-ordinator was Jean-Daniel Vigny, now head of the human rights department in the Swiss Foreign Ministry.

10. Based on the author's notes.

11. Greece's reaction to the autonomy clause was because of the so-called 'Muslim minority', comprised mainly of ethnic Turks, residing fairly compactly in eastern Thrace. The fear was that a provision on autonomous rule would lead to calls for autonomy and that this would be a stepping stone to secessionist self-determination, with the active assistance of Turkey. The reaction on NGOs was basically emotional and linked with the activity of Yugoslavian Macedonian NGOs on the margin of the meeting in Copenhagen.

12. Athens at a high level was finally convinced by the Greek delegation, which suggested the idea of following the Bulgarian line of making an interpretative statement. It also pointed to the statement which the chief co-ordinator, in one more effort to meet the Greek difficulties, undertook to make when introducing the Document of Copenhagen in the plenary, namely that it was a factual statement.

13. Ambassador Helmut Tuerk's speech of 28 June 1990 in plenary.

14. Greece, referring to four of the list of six rights of persons belonging to national minorities, paragraphs 32.3–6, stated that they 'should be in accordance with the relevant provisions of international human rights law and should respect, *inter alia*, the rights and freedoms of others and the principle of territorial integrity of the States concerned'. Bulgaria stated that the absence of a definition of national minority 'cannot be construed either as exempting any participating State from compliance with the international standard' (this was probably in order to point a finger at Turkey or perhaps Yugoslavia) and concluded that in implementing the provisions

> Bulgaria declares that this shall not in any way prejudice the right of the freely and democratically elected Parliament in Bulgaria to consider those provisions and to determine the appropriate legal and other means for their implementation in accordance with the sovereign will of the Bulgarian people.

See CSCE Conference on the Human Dimension, Copenhagen Meeting, Journal No. 18, 28 June 1990.

15. It was stated that 'In Turkey's concept, the term "national minority" only encompasses population groups whose status is subject to bilateral or multilateral

199

international instruments', and that the provisions of the document 'shall be applied in conformity with its Constitution and national legislation'. In other words, the national minority clauses did not apply to the great bulk of ethnic minorities in Turkey, notably the Kurds, of whom there were at least ten million. Document CSCE/CHD/Inf.7/ Copenhagen, 28 June 1990.
16. Thomas Buergenthal, 'The Copenhagen Meeting: A New Public Order for Europe', *Human Rights Law Journal*, 217 (1990); Thomas Buergenthal, 'Copenhagen: A Democratic Manifesto', *World Affairs* 153, No. 1 (Summer 1990), pp. 5–8; Jean-Daniel Vigny, 'Le Document de la Réunion de Copenhague sur la dimension humaine de la CSCE/Introduction et commentaires', *Revue Universelle des Droits de l'Homme*, 2, No. 9 (22 October 1990), pp. 309–10; Theodor Meron, 'Democracy and the Rule of Law', *World Affairs*, 153, No. 1 (Summer 1990); Victor-Yves Ghebali, 'Le thème des droits de l'homme dans le processus de la Conférence sur la Securité et la Co-opération en Europe', *Le 'noyau intangible' de la protection des droits de l'homme*, Actes du Colloque de Fribourg (Fribourg, 1991), pp. 191–2. A more balanced view on this subject is to be found in Arie Bloed, 'A New CSCE Human Rights "Catalogue"', in Bloed and van Dijk, op. cit., pp. 67, 72–3.
17. Buergenthal (Summer 1990), op. cit., pp. 6–7; Buergenthal, 1990, op.cit; Emmanuel Decaux, 'La Réunion de Copenhague de la Conférence sur la dimension humaine de la CSCE', *Revue Générale de Droit International Public*, No. 4 (October–November 1990).
18. See nn 16 and 17 in this chapter for more details on the legal significance of the chapter on rule of law.
19. Among legal texts there are Article 27 of the UN Covenant on Civil and Political Rights, and various non-discrimination clauses, which among other things exclude discrimination as to 'ethnic origin' in Article 1 of the UN International Convention on the Elimination of All Forms of Racial Discrimination, 'association with a national minority' in Article 14 of the Convention for the Protection of Human Rights and Fundamental Freedoms of the Council of Europe, and 'ethnical' and others in Article II of the UN Genocide Convention of 1948.
20. Hazewinkel, op. cit., p. 133.
21. Kalevi J. Holsti, 'Who Got What and How: The CSCE Negotiations in Retrospect', in Robert Spencer (ed.), *Canada and the Conference on Security and Co-operation in Europe* (Toronto: University of Toronto Press, 1984), p. 152.

CHAPTER TEN: VIENNA AND PARIS: PROCLAIMING THE
'NEW EUROPE' AND THE NEW CSCE

1. Eduard Shevardnadze, *The Future Belongs to Freedom* (London: Sinclair-Stevenson, 1991), p. 137. President Gorbachev first suggested the summit idea to President Mitterrand who, according to the *Economist*, 'snatched at the chance of holding it in Paris'. It was also supported by German Foreign Minister Genscher, who through the years has been the main partisan of the CSCE among top politicians (the CSCE is known in Germany as 'Genscher's baby'). See *The Economist*, 24 November 1990, p. 63, 9 December 1989, p. 54, and 17 November 1990, p. 20.
2. The '12' initiative had not been appropriately co-ordinated with their other NATO allies, partly due to the fact that the presidency of the '12' was then held by Ireland, a non-NATO member, a fact which in particular annoyed the United

States, which was the least enthusiastic about the summit, feeling that it was somewhat premature.

3. Victor-Yves Ghebali, 'La Charte de Paris pour une Nouvelle Europe', *Défense Nationale*, 47 (March 1991), pp.73–4; Document of the Copenhagen Meeting…', p.26 (in the English edition); DOC/E, 22 March 1990 (Ireland).

4. NATO Press Communiqué S–1(90)36, 6 July 1990, pp.5–6; Shevardnadze, op. cit., p.141; DOC/E, 22 March 1990 (Ireland); non-paper by France, 'Institutional Arrangements' (19 July 1990).

5. The co-ordinator was Stefan Lehne.

6. CSCE Committee for the Preparation of a Summit Meeting in Paris, Vienna 1990, CSCE/GVA.1 (11 July 1990). This was one of the few proposals to be tabled officially. Most of the others were in the form of non-papers.

7. Non-paper presented by the delegations of Austria, Cyprus, Finland, Liechtenstein, Malta, San Marino, Sweden, Switzerland and Yugoslavia (13 July 1990).

8. Non-paper by France, 'Institutional Arrangements' (19 July 1990).

9. 'U.S. Delegation' (20 July 1990).

10. 'Working Paper by Canada: Basic Elements for One or More Documents' (20 July 1990).

11. France, 'Schéma pour la préparation des principaux éléments de la première partie d'un ou deux des documents(s) du sommet' (20 July 1990).

12. Italy–European Community, 'Elements for One or More Summit Documents', NP-B1 (19 July 1990).

13. Ad Hoc Group on Draft Elements of One or More Summit Documents, Co-ordinator's Non-paper (23 July 1990); ibid. (26 July 1990), revised; DOC/G, 27 July 1990; statement by Ambassador Antonio Armellini, Head of the Italian Delegation, on behalf of the European Community and its Member States at the Plenary Meeting of the Preparatory Committee for the CSCE Paris Summit (Vienna, 27 July 1990).

14. Ghebali, op. cit., p.75.

15. Based on the various texts mentioned.

16. DOC/E, 1 September 1990; DOC/E, 1 September 1990 (same date as the other); DOC/E, 1 August 1990 (UK); DOC/E, 4 August 1990 (Italy); DOC/E 23 August 1990 (France).

17. Based on discussions with several participants.

18. Based on several texts and discussions with participants.

19. Ibid.

20. One of the incidents during the negotiations that is worth mentioning was the question of what word to use at the end of the very first preambular paragraph, a very important one, introducing the whole text. It started with 'We the Heads of State or Government … have assembled in Paris at a time of profound change and historic expectations. The era of confrontation and division of Europe is ended. We declare that henceforth our relations will be founded on … [space] and co-operation'. The French word '*concorde*' was suggested, to which the British delegate pointed out that the English equivalent was precisely the same word (concord). But this did not go through, because the United States delegate retorted that the only such word he was aware of was a type of aircraft. The void was finally filled by the word 'respect'. I would like to thank Emil Golemanov for this *vignette*.

21. See international press at the time, for example, *The Economist*, 24 November 1990, pp.63–4, 69.

22. Ghebali, op. cit., p. 74.
23. 'Charter of Paris for a New Europe', Paris 1990, p. 13 (English version).
24. Ghebali, op. cit., p. 77. Note that since 'culture' and 'migrant workers' were given separate sub-chapters of their own several delegations have claimed in subsequent CSCE meetings that they therefore do not form part and parcel of the human dimension (which could be said for NGOs as well, for they have a chapter of their own). Others, of course, have strongly objected to such a view.
25. 'Charter of Paris for a New Europe', 'Supplementary Document to Give Effect to Certain Provisions Contained in the Charter of Paris for a New Europe', pp. 17–18, 20.
26. Ibid., pp.17–18, 20.
27. Ibid.

CHAPTER ELEVEN: BEYOND PARIS AND UNTIL THE EVE OF HELSINKI-II

1. The presentation of the Cracow Symposium is based on the author's notes taken during the meeting.
2. 'Document of the Cracow Symposium on the Cultural Heritage of the CSCE Participating State', Cracow, 1991.
3. The *Journal de Genève* reported regularly on the meeting, though it was often inaccurate and biased in its commentaries. See, for example, *Journal de Genève*, 13–14 July 1991.
4. The Pentagonale proposal, REMN.2, consisted of four chapters: preamble, normative provisions, confidence-building measures and procedures.
5. The '12' proposal (REMN.14) had, after a long preamble, six chapters: equal opportunity, protection of identity and creation of conditions for the promotion of identity, effective participation in public affairs, transboundary co-operation, information, and furthering of implementation of commitments.
6. The Franco-Hungarian proposal, REMN.11, was launched for symbolic reasons to indicate that even countries with such different approaches on national minorities could reach agreement. (Based on discussions with the originators of the idea.)
7. See, for example, the assessment of the US Commission on Security and Co-operation in Europe, in 'The Geneva CSCE Experts Meeting on National Minorities', August 1991, pp.9–10. The full title of the document is 'Report of the CSCE Meeting of Experts on National Minorities, Geneva 1991'.
8. Based on the hurried communications between capitals following the coup.
9. See *International Herald Tribune*, 11 and 12 September 1991.
10. DOC/E, 6 and 14 November 1991 (Netherlands Presidency).
11. CSCE, Conference on the Human Dimension, Moscow Meeting 1991, Journal No.18, 3 October 1991.
12. See note 10 above.
13. Full title 'Document of the Moscow Meeting of the Conference on the Human Dimension of the CSCE'.
14. It was pointed out by this author that the traditional inter-governmental character of the CSCE should not be diluted by active NGO participation in CSCE meetings, as in the UN Commission on Human Rights, particularly at a time when cool-headed problem-solving was necessary in order to cope with complex issues.
15. Paragraphs 3, 4 and 10 of the 'Document of the Moscow Meeting ...'. For the

workings of the mechanism, I am particularly indebted to legal expert Mania Telalian, the Greek negotiator in the drafting group on mechanism.

16. Ibid., paragraph 5.
17. Ibid.
18. Ibid., paragraph 7.
19. Ibid., paragraph 11.
20. Ibid.
21. Ibid., paragraph 12.
22. Ibid., paragraph 13.
23. Commission on Security and Co-operation in Europe, 'The Oslo Seminar of Experts on Democratic Institutions', Report prepared by the Staff of the Commission (1991), pp.4–6, p.19.
24. The mandate from the Charter of Paris was unclear, speaking in terms of a 'summing up' of the meetings to be taken into account by the Council of Ministers, and there was no hint as to the length of the document or whether it would have an operational part with recommendations and/or new commitments.
25. This was done even though several states were unhappy that a precedent would be created by having for the fourth time in the same year the host country acting as drafter/co-ordinator (previously in Cracow, Geneva and Moscow).
26. The Austro–Italian paper contained the following tasks for the ODI: (a) points 2 and 3 of the Vienna CHD mechanism; (b) the various practical-procedural tasks of the Moscow rapporteurs/good offices; and (c) tasks aimed at involving individuals and NGOs on the CSCE human dimension and its implementation. The United States paper also included the task of the Moscow mechanism but it was otherwise concerned with making the office a venue for advice and assistance on democratic institutions, a data bank of sorts and a place from which to send experts. The proposal by the OFE had, in addition to the above, also the convening of meetings related to democratic institutions.
27. The veteran Ambassador Saliba of Malta (who was the one who in the early days delayed CSCE meetings by not giving Maltese consent) was furious, calling the meeting 'the most Kafkaesque' CSCE meeting he had ever attended.
28. The French insistence in Oslo was more perplexing than in Moscow, for there had followed, in the meantime, the NATO Rome Declaration, issued by the heads of state and government on 8 November, clearly stating the enhancement of the role of the OFE to transform itself 'into a broadly focused Office of Democratic Institutions to promote co-operation in the field of human rights, democracy and the rule of law'. NATO, Press Communiqué, S-1 (91)86, 8 November 1991, p.6. The idea was also included in the non-paper of the CSO Prague Meeting: CSO, Non-Paper, Prague, 24 October 1991.
29. 'Commission', op. cit., p.1; DOC/E, 22 November 1991.
30. 'Commission', op. cit., p.6.
31. Based on discussions with participants. See also 'Prague Meeting of the CSCE Council, 30–31 January 1992, Summary of Conclusions', Prague, 31 January 1992; CSCE, sixth Meeting of the Committee of Senior Officials, Prague 1992, Journal No.1, Annexe 2 (27 January 1992).
32. Prague Meeting of the CSCE Council, 30–31 January 1992, Summary of Conclusions.
33. 'Interim Report of the CSCE Rapporteur Mission on the Situation in Nagorno Karabakh', 25 February 1992.
34. Summary of Conclusions, op. cit.

35. 'Prague Document on Further Development of CSCE Institutions and Structures', Prague Council Meeting, Prague, 30 January 1992.
36. Ibid.

CHAPTER TWELVE: CONCLUDING REMARKS

1. Luigi Vittorio Ferraris, *Report on a Negotiation. Helsinki–Geneva–Helsinki 1972–1975* (Alphen aan den Rijn: Sijthoff & Noordhoff, 1979), p.79.
2. Max M. Kampelman, *Three Years at the East–West Divide* (New York: Freedom House, 1983), p.122.
3. 'The Charter of Paris for a New Europe', p.13.
4. Jeanne Kirk Laux, 'Human Contacts, Information, Culture, and Education', in Robert Spencer (ed.), *Canada and the Conference on Security and Co-operation in Europe* (Toronto: University of Toronto Press, 1984), pp.260–3; Vojtech Mastny, *Helsinki, Human Rights and European Security* (Durham: Duke University Press, 1986), pp.15–16; Geoffrey Edwards, 'Human Rights and Basket III Issues: Areas of Change and Continuity', *International Affairs*, 61 (Autumn 1985), pp.631, 633–40.
5. Max M. Kampelman, *Entering New Worlds. The Memoirs of a Private Man in Public Life* (New York: Harper Collins, 1991), p.275.
6. Victor-Yves Ghebali, 'Le rôle de la Communauté Européenne dans le Processus de la CSCE', *Revue du Marché Commun et de l'Union Européenne*, No.343 (January 1991), pp.8–13; Victor-Yves Ghebali, 'The CSCE in the Post-Cold War Europe', *NATO Review*, 39, No.2 (April 1991), pp.8–11.
7. 'French Memorandum on Post-Helsinki Security Negotiations', 10 February 1992.
8. DOC/E, 26 February 1992.
9. The United States stance was obvious from the answers given by Ambassador Kornblum (the designated United States head of delegation at Helsinki-II) to questions posed by this author and other commentators via the USIA network on the eve of Helsinki-II (USIA, EUR, 27 February 1992). See also DOC/E, 19 and 28 February 1992.
10. On the 'down-side' of ethnic conflict in the CSCE region see, for example, Dennis J.D. Sandole, 'The Conflict Prevention Centre: Prospects for Cooperative Conflict Resolution in the New Europe', paper presented at the International Institute for Peace, Vienna, 9–10 March 1991.

POSTSCRIPT: HELSINKI-II AND ITS AFTERMATH

1. For more details on the Human Dimension at Helsinki-II see Rob Zaagman, 'The Human Dimension in Helsinki: Institutional Aspects', *Helsinki Monitor*, 3, No. 4 (1992); and Alexis Heraclides, 'Helsinki-II and the Human Dimension: Normative Commitments the End of an Era?', *Helsinki Monitor*, 3, No. 4 (1992).
2. The filling of gaps was mentioned by this author early on in Working Group 3 and was later popularized as 'gap-filling' by the Austrian delegate, Dr Thomas Buschbaum, who became the coordinator on the structures of the human dimension.
3. 'CSCE Helsinki Document 1992. The Challenges of Change' (July 1992), p.2.
4. 'Summary of Conclusions of the Stockholm Council Meeting' (15 December 1992), pp.13–15.

SELECTED BIBLIOGRAPHY

Acimovic, Ljubivoje, 'Follow-Up to the Conference', in Vojtech Mastny, *Helsinki, Human Rights, and European Security* (Durham: Duke University Press, 1986).

Andren, Nils and Karl E. Birnbaum (eds.), *Belgrade and Beyond: The CSCE Process in Perspective* (Alphen aan den Rijn: Sijthoff & Noordhoff, 1980).

Arangio-Ruíz, Gaeteno, 'Human Rights and Non Intervention in the Helsinki Final Act', *Recueil des Cours*, Hague Academy of International Law, IV (1977).

Bastid, Susan, 'The Special Significance of the Helsinki Final Act', in Thomas Buergenthal (ed.), *Human Rights, International Law and the Helsinki Accord* (Montclair, NJ: Allanheld, Osmun, 1977).

Birnbaum, Karl E., 'East–West Diplomacy in the Era of Multilateral Negotiations: The Case of the Conference on Security and Co-operation in Europe (CSCE)', in Nils Andren and Karl E. Birnbaum (eds.), *Beyond Détente: Prospects for East–West Co-operation and Security in Europe* (Amsterdam: Sijthoff, 1976).

Bloed, Arie, 'A New CSCE Human Rights "Catalogue": The Copenhagen Meeting of the Conference on the Human Dimension of the CSCE', in A. Bloed and P. van Dijks (eds.), *The Human Dimension of the Helsinki Process* (Dordrecht: Martinus Nijhoff, 1991).

Bloed, A. and P. van Dijk (eds.), *The Human Dimension of the Helsinki Process* (Dordrecht: Martinus Nijhoff, 1991).

Buergenthal, Thomas, 'International Human Rights Law and the Helsinki Final Act: Conclusions', in Thomas Buergenthal (ed.), *Human Rights, International Law and the Helsinki Accord* (Montclair, NJ: Allanheld, Osmun, 1977).

——, 'The Copenhagen Meeting: A New Public Order for Europe', *Human Rights Law Journal*, 217 (1990).

Cassese, Antonio, 'The Helsinki Declaration and Self-Determination', in Thomas Buergenthal (ed.), *Human Rights, International Law and the Helsinki Accord* (Montclair, NJ: Allanheld, Osmun, 1977).

Crawford, James, *The Creation of States in International Law* (Oxford: Clarendon Press, 1979).

Decaux, Emmanuel, 'La Réunion de Copenhague de la conférence sur la dimension humaine de la CSCE', *Revue Générale de Droit International Public*, No. 4 (October–November 1990).

——, *La Conférence sur la Sécurité et la Co-opération en Europe (CSCE)* (Paris: Presses Universitaires de France, 1992).

Edwards, Geoffrey, 'Human Rights and Basket III Issues: Areas of Change and Continuity', *International Affairs*, 61 (Autumn 1985).

Eickhoff, Ekkehard, 'Assessment of the Meeting of Experts' translated from *Europa-Archiv*, 19 (1985), in Vojtech Mastny, *Helsinki, Human Rights and European Security* (Durham: Duke University Press, 1986).

Fawcett, J.E.S., 'The Helsinki Act and International Law', *Revue Belge de Droit International*, 8, 1 February 1972.

Ferraris, Luigi Vittorio, *Report on a Negotiation. Helsinki–Geneva–Helsinki 1972–1975* (Alphen aan den Rijn: Sijthoff & Noordhoff, 1979).

Frowein, Jochen Abr., 'The Interrelationship between the Helsinki Final Act, the International Covenants on Human Rights, and the European Convention on Human Rights', in Thomas Buergenthal (ed.), *Human Rights, International Law and the Helsinki Accord* (Montclair, NJ: Allanheld, Osmun, 1977).

Ghebali, Victor-Yves, 'Les résultats de la Réunion de Madrid sur les suites de la CSCE', *Défense Nationale* (December 1983).

——, *La diplomatie de la détente: la CSCE d'Helsinki à Vienne (1973–1989)* (Brussels: Emile Bruylant, 1989).

——, 'La Charte de Paris pour une Nouvelle Europe', *Défense Nationale*, 47 (March 1991).

——, 'Le thème des droits de l'homme dans le processus de la Conférence sur la Sécurité et la Co-opération en Europe', *Le 'noyau intangible' de la protection des droits de l'homme*, Actes du Colloque de Fribourg (Fribourg, 1991).

Greenwald, G. Jonathan, 'Vienna – A Challenge for the Western Alliance', *Aussenpolitik*, 38, No.4 (1987).

Hazewinkel, Harm, 'Paris, Copenhagen, and Moscow', in A. Bloed and P. van Dijk (eds.), *The Human Dimension of the Helsinki Process* (Dordrecht: Martinus Nijhoff, 1991).

Henkin, Louis, 'Human Rights and "Domestic Jurisdiction"', in Thomas Buergenthal (ed.), *Human Rights, International Law and the Helsinki Accord* (Montclair, NJ: Allanheld, Osmun, 1977).

Heraclides, Alexis, 'Helsinki-I: From Cold War to "A New Europe". The Human Rights Phase of the Conference on Security and Co-operation in Europe, 1975–1990', The Greek Institute for International and Strategic Studies, Occasional Paper No. 2 (August 1991).

——, *The Self-Determination of Minorities in International Politics* (London: Frank Cass, 1991).

——, 'The CSCE and Minorities. The Negotiations behind the Commitments, 1972–1992', *Helsinki Monitor*, 3, No. 3 (1992).

Holsti, Kalevi J. 'Who Got What and How: The CSCE Negotiations in Retrospect', in Robert Spencer (ed.), *Canada and the Conference on Security and Co-operation in Europe* (Toronto: University of Toronto Press, 1984).

Jonathan, Gerard Cohen and Jean-Paul Jacqué, 'Obligations Assumed by the Helsinki Signatories', in Thomas Buergenthal (ed.), *Human Rights, International Law and the Helsinki Accord* (Montclair, NJ: Allanheld, Osmun, 1977).

206

Selected Bibliography

Kampelman, Max M., *Three Years at the East–West Divide* (New York: Freedom House, 1983).

——, 'Reflections on the Madrid CSCE Review Conference', in Leon Sloss and M. Scott Davis (eds.), *A Game for High Stakes: Lessons Learned in Negotiating with the Soviet Union* (Roosevelt Center for American Policy Studies, 1985).

——, *Entering New Worlds. The Memoirs of a Private Man in Public Life* (New York: Harper Collins, 1991).

Kovrig, Bennett, 'European Security in East–West Relations: History of a Diplomatic Encounter', in Robert Spencer (ed.), *Canada and the Conference on Security and Co-operation in Europe* (Toronto: University of Toronto Press, 1984).

Laux, Jeanne Kirk, 'Human Contacts, Information, Culture, and Education', in Robert Spencer (ed.), *Canada and the Conference on Security and Co-operation in Europe* (Toronto: University of Toronto Press, 1984).

Legvold, Robert, 'The Problem of European Security', *Problems of Communism*, No. 23 (January–February 1973).

Lehne, Stefan, *The Vienna Meeting of the Conference on Security and Co-operation in Europe, 1986–1989* (Boulder, CO: Westview Press, 1991).

——, *The CSCE in the 1990s: Common European House or Potemkin Village?* (Luxemburg: Austrian Institute for International Affairs, 1991).

Lyon, Peyton V., 'Canada at Geneva, 1973–1975', in Robert Spencer (ed.), *Canada and the Conference on Security and Co-operation in Europe* (Toronto: University of Toronto Press, 1984).

Maresca, John J., *To Helsinki: The Conference on Security and Co-operation in Europe, 1973–1975* (Durham: Duke University Press, 1985).

Mastny, Vojtech, *Helsinki, Human Rights and European Security* (Durham: Duke University Press, 1986).

Meron, Theodor, 'Democracy and the Rule of Law', *World Affairs*, 153, No. 1 (Summer 1990).

Mottolla, Kari (ed.), *Ten Years After Helsinki: The Making of the European Security Regime* (Boulder, CO: Westview Press, 1986).

Prévost, Jean-François, 'Observations sur la nature juridique de l'Acte Final de la Conférence sur la Sécurité et la Co-opération en Europe', *Annuaire Français de Droit International*, 21 (1975).

Rotfeld, Adam Daniel, 'Introduction: The New Dimensions of the CSCE Process', in Halina Ognik and Adam D. Rotfeld (eds.), *Cultural Heritage and the CSCE Process* (Warsaw: Polish Institute of International Affairs, 1991).

Roucounas, Emmanuel, *Engagements parallèles et contradictoires*, in *Recueil des Cours*, Hague Academy of International Law (Dordrecht: Martinus Nijhoff, 1987).

Russell, Harold S., 'The Helsinki Declaration: Brobdingnag or Lilliput?', *American Journal of International Law*, 70, 1976.

Schachter, Oscar, 'The Twilight Existence of Non-Binding International Agreements', *American Journal of International Law*, 71, 1977.

207

Schlager, Erika B., 'The Procedural Framework of the CSCE: From the Helsinki Consultations to the Paris Charter, 1972–1990', *Human Rights Law Journal*, 12, Nos. 6–7 (12 July 1991).

Shevardnadze, Eduard, *The Future Belongs to Freedom* (London: Sinclair-Stevenson, 1991).

Sizzoo, Jan and Rudolf Th. Jurrgens, *CSCE Decision-Making: The Madrid Experience* (The Hague: Martinus Nijhoff, 1984).

Skilling, H. Gordon, 'The Belgrade Follow-up', in Robert Spencer (ed.), *Canada and the Conference on Security and Co-operation in Europe* (Toronto: University of Toronto Press, 1984).

——, 'The Madrid Follow-up', in Robert Spencer (ed.), *Canada and the Conference on Security and Co-operation in Europe* (Toronto: University of Toronto Press, 1984).

Spencer, Robert, 'Canada and the Origins of the CSCE', in Robert Spencer (ed.), *Canada and the Conference on Security and Co-operation in Europe* (Toronto: University of Toronto Press, 1984).

Staden, Berndt von, 'From Madrid to Vienna: The CSCE Process', *Aussen-politik*, 37, No. 4, 1986.

Tornopolsky, Walter, 'The Principles Guiding Relations between Participating States: Human Rights and Non-Intervention', in Robert Spencer (ed.), *Canada and the Conference on Security and Co-operation in Europe* (Toronto: University of Toronto Press, 1984).

Tretter, Hannes, 'Human Rights in the Concluding Document of the Vienna Follow-up Meeting of the Conference on Security and Co-operation in Europe of 15 January, 1989', *Human Rights Law Journal*, 10 (1989).

Velliadis, Hannibal, 'The Madrid Conference and the Consensus Building Process in Decision-Making', *Hellenic Review of International Relations*, 2, No. 1 (1981).

Vigny, Jean-Daniel, 'Le Document de la Réunion de Copenhague sur la dimension humaine de la CSCE/Introduction et commentaires', *Revue Universelle des Droits de l'Homme*, 2, No. 9 (22 October 1990).

Vincent, R.J., *Human Rights and International Relations* (London: Cambridge University Press, 1986).

Wells, Samuel F., Jr. (ed.), *The Helsinki Process and the Future of Europe* (Washington, DC: Wilson Center Press, 1990).

Wyatt, Marylin (ed.), *CSCE and the New Blueprint for Europe* (Washington, DC: Georgetown University Press, 1991).

INDEX

Index

211

113, 116, 117, 121, 123, 124, 136, 140, 141; Geneva Conference (1973–75), 20, 21, 24, 30, 33, 34; Madrid Meeting, 57, 63, 64, 65; *Ostpolitik* of, 3; self-determination, 30, 31, 32; Soviet bilateral treaty with, 5; Vienna Meeting, 85, 86–7, 88–9, 96, 97, 98, 105; *see also* Berlin; Bonn; Germany (post-reunification)

German reunification, 24, 30, 136, 143

Germany (post-reunification), 143, 175; Geneva Meeting, 151, 153–4, 155, 156, 161; Moscow CHD Meeting, 158, 159, 160, 161–2; Oslo Seminar, 168

Ghebali, Victor-Yves, 19, 145

Gibraltar, 30

Giscard d'Estaing, President Valéry, 191n

Goldberg, Justice Arthur, 52, 53, 55, 61, 191n

Gonzalez, Premier Felipe, 65

Gorbachev, Mikhail, 75, 96, 136, 157, 200n

Goubenko, Soviet Minister for Culture, 148–9

Greece, 45, 47, 49, 57, 58, 60, 63, 71, 72, 113, 117, 140, 143, 148, 149, 150, 155, 156, 158, 190n, 193n; Albanian clash with, 158; Copenhagen Meeting, 121, 122, 123, 124, 125, 126, 127, 199n; Cyprus crisis, 23, 41, 49, 76, 94, 111; Geneva Conference (1973–75), 21, 23, 25, 26, 29, 30, 32; Helsinki-II, 179; Macedonian dispute, 120, 158; Mersin dispute, 94–5; Moscow CHD Meeting, 157, 158, 159, 161, 162; Muslim minority in, 158, 199n; Vienna Follow-up Meeting, 85, 86, 88, 97, 105; *see also* Athens Meeting

Gromyko, Andrei, Soviet Foreign Minister, 20, 24

Guvendiren, Ekrem, Turkish Ambassador, 194n

Haig, Alexander, US Secretary of State, 63

Hajek, Professor Yiri, 117, 119, 122, 174

Hamburg Scientific Forum (1980), 55

Havel, Vaclav, 116, 117, 119, 174

Helsinki, Commemoration of 10th Anniversary of the Final Act (1985), 75, 88

Helsinki CSCE Conference (Phase 1, July 1973), 10, 19–20; Blue Book adopted at, 7, 10, 11–18, 19, 21–7; ceremonial opening, 19–20; *see also* Geneva CSCE Conference (Phase 2)

Helsinki CSCE Conferece (Phase 3, July–August 1975), 19; signing of Final Act at, 1, 2, 6, 19, 20, 32, 35–40, 41

Helsinki (Dipoli), Multilateral Preparatory Talks (1972–73), 5, 7–11, 19, 21, 34, 56

Helsinki Final Act, 21, 22, 23, 25, 27, 42, 54, 67, 68, 102, 145, 147, 173, 174; human dimension in, 38–40, 53, 70, 74; significance, normative character and content, 35–8; signing of (August 1975), 2, 6, 19, 20, 32, 35–40, 41

Helsinki monitors, 62, 64, 68, 74, 87, 89, 103

Helsinki Summit (August 1975), signing of the Final Act, 1, 2, 6, 19, 20, 32, 35–40, 41

Helsinki-II CSCE Summit Meeting (July 1992), 179, 180

Helsinki-II Document (1992), 180

Helsinki-II: Fourth CSCE Follow-up Meeting (March–June 1992), xvi, 1, 11, 13, 109, 110, 133, 162, 167, 175, 176, 177–80; Preparatory Committee, 169; Prague guidelines for, 169–71, 175

Heraclides, Dimitris, Greek Ambassador, 55

Hexagonale, 151

High Commissioner on National Minorities, 177, 180

Hoffburg Palace, Vienna, 82

Holsti, Kalevi J., 19, 43

Holy See, 1, 28–9, 52, 58, 60, 61, 72, 104, 117

Hoyer, Congressman Steny H., 167

human contacts, 32, 34, 37, 38, 61, 65, 67–8, 81, 83, 88, 91, 101, 102, 105, 129; Bern Meeting of Experts on, 47, 50, 66, 68, 70, 75–80, 83, 86, 105, 151, 153, 154, 163

Hungarian minority (in Romania), 108, 111, 178

Hungary, 47, 54, 57, 58, 71, 108, 109, 110, 112, 113, 117, 142, 148, 149, 150; Copenhagen Meeting, 120, 121, 123, 125, 127, 133, 134; Croatia/Slovenia issue, 163; Geneva CSCE Conference (1973–75), 29, 31, 32; Geneva Meeting (1991), 151, 152, 154, 155, 156; Helsinki-II, 179; Moscow CHD Meeting, 158, 159, 160, 161, 162; Oslo Seminar, 168; Soviet intervention in (1956), 3; Vienna Follow-up Meeting, 83, 84, 91, 92, 105; *see also* Budapest Cultural Forum

Hurr, Philip, 83

Iacovou, George, Cypriot Foreign Minister, 111

Iceland, 118, 151

IGO (Intergovernmental Organization), xv

Index

information, press, freedom of (journalists' rights), 32, 34, 65, 68, 99, 159–60, 180; London Forum on (1989), 45, 107, 108–10
Ionesco, Eugene, 6
Ireland, 8, 45, 53, 57, 71, 72, 86, 116, 118, 125, 148, 158, 159, 160, 201n
Israel, 20, 52, 78
Italy, 8, 46, 53, 57, 71, 72, 86, 88, 109, 115–16, 118, 138, 141, 148, 150, 153, 155, 156; Copenhagen Meeting, 121, 122, 123, 125; Geneva Meeting (1991), 153, 155, 156; Geneva Conference (1973–75), 20, 26, 28, 29, 31, 33; Helsinki-II, 179; Moscow CHD Meeting, 158, 159, 160, 161; Oslo Seminar, 168

Jazz Section, Czechoslovakia, 84
Jews, 179; Soviet, 46, 52, 78
Jivkov, President Todor, 42
Joint Declaration of Twenty-Two States (1990), 145

KAL (Korean Airlines) incident, 66
Kampelman, Max M., US Ambassador, 58, 59, 61, 69, 83, 120, 152, 172, 174, 192n, 193n
Karandreas, Nicos, Greek Ambassador, 184n
Karlovy Vary, Warsaw Pact Meeting (1967), 4
Kashlev, Yuri, Soviet Ambassador, 76, 84, 95, 98
Kazakhstan, 1, 169–70
Kirgistan, 1, 169–70
Kissinger, Henry, US Secretary of State, 5, 6, 24, 34
Kohl, Chancellor Helmut, 98
Kondrashev, Sergei, 61, 194n
Kornblum, John, US Ambassador, 204n
Kosovo, Albanians of, 47, 117, 155, 158, 167, 178
Kovalev, Anatoly, 85
Kuhn, Thomas, 43
Kurdistan Workers' Party (PKK), 178
Kurds, 47, 108, 112, 115, 118, 178
Kuznetsov, Pavel, 117

Latvia, 149, 157; see also Baltic states
Laurent, J., Belgian Ambassador, 182n, 195n, 197n
Legvold, Robert, 5
Lehne, Stefan, 91, 93
Liechtenstein, 1, 71, 72, 109, 117, 151, 152
Limassol, NNA Meeting (1987), 93
Lipatti, Valentin, Romanian Ambassador, 23

Lithuania, 149, 157; see also Baltic states
London Declaration on a transformed North Atlantic Alliance, 137, 139, 140
London Information Forum (1989), 45, 107, 108–10
Luxembourg, 52, 53, 57, 116, 118, 158, 159, 160

MAC ('mutually acceptable conditions'), 9
Macedonia (Yugoslavia), 120, 158, 169
Macedonian minority in Greece and Bulgaria, 120
Madrid Concluding Document (1983), 8, 26, 44, 66–9, 74, 101, 102
Madrid Preparatory Meeting (1980), 54, 56–8; 'stopping the clock' device at, 57
Madrid Second CSCE Follow-up Meeting (1980–83), 50, 54, 55–6, 58–66, 69, 81; Western 'eloquent silences' at, 63–4
Mali Federation, 14
Malta, 10, 20, 29, 50, 54, 60, 61, 66, 117, 149, 150, 168; see also Valletta Meetings
Marchenko, Anatoly, 84
Marcuse, Herbert, 41
Maresca, John J., US Ambassador, 24, 138
Mastny, Vojtech, 40, 43, 64
Mazilu, 117
MBFR (Mutual and Balanced Force Reduction), 4, 5
Mediterranean issue, 20, 54, 66, 177; Valletta Meeting on (1979), 54, 55
Mersin dispute, 94–5
migrant workers, 72, 102, 121, 124, 130, 151, 155, 159, 161, 162, 178, 180
military service, conscientious objection to, 127, 129
minorities, national, 9–10, 18, 20, 28, 29–30, 37, 68, 72, 73, 91, 102, 105–6, 113, 137, 142–3, 170; Albanians of Kosovo, 47, 155, 158; Copenhagen Meeting and Document on, 120, 121, 122, 123–8, 128, 130–3, 140; Geneva Meeting of Experts on, 116, 121, 142–3, 150–6, 161, 163; Helsinki-II, 177, 178, 180; Hungarians in Romania, 108, 111, 178; Kurds, 47, 108, 112, 115, 118, 178; Macedonian, 120; Moscow CHD Meeting on, 158, 159, 161, 162, 164; Muslims in Greece, 158, 199n; Muslims/Turks in Bulgaria, 71, 76, 80, 83, 100, 108, 110, 111, 133, 158; Roma/gypsies, 133, 151, 159, 160, 178
minority languages, teaching of, 124–5, 127, 132
Mintoff, Dom, Maltese Prime Minister, 66
Mitterrand, President François, 99, 110,

213